and Vices

Sports hav
ing link be
compreher
wider soci

The prir
of sports
gymnasia
that sports
education
– a valuab
Includir
key ethica

- The d
- Defin
- Dopir
- Biom
  coach
- Racis
- The p

Writter
also powe
tial readir
losophy c

Mike Mc
History
Universit
Association for the Philosophy of Sport and the Founding Chair of the British
Philosophy of Sport Association. He is series co-editor of Routledge's suc-
cessful 'Ethics and Sport Series' and is Editor of the international journal
Sport, Ethics and Philosophy.

Sports, Virtues and Vices
Morality plays

Mike McNamee

Routledge
Taylor & Francis Group

LONDON AND NEW YORK

First published 2008
by Routledge
2 Park Square, Milton Park, Abingdon, Oxon OX14 4RN

Simultaneously published in the USA and Canada
by Routledge
270 Madison Ave, New York, NY 10016

*Routledge is an imprint of the Taylor & Francis Group,
an informa business*

© 2008 Mike McNamee

Typeset in Sabon
by Swales and Willis Ltd, Exeter, Devon
Printed and bound in Great Britain by Antony Rowe Ltd,
Chippenham, Wiltshire

British Library Cataloguing in Publication Data
A catalogue record for this book is available
from the British Library

Library of Congress Cataloging in Publication Data
A catalog record has been requested for this book

ISBN 10: 0–415–19408–3 (hbk)
ISBN 10: 0–415–19409–1 (pbk)
ISBN 10: 0–203–09010–1 (ebk)

ISBN 13: 978–0–415–19408–2 (hbk)
ISBN 13: 978–0–415–19409–9 (pbk)
ISBN 13: 978–0–203–09010–7 (ebk)

To the girls: Cheryl, Megan and Ffion, with love

Contents

Preface

The book is comprised of essays, many of which were presented or published between 1992 and 2007. While some of them are unpublished in their present form, all of them, bar the final chapter of this book, have undergone significant revisions from their earlier forms as papers and articles.

In Part I, I set out the groundwork for the book. Some remarks from Chapter 1 were collected in a conference proceedings of the International Association for the Philosophy of Sport (1995b) under the title 'Sport: relativism, commonality and essential contestability' though I have substantially changed my understanding of conceptual analysis since then and limited the scope of my ambitions as a result. An early version of Chapter 2 was published under the heading 'Physical education and the development of personhood' in the *Physical Education Review* (1992). I have removed all discussion of educational and physical educational relevance from the paper and indeed I have softened up the cognitive-linguistic emphasis a little in relation to work that was published later in moral psychology and philosophical anthropology. Chapter 3 is adapted from "Sporting practices, institutions and virtues" published in the *Journal of the Philosophy of Sport* (1995a) while Chapter 4 is a significantly revised version of 'Ethics, psychology and sports: back to an Aristotelian "museum of normalcy"' which appeared in the *International Journal of Sport and Health Science* (2003) and was written with Carwyn Jones and Joan Duda. I have removed portions of the empirical psychology of the original article and have adapted the chapter to fit specifically with the virtue-ethical framework of the book, and I happily record my appreciation for their earlier collaboration.

In Part II, on the virtues and vices of sports, I gather together and revise various chapters that deal specifically with the virtue ethics of sports. Chapter 5, 'Celebrating trust: virtues and rules in the ethical conduct of sports coaches' (1998) was published in *Ethics and Sport* edited by myself and Jim Parry, the first book in our series of the same name. The essay has been revised in a number of ways showing the continuity between modern codes and the ancient sixth-century BC Hippocratic Oath and third-century BC Beroia Law for *gymnasiarchos* in Ancient Greece. A version of Chapter 6, like Chapter 4, was published jointly as 'The moral economy of racism and racist rationalisations in sport' with Jonathon Long in the *International Review for the Sociology of Sport* (2004) whom I thank here. Originally the paper was split along methodological lines: half articulation of conceptual and ethical aspects of racism, and half comment on rationalisations sportspersons used for their racism based on empirical research he had conducted with colleagues over a decade. I have omitted direct reference to that substantial body of empirical research and have developed the virtue-ethical aspects of racism with respect to the racist act/racist character distinction and also included discussion of role modelling in relation to racism and racial stereotypes.

The following chapters (7 and 8) appeared first in the *Journal of the Philosophy of Sport* (2002, 2003a respectively). While 'Hubris, humility and humiliation' remains fairly intact, the subsequent chapter '*Schadenfreude* in sport' underwent very substantial revision when I published another version of the ethics of *schadenfreude* in healthcare contexts in *Medicine, Healthcare and Philosophy* (2007b). A perceptive and helpful reviewer forced me to give a much more sympathetic account of Kant's conception of the emotions than I had done originally in the former article and I have included those revisions in the chapter here.

The final part of the book (III), rather like the final chapter of Part II, reflects work over the last few years where I have attempted to explore the interfaces between medical ethics and sports ethics. Chapter 9, 'Suffering in and for sport' (2005a) appeared first in an anthology from the 'Ethics and Sports Series' entitled *Pain and Injury in Sport* and is only slightly altered. While Chapter 10 has not been previously published, I draw upon some portions of an essay on slippery slopes that was published jointly with Steve Edwards as 'Transhumanism, medical technology, and slippery slopes', in the *Journal of Medical Ethics* (2006) and a report written for the UK Parliament Select Committee on Science and Technology entitled "Ethical issues regarding human enhancement technologies" (2006) (www.publications.parliament. uk/pa/cm/200607/cmselect/cmsctech/67/67we16.htm; accessed 1.1.08). The final essay deals with a subject that strikes to the very heart of ethics more generally and the future of sports specifically: the uses and abuses of biotechnology to transfigure our very conception of the human. I draw from some remarks from the former essay and also a talk I gave at the Thomas More Institute (2006) in the writing of Chapter 11: 'Whose Prometheus?: Transhumanism, biotechnology and the moral topography of sports medicine' (2007a), which was published in the journal that I launched as editor in 2007: *Sport, Ethics and Philosophy*.

I thank the various Editors for their kindness in allowing the part reproduction of those papers and the many reviewers who gave freely and generously of their wisdom. Naturally, all mistakes remain of my own making and responsibility.

Acknowledgements

Like any book that has been a long time in the writing (and like this book that is considerably late in the making) I have many people that I wish wholeheartedly to thank. Sadly, there are simply too many of them to list without descending into a sentimental Oscar-winning-style appreciation speech. Those friends not specified here I hope will content themselves with my unfailing, though unspecified, appreciation.

Perhaps the first place to start is with thanks to two Editors I have worked with at Routledge, Samantha Grant and Simon Whitmore, whose patience and support have been considerable. I am immensely grateful too, for what I learnt in the supervision of many Doctoral students it has been my pleasure to work with. Among them Andrew Bloodworth, Carwyn Jones and Heather Sheridan deserve special mention. Equally, I have to thank Jim Parry with whom I have enjoyably worked for many years as the Series Editor of 'Ethics and Sport'.

My colleagues in the Centre for Philosophy, Law and Healthcare at Swansea University – Steven Edwards, Thomas Schramme and Hugh Upton – have been both a source of intellectual stimulation and exemplary collegiality. I have learnt from all of them and enjoyed every minute in their insightful and warm company.

Sigmund Loland, Rektor of the Norwegian School of Sport Sciences, kindly afforded me the opportunity to gather a draft of the whole book while on a sabbatical there in 2006. I also happily record my gratitude to Graham McFee with whom I have shared much of the book, in different stages of its development as individual papers or chapters. His genial company has, as the Irish poet Seamus Heaney once remarked, always seemed like a cure one never noticed happening.

Finally, it is a pleasure to record my love and appreciation to my wife, Cheryl, and our beautiful daughters, Megan and Ffion, without whose forbearance the book would never have been finished and without whom it would not have been worthwhile.

Introduction
Ancient rituals and modern morality plays

In Medieval Europe, the Roman Catholic Church was the dominant social and political institution as well as the seat of learning. The vast majority of the populace, however, were illiterate and the possibility of their understanding or even following its principal ceremony, Holy Mass, conducted in Latin, was unthinkable. One fairly widespread way of reducing the mysteriousness of religious morality was the enactment of morality plays. The precise details of this cultural practice is unknown, so I offer here the merest sketch to make the point I wish to at the beginning of this book on the ethics of sports. Around this time, travelling circuses not only brought entertainment to the masses, but typically included in their show a morality play. Here good and evil were played out on a stage where what was at stake was the very soul of the principal character: Everyman. Though crudely analogous, it is my contention that sports, among other things, now fulfil this role or function on a global scale. In a world where the Enlightenment myth of shared morality is assaulted on every side by anthropologists, cultural commentators and philosophers alike, sports offer a cognitively simple canvas of good and evil writ large in the everyday contexts of the arena, the court, the field and, of course, the back pages of our newspapers and the screens of our televisions. Just as the moralising point of the medieval plays was not dramatically dense, one needs neither complex cognitive nor moral vocabularies to understand cheating and courage, nor fair and foul play in the varied forums of sport. Indeed, sports, I will argue, offer our best vehicles for moral education in the light of the clash of moral cultures that the present world throws up.

While different philosophical approaches have been developed in sports ethics, the aim of this book is to situate ethics at the heart of sports and to do it via virtue-ethical considerations derived in large measure from the gymnasia of Ancient Greece.

Book synopsis

The book comprises three parts. The first provides a foundation. It sets out an account of what we need to understand about sports and sports ethics to develop a virtue-ethical account. The second part develops an account of why rules and rule books do not supplant virtues and opens the way for a close consideration of a family of vices and virtues that are to be found in sport throughout all levels of competition. The final part links the virtues and vices that attend the pursuit of excellence with respect to suffering and the harm that elite sports foster. I discuss the greed and shame that attend those who cheat by doping, and finally the future of sports and how this may be undermined by recent advances in biomedical technology aligned to the vices that have traditionally attended sports' limited focus on a technical excellence. I offer below a thumbnail sketch of each chapter.

In Chapter 1, I give an account of the nature of sports. I highlight the ethical core of sport and relate it to its gratuitous logic (Suits, 1978), the very fact that in engaging in sports we undertake activities, the pursuit of which are rendered more difficult by the rules that define the activity and which we agree to be governed by in pursuit of athletic victory. I offer a critique of those essentialists who seek to find some kind of closure to the analysis of the concept of sport simply by defining it in terms of necessary and sufficient conditions. I offer an account of sports as an open concept that nonetheless has a form of rule-governed gratuitous activities demanding and developing embodied capacities in the ethically defensible pursuit of the ends of victory in a shared contest.

In Chapter 2, I argue that we cannot have a substantive normative account of sportspersonship without a theory of personhood. Charles Taylor's work on the philosophy of agency is used to articulate personhood as the capacity for strong evaluation – or qualitative discrimination – among one's ends, goals and identities, arising partly from our ethically informed emotional lives. Contrary to the everyday understanding of sportspersonship where one plays with ruthless efficiency to reach the goal while bending all possible rules to one's advantage, I hold that sportspersonship is crucially related to this normative capacity of distinguishing between goals that are desirable, noble, valuable and worthy from those which are not.

Developing on from the account of sports and sportspersons, in Chapter 3 I situate the ethics of sports within a critical account of social practices first developed in the work of Alisdair MacIntyre. It is in sports, conceived historically as social practices, that the virtues can be developed and sustained by sportspersons, administrators, coaches and officials, in pursuit of the internal goods of sports and their institutional promotion and protection. In the last chapter of this section, Chapter 4, I give a more fine-grained account of ethical development in and through sport that pays close attention to the emotions in harmony with our considered perceptions and judgements of right and wrong, good and bad, and that are formed first by habitualised training and emulation. This paves the way for more detailed discussion of particular vices and virtues.

In Chapter 5, which initiates Part II, I argue that rule-based moralities underdetermine moral action. In particular I show how they can foster an attitude of moral minimalism, the like of which is often crystallised in codes of conduct. This institutionalised response to ethical difficulty and the attitude it often spawns are not new. Indeed it is to be found in third-century BC Greek Beroia Law for the *Gymnasarchoi* who had authority over the conduct of athletes and instructors in the gymnasium. In considering more contemporary examples of rule-based codes, I show how the fetish for codes of conduct can in fact undermine the very trust in human character and conduct that they were supposed to foster. I close the chapter with a consideration of the virtue of trust which, though it does not replace institutional needs for rules and sanctions, can better underscore the types of action the rule book attempts crudely to foster.

In Chapter 6, I offer an account of racism as a vice. While the sociological and political anti-racist literatures often present us with a simplistic dichotomy (either one is racist or not racist) I offer a dispositional account that holds that one cannot typically be considered a racist on the basis of a one-off act or utterance. Developing this account I present a richer catalogue of the vices that attend our attitudes towards otherness and reinforce the idea of a responsibility for feelings of dominance over and antipathy to racialised others in sports. Focusing on the fact that the ethos of certain sports may still harbour racist sentiments, I offer an example of moral courage of two cricketers who risked limb and livelihood in their public denunciation of racist norms outside the sub-cultures of sports.

In Chapter 7, I develop the theme of feelings of superiority over others that are often thought to be a precondition of success in elite sports. I offer a critical revision journalistic idea that teams and athletes who lose in certain ways are thereby humiliated. Against the hubris typical of certain sports stars, I argue for greater humility and empathy in sports winning and losing. In Chapter 8 I continue this train of thought in relation to our attitudes towards losers whom we may think deserve their humiliation and whose suffering is somehow merited. I attempt to render problematic the celebration of the suffering of those who are humiliated despite their responsibility for it, as in cases of doping and other forms of cheating or poor conduct.

These chapters culminate in what I take to be a deep and serious problem in sports, its relation to suffering. A common picture of the logic of sports is twofold: winners rejoice, losers suffer. In Chapter 9 I give an account of the ethical nature and significance of suffering by exploring the common ground between the experience of losing in sports and undergoing serious illness. It seems to me that considering an applying scholarship from medical ethics may, with the appropriate changes, help us better understand our responses to vulnerability and promote shared understanding of our humanness in and outside sport.

In Chapter 10, I offer an original line of discussion in an often tired debate. I first sketch the typical arguments regarding the im/permissibility of doping (e.g. fairness, harm, paternalism, and so on). Due to the inherent conceptual vagueness of un/acceptability of illicit means of preparation and performance in sports it seems that we cannot logically determine a point at which we can say doping is wrong. In contrast, I argue in defence of the bans on certain

pharmacological means of performing enhancement via the notion of slippery slopes. Moreover, developing the aretaic position in sports ethics, I offer two vices that characterise cheats who dope and which underwrite our perception of the undesirability of those who cheat thus. I return, as I do throughout the book, to the Greek catalogue of vices and virtues. We can understand the wrongness, or baseness, of the character of those who dope, as an example of what the ancient Greeks called '*pleonexia*' (loosely understood as greed aligned to the desire for more than is one's due) and the loss of '*aidos*' (shame) to be understood literally as the shamelessness of athletes who, on being caught, are merely embarrassed or fretful over their loss of external goods (salary, sponsorship, status and other financial rewards). I argue that although the World Anti-Doping Association is inevitably based in a catch up game, their task, although analogous to the struggle of Sisyphus, is both admirable and necessary.

In Chapter 11, I present two versions of the myth of Prometheus in order to consider the normativity of elite sports and what is becoming ever more closely aligned to it, the practice of sports medicine. It is often said that those who would promote genetic engineering in and out of sports are engaged in a Promethean enterprise. I present two contrasting accounts of the myth (Hesiod v Aeschylos) to bring to light dispositions favourable and unfavourable to those who seek to challenge and revise the very nature of humans themselves in order to gain excellence whether in or beyond sports. I then argue that these human-enhancing ideologues may well use elite sports as the vehicle for legitimating otherwise unacceptable technological libertarianism and how their pursuit is contrary to the spirit of sports and the flourishing of sportspersons therein.

Sport, ethics and Ancient Greece: a methodological note

Although the title of this book indicates a Christian context, I argue throughout the book that the context of the virtues in Ancient Greece offers us instructive examples for our conduct and character in sport in (post)modernity. True, there is much overlap between Aristotelian ethics and, via St Thomas Aquinas, later Christian ethics. A critic might well latch on to Woody Allen's remark that my posture in this book is predicated on the belief that "nostalgia ain't what it used to be". Some methodological notes are therefore required in order at least to forestall this objection.

It seems to me that there is sufficient continuity in the human condition that certain vices and virtues are historically present irrespective of the age in which they are commented upon. They are so deeply embedded within our language and social life as to be unavoidable. I take the spirit of this posture directly from Peter Strawson who writes:

> [H]uman commitment to participation in ordinary interpersonal relationships is, I think, too thoroughgoing and deeply rooted for us to take

seriously the thought that a general theoretical conviction might so change our world that in it, there were no longer any such things as interpersonal relationships as we normally understand them.

(Strawson, 1968: 86)

The position presented is close to that of Hart (1961) who once remarked that human society is not a suicide club. Our present concern with a given aspect of the continuation of social existence – ethical action in sports – is also embedded in our very thought and language. Consider the metaphors that derive from sport which find wider application in our daily lives: "playing with a straight bat"; "keeping one's eye on the ball"; "a level playing field"; "moving the goalposts"; or the widespread usages of a "slam-dunk", "home-run" or "strike out" and so on. Reaching deeper, one need only look to generalisations concerning human nature to derive certain necessary ideals of character and conduct that any society must seek to uphold.

Notions such as blame, praise, responsibility, courage, cowardice, vice and so on, are likely to occur in all modern societies by virtue of the sorts of social creatures that human beings are and the forms of social organization they construct. The language of human action presupposes their import; but what exactly they mean and how they are interpreted will of course be instantiated differently over time within and between cultures, classes and sexes. Bringing complex and incomplete notions such as justice, freedom, politics, power, education and those of which the wholesale term "social concepts" has been applied into some meaningful characterisation of human nature and association has the effect of allowing an objective grounding for the inevitable disputes as to their meanings whilst appreciating the great significance of variability in their interpretation. Sports do not enjoy this complexity though their sophistication is often underplayed.

Of course the caveat has also to be made that the precise contours of ethical ideals and the virtues – wise and particular patterns of action, feeling, judgement and perception – that shape them and are shaped by them in their pursuit, are nuanced in ways that must be understood within a historical frame. Thus regret and responsibility, trust and truthfulness, these are not historically conditioned social constructions that could be swept away in any particular historical epoch or cultural settings. They are not mere social constructions but presuppositions of the very idea of a community or society.

So the power of Hampshire's view that there should be a "no shopping principle" when it comes to adopting and adapting moral notions from various cultures and historical epochs, should not, I think, take as its target those historical ideas and ideals that I have drawn from the settings of Ancient Greece. I hope that in drawing deeply and frequently from the quarry (though not the supermarket) of Ancient Greek culture I have resisted the idea that all we need in sport, as elsewhere, is the simple reincarnation of an earlier epoch when all was well. All was palpably not well. It takes no prescience to rebuke the naive memory makers, the reactionaries, that ancient Greek life was very often elitist, sexist and xenophobic among its many unethical postures. Much of what has motivated the book has been a task of reconstructing the point of ancient virtues, myths and models, not merely reviving them.

In this book, I have been guided, though perhaps not enough or not subtly enough, by philosophers who have challenged the liberal paradigm of moral progress. The point is made by moderns, as Williams (1985) points out, that the word "morality", that peculiar institution as he called it, with its universalising scope of duties owed to all humankind was not present in Ancient Greek times. And though he is sceptical of this claim, he argues that progress was indeed made even in the epoch of Ancient Greece. Although MacIntyre brilliantly captures the more limited role of morality of the time, where what one is defines what one ought to be and do, Williams claims that the notion of aretē, or excellence, was not strictly determined by social position, that there existed some possibility to achieve this state irrespective of the perception that only certain classes of persons could attain it.

It is not, then, that there are no differences between these historical cultural junctures nor that they are insignificant, yet it still is true, I believe, that we have much to learn from them in order to make our sports better, our sportspersons more excellent in the ethical and technical senses of that word, and thus possible that our lives may go better too. Williams puts the general point eloquently:

> Still more there are differences, differences we must approve, between ourselves and the ancient Greeks. The question is how these differences are to be understood. My claim is that they cannot best be understood in terms of a basic shift in ethical conceptions of agency, responsibility, shame, or freedom. Rather, by better grasping these conceptions themselves and the extent to which we share them with antiquity, we may be helped to recognize some of our illusions about the modern world, and through this gain a firmer hold on the differences that we value between ourselves and the Greeks. It is not a question of reviving anything. What is dead is dead, and in many important respects we would not want to revive it even if we knew what that could mean. What is alive from the Greek world is already alive and is helping (often in hidden ways) to keep us alive.
>
> (Williams, 1993: 7)

I am conscious that I have not come anywhere near exhausting the ethics of sports even from an aretaic perspective. I hope only to have sown the seeds of doubt that all sports ethics should be conceived of either in deontological or consequentialist frameworks. I hope also to have shown that there is much to be gained from considering the value of sports from within a perspective informed critically by the contestual nature of Ancient Greek life, and in doing so to have offered a better understanding of the characters that perform nightly on our screens in the modern morality plays.

Part I

Sports, persons and ethical sport

1 What is this thing called sport?

Introduction

In a book devoted to the ethics of sports, one might properly expect a clear account of what sports are, what ethics is and how – if at all – they are related. What form those clarifications take, however, is a matter of some dispute. While I will develop a virtue-ethical account of sports that unfolds throughout the course of the book, this chapter focuses on what sport is taken to mean. I will argue that attempting to locate some transhistorical essence of the concept sport simply by reducing its complexity and variety to a set of necessary and sufficient conditions is not a helpful way to proceed. I conclude the chapter with an account of sports that I hope is sufficiently uncontentious (at least) for the purposes of the book. I understand sports in a rather more open-ended way than many authors who have attempted to circumscribe the concept. I argue that sports are best understood ritually as rule-governed contests with a gratuitous logic, and which necessarily embody an ethical dimension.

Defining sports as games

On the national holiday that occurs each year at the end of August, the World Championships for a not very well-known sport is hosted in the smallest town in Great Britain: Llanwrtyd.[1] In the heart of rural Wales, the smallest of the nations that comprise Great Britain, the championships take place in a stretch of water in the middle of a dense peat bog (Waen Rhydd) on the outskirts of the town. It is that much heralded sport called 'Bog Snorkelling'. For those of you unfamiliar with the activity, the following account is offered on their web site (see Llanwrtyd Well Coming Events, 2007):

> Competitors have to complete two lengths of a 60 yard [50m] trench cut through the peat bog in the quickest time possible, wearing snorkels and flippers (wet suits optional but advisable) but without using any conventional swimming strokes.

One can imagine addicts of baseball, devotees of basketball and aficionados of cricket arise in shared outrage. You cannot 'call that a sport' they surely will protest. Well, 'why ever not?' the bog snorkellers might respond. One common way of settling this matter, or the host of similar conceptual border disputes that are vented frequently in the media (such as the sporting status of darts, ice-dance, pool, river-swimming, synchronised swimming and so on) is by defining what sports essentially are and then applying that definition to the disputed activity. The problem at the heart of the definitional project is almost as old as philosophy itself. Aristotle thought that a definition was a phrase signifying a thing's essence. This common approach allows us to think of a definition then as a kind of conceptual abbreviation. Defining might be thought of as an activity where the complex (or at least many similar) things are analysed into simpler (constitutive) elements. Consider the following simple examples: a bachelor is an unmarried male; a mother is a female parent; a fortnight is fourteen days; a triangle is a plane three-sided object whose internal angles add up to 180 degrees.

Technical terms such as these, possessed of a certain determinacy, present us with a definitional task that seems straightforward. On first inspection at least, other concepts such as 'art', 'democracy' and 'education'[2] seem considerably less promising candidates for definitions. For our present purpose, understanding sport by way of defining it will take us to consider its conceptual cousin 'game' of which Wittgenstein (1953) famously remarked there was no essence. In order to test out the value of each of any definition we might look for tests of inclusion and exclusion. Does the definition allow things other than those properly belonging to the class to be defined or does it fail, in the opposing direction, by ruling out cases which it is agreed should fall in the class? In each of the conceptually simple cases above (bachelor, mother, fortnight, triangle) what is being defined corresponds to the thing falling under the definition. This activity seems reasonable enough, one might think, therefore the application of it to sport should not trouble us too much.

While most adults would have little difficulty in recognising as sports those commercialised activities that appear regularly on the back pages of newspapers or on prime time weekend viewing such as baseball, football or tennis, others might be less clear. Consider the example above: should bog snorkelling be properly classified as a sport? Well, if we looked at what these examples had in common we could attempt to see whether there was anything by way of necessary conditions (conditions that were necessary for the ascription of the term sport properly to the activity in question) which jointly would be sufficient (for the proper ascription). Working through such an example as this might lead us to a position, often attributed to Wittgenstein, and loosely labelled 'anti-essentialism'. Here is what Wittgenstein famously had to say:

> Consider for example the proceedings that we call "games." I mean
> board-games, card-games, ball-games, Olympic games, and so on. What

is common to them all?-Don't say: 'There must be something common or they would not be called "games"' – but look and see whether there is anything common to all. – For if you look at them you will not see something that is common to all, but similarities, relationships and a whole series of them at that. To repeat: don't think, but look! . . .

And the result of this examination is: we see a complicated network of similarities overlapping and criss-crossing: sometimes overall similarities, sometimes similarities of detail.

(Wittgenstein, 1967: §66–7)

The idea of recognising family resemblances rather than attempting forlornly to locate a conceptual essence is often accorded great status within the thought of the later Wittgenstein. In contrast to the picture theory of meaning which he advocated in the *Tractatus Logico Philosophicus*, where words supposedly stood for some *thing* in external reality, Wittgenstein begins to develop a more subtle and complex appreciation for the complexity of the relations between language, thought and the world. The earlier picture theory of meaning was based upon the idea that the sum world was the sum of all facts that could be captured in propositions. Facts represented the world and did so in a pictorial way. Coming to understand these propositions, how words captured the world, meant that philosophers were required to grasp the meaning of words by analysing what was essential to them. The idea of generality and diversity in language is brought about in his posthumously collected lectures *Philosophical Investigations* by several variations of the family metaphor such as 'family of meaning' (1953: §77), 'family of structures' (§108), 'family of cases' (§168) and 'family of language games' (§179), and most famously 'family resemblances' (McFee, 2003a). What lay behind the deployment of the familial metaphor was Wittgenstein's foil against those who craved such generality in meaning. This notion, after Bambrough (1968: 189), is commonly illustrated in the following manner where numbers 1–6 are the names of certain games and the letters beneath them are their observable features or characteristics:

1	2	3	4	5	6
abcde	bcdef	cdefg	defgh	efghi	fghij

It can be seen from this representation of the family resemblance idea that there is a very strong set of resemblances between one grouping and the next (i.e. between 1 and 2, 2 and 3 and so forth) but that there is no single common element that holds all groups together. So Wittgenstein tells us to consider things we call games that are as diverse as chess, football, patience, the Olympic Games and children's games. Contra the idea set out in the *Tractatus Logico Philosophicus* Wittgenstein does not accept that a definition can be given for the essence of language. Rather, the metaphor shows us that of words in general, and 'games' in particular, 'these phenomena have no one thing in common which makes us use the same word for all, – but they are related to one another in many different ways' (1953: §65). Wittgenstein uses the analogy that the concept of 'games' is held together by the similarities that hold between members of a family; build, features, colour of eyes, gait, temperament and the like. One member of the family may share the same colour eyes as his brother, yet have the build of his father, the gait of his mother and so forth. Wittgenstein offers, perhaps, a better analogy by asking us to consider a thread; the thread is held together not by a single fibre that runs the entire length, but by the criss-crossing, overlapping and inter-twining of many fibres.

Many critics have, however, latched on to what appears to be a throw-away line of Wittgenstein in §66: 'don't think, but look!' For if we do not think how are we to know what to look at, where to look for it, and how do we recognise whatever it is when we see it? Or, as Baker and Hacker put it most philosophers criticising Wittgenstein on this point have found his answers 'either non existent or inadequate' (Baker and Hacker, 1980: 332 cited in McFee, 2003a: 21).

This simple line of criticism belies a more fundamental objection to the idea of family resemblances as a family of meanings for a given concept. If this artificial construction of Wittgenstein's suggestion is followed through one could conceivably end up with the following:

7	8	9	10	11	12
ghijk	hijkl	ijklm	jklmn	klmno	lmnop

While it is clear that 7 is closely related to 8 and, likewise, 8 to 9, it is not immediately apparent what resemblances 1 has in common with 9, 10, 11 or 12? It can be seen that 1, 2, 3, 4, 5 and 6 are clearly related to each other. But what similarities have these in common with 9 other than empirical traits shared with other groups that might ordinarily be considered quite disparate? Kovesi puts the point less abstractly:

> The similarities are connected like threads in a rope. The family resemblances between games illustrate this picture well. But I do not see any foundation for a claim that we call both football and chess games because football is played with a ball, and so is tennis, while tennis is played by two people, and so is chess.
>
> (Kovesi, 1972: 22)

One might anticipate the following response: 'It is only when we know that these individuals *are* members of a family that we test them to see if they have empirical similarities.' On this reading the resemblances themselves do not make them members of the family. Rather it should be said that they *are* members of the family *and* they have resemblances. The 'family resemblances' idea is simply an analogy to prove that there is no single essence or essential characteristic within a given concept.

Within the philosophy of sport literature, a celebrated attempt to define sports by way of a definition of games was given by Bernard Suits.[3] Suits argued for a definition of game that met the demands of inclusivity and exclusivity without remainder. He conceived of his thesis as a direct response to Wittgenstein's challenge to 'look and see' and a refutation of his anti-essentialist line of thinking. It was argued by Suits that all sports were a type of game. His account was not circular for he also argued that there were certain games that were not sports. This looks like a strong contender to establish whether, for our purposes, bog snorkelling should indeed be classified a sport. The elements of his definition act as individually necessary and jointly sufficient conditions of the concept 'sport'. This is the very thing that Wittgenstein had denied. That is to say, that for any X to count as a sport it must contain all necessary elements and that, moreover, any activity that contained them was sufficient to be classified a sport.

Suits argued that for an activity to be called a game it must have (1) a *pre-lusory goal* (that is to say a goal specified prior to the contest such as scoring more goals, jumping the furthest, and so on); (2) a set of *means* that limited the ways in which the goal could be legitimately achieved; (3) *rules* that define the activity and specify permissible and impermissible means in the achievement of the pre-lusory goal; and (4) a disposition that the game player must adopt in their attempt to achieve the pre-lusory goal.

This disposition to achieve the pre-lusory goal (as opposed to any further goals the sportsperson may individually hold) is called the 'lusory attitude': 'the knowing acceptance of constitutive rules just so the activity made possible by such rules can occur' (Suits, 1998). Anyone failing to hold such a disposition is simply not *playing* sport even where they share the same field, or court, or track with others so engaged. In a wonderfully pithy summary Suits (1978) holds: 'Playing a game is the voluntary attempt to overcome unnecessary obstacles.' Now all this seems apposite for sports. It seems, if we take paradigmatic examples such as football or hockey they certainly fit the bill.

How are we to know that the definition offered is authoritative in the settling of the conceptual dispute? One difficulty with the idea, that is to say the whole enterprise, is to consider the idea of conceptual revision. Suits, like so many others in different contexts, offers an analysis of the concept in a way that is ahistorical. It is as if the concept has been crystallised in time by the analysis. One way of challenging the thesis, then, will be to look back at examples of activities we might recognise as games but that do not fit the features of the activity thus defined.

No one, I think, would call an activity a game were it not rule-governed. And games typically have a purpose or a goal that is specified in the game. And not any means could constitute a legitimate way of achieving the ends of the activity lest we have mayhem. And games may be manic, but not mayhem. Could we not, it might be said, imagine players making up rules as they go along, and deciding on the precise goal and its manner of achievement as they went along their merry way? It is unlikely to be sure, but it is not logically impossible. Consider now a much stronger objection. Suits argues that the lusory attitude is a necessary condition for a game. That is to say, for any X to be a game it must be played and played in a certain way. Contrast this lusory attitude with an account from (not a philosopher but a classicist) David Young who criticises Harris's account of Ancient Greek athletics:

> The glaring difference between Harris' ideal amateur sport and Greek athletics lies in the seriousness of the latter. They were not a diversion or recreation. They were not play. The Greek verb *paizen*, "to play" in Greek comes from the word *pais*, "child." Etymologically, at least, "to play" means to act like a child and in a sportive way. The Greeks sometimes apply the verb to playing music, to dancing and playing games (such as board games or drinking games) to playing ball, to jesting and to what we call mere "horseplay." Yet I know of no text that uses the verb *paizen*, "play", for athletic contests. They were not associated with childhood behaviour. [. . .] a boy athlete was acting like a man, not the other way around. Neither game nor play, Greek athletics were a serious business and an organized adult activity.
>
> (Young, 1984: 171–2)

Here then, we have at least a plausible candidate for an exception to what should be an exceptionless class: that is after all the point of developing necessary and sufficient conditions. Of course, one can just say if these activities were not play-like then they cannot have been games. But to stipulate such a meaning is itself like offering a prescriptive definition. Why should one not offer a definition that bore no reference to the motivations of the gamewrights? Analysis is supposed to offer more than mere prescriptive definitions. Might it not be the case that modern sports, in the Western world at least (for I have said nothing of similar activities whether in antiquity or the present[4]), have come to embrace the lusory attitude? Young (1984) is highly critical of the romantic writings of De Coubertin that try to link the aristocratic amateur sensibility of playing the game for its own sake to a constructed tradition that harked back to Ancient Greece.

Well, *if* this is the case then we have to acknowledge not some timeless essence but a meaning that is shared *and* revised over time. I will develop this idea below. Another move might be to say that Greek athletics is not the same as sports. But that would beg another argument: what kinds of activities are sports?

Suits' definition of 'sports'

Suits' original argument has it that all sports are games but that they are games of a particular kind. He argues that in addition to being games, there are four necessary conditions for sports that, taken together, are sufficient:

1   That the game be a game of skill;
2   That the skill be physical;
3   That the game have a wide following;
4   That the following achieve a wide level of stability.

The first condition rules out games that are entirely based on, say, luck or chance such as lotteries. By holding that the skill is physical Suits attempts to rule out card games or board games such as chess. It is interesting to note, however that in Cuba, for example, chess is considered a sport. So that necessary condition appears not to hold or else the relevant Cuban institutions are ill-conceived in designating it thus. For the moment let us set this aside for it is true of certainly most sports that we think of them as requiring and cultivating physical skills. How does our example of bog snorkelling fare? Let us say that bog snorkelling is a game. And it certainly fits the condition of being physical. Does it further satisfy these conditions in order for it to fall under the definition, or within the class of sports?

Suits' final two necessary conditions have a vagueness about them which is not apparent in the first two. It is true that one could argue for chess players the skills involved do entail moving the pieces around the board according to its constitutive rules but one can easily imagine a disabled chess player who was physically unable to so move the pieces and had someone else to move them without this negating the general claim. One can imagine a tightening up of this condition to the effect of specifying the relation of physical skill to the achievement of the pre-lusory goal where the skill of the player was internally related to the achievement. Yet here we can imagine that the champion bog snorkeller will have to have efficient techniques (though not those recognised in swimming) to transport themselves efficiently up the bog. What does it mean to say that activities without a wide following are not sports, or that those without a wide level of stability cannot so be classified?

Suits makes it clear that what he is ruling out are mere fads. But what is logically improper about imagining a sport that does not persist substantially over time? There is considerable dispute now over what was once called 'blood sports' or 'field sports' or 'country sports' such as fox hunting or badger baiting or cock fighting. And then of course there is bull fighting. Now of the former there is considerable dispute as to whether these activities should be called sports by some who feel that the designation sport somehow legitimates otherwise barbarous activities. Fox hunting has now been made illegal in the UK: does that mean it is not a sport?; can sport be only legally permissible activities? And this is to say nothing of boxing. What about the idea that bull fighting, being confined to the Iberian cultures, has an insufficiently wide following to enable it to be classified a sport? One can imagine bog snorkelling enthusiasts arguing that the rules of the activity have been laid down for a given number of years. Its World Championships include over one hundred participants from places as far flung from Great Britain as Australia and Russia. Its spectators attend in significant numbers and it is sponsored commercially.[5] All these simple criticisms seem legitimate objections to the idea of a once-and-for-all crystallising of the essence of sport in any way, not merely the manner in which Suits has.

What is to be gained then from a definition of sport which apparently captures its transhistorical essence? Very little it seems to me.

Sport, language and conceptual revision

So, what is this thing called sport? Part of this answer must be historically specific; part not. Let us be clear that, consistent with the above, in offering an account of sport for the purposes of this book, I am not setting out a timeless account, an ahistorical core or essence. What is formal to my account, as any other, is always open to revision. And to reconfirm, part of this openness is that the practitioners themselves will reflexively conceive and re-conceive the particularities of sports in the light of new circumstances. A cursory etymological examination shows how this is so. In English the word sport appears in the fifth century while many languages have no word for 'sport' and many languages simply used slightly modified versions of the English word 'sport' (Sansone, 1988): *spòrs* (Gaelic); *supōtsu* (Japanese); *spor* (Turkish). The archaic English word disport which in turn comes from the Old French *desport* (Sansone, 1988).

If Greek athletics were considered deadly serious attempts to attract glory to one's name and honour to oneself and family, it seems clear that the Anglo-French usage is linked to something less serious and more diversionary or recreational. This is attested to in various places from the King James's translation of the Bible (Proverbs, 10.23: 'It is as sport to a fool to do mischief' and in Judges, 16.25: 'And it came to pass, when their hearts were merry, that they said, Call for Samson out of the prison house; and he made them sport; and they set him between the pillars') (cited in Sansone, 1988: 4). Does this mean that we have different concepts in operation? I think not. It is more simply the case that activities we can recognise as sports have a long and varied history though the specific designation is less antique. It is also widely suggested that in its current form sport refers to a family of activities that is closely associated with the industrial revolution (Eichberg, 1990; Guttman, 1978; Holt, 1989; Mangan, 1986).

One way of distinguishing these activities is to refer to them as 'modern sports'. While this does help to clarify the genesis of certain activities codified largely in seventeenth- and eighteenth-century Britain (think of Association Football (that is, soccer), field hockey, rugby, tennis and so on), there are sufficient similarities with wrestling contests in Ancient Greece, or in the footraces of the Apache Indians, or even in Mayan ball games for us to recognise their family resemblances and talk about them in the same breath. We may, moreover, see their codification as a particularly important conceptual revision. Or, to take a more local example, consider Connolly's discussion of the formation of a concept of foul in basketball:

> Suppose a friendly group of Americans compete together each week in a game something like our game of basketball. The rules governing the game differ from ours in one significant respect: it is permissible for the offense to block, tackle or push members of the defense while trying to score a basket, and the defense can reply in kind. In fact, short of maiming or injuring opposing players, 'anything goes' in this game of basketball. . . .
>
> Suppose, now, a British gentleman of high character and charismatic personality, invited to join the weekly game, begins to describe as "foul play" various practices of holding, hacking, bumping and pushing opposing players. Overwhelmed by his reasonableness and character – he himself never indulges in "foul play" – the American players gradually begin to reciprocate. They incorporate into their play the precept, "Try to avoid, bumping, pushing . . . opposing players" and they characterize a player as indulging in "foul play" when he stoops to such conduct.
>
> The term "foul play" gradually comes to be a means of describing a certain open-ended range of behavior within the game *and* an expression of reproach in the light of that description. Gradually the concept is refined and sharpened through the accumulation of shared experience.
>
> (Connolly, 1993: 181–2)

What Connolly describes in his artificial example is meant to show how conduct in politics is altered by the reflexive understandings of the political actors themselves. And so it is with sports. Conceptual revisions must be understood historically too. But there must be a limit to the range of revisions possible for the social activity to retain its referent: sport.

We could recognise a given activity to be a sport without this condition while we could not recognise as a sport an activity that enshrined a problem, in a rule-governed manner that was in some way inefficient and artificial and to be pursued by inefficient means. And this understanding or self-understanding of the activity so conceived represents a shift from traditional folk activities to which the label sports might be withheld (see Eichberg, 1990). Of course, in light of the example above, it is possible that this trend towards codification, seriousness of intent within a playful structure, and morally limited means of securing the goal, might be reversed. After all, it was not merely some lofty goal of British aristocrats that wrought the change to a more codified and ethical pursuit of excellence but the needs of the gambling economy for relatively fair contests whose outcomes might be reasonably guessed upon and where chance or "foul play" ought not to be too influential in the determination of the outcome.

It seems moreover that Morgan (1994), following Suits (1978), may best have captured this notion of accepting morally limited means by the term 'gratuitous logic'. This term felicitously brings out not merely the artificiality of sporting actions, their non-necessity we might say, and the instrumental inefficiency that is characteristic of them too. It extends beyond this to the normative dimension of sports and sporting acts. That this is historically specific need not be denied. It is clear that such a notion is woven into certain prevailing morals of Victorian Britain (harking back *mistakenly* to an aristocratic Greece[6]) where it was canonized in one form or another as 'muscular Christianity'. But to move much further in that direction would not be to cash out what is minimally central to the concept but to give a full-blown account of sport and that is not my aim here.

Nevertheless, the notion of gratuitous logic is not sufficient for the account of sport I want to deploy as the context for the ethical discussion that follows. I want to add three further specifications; first the nature of the gratuitous act must involve physicality centrally in the achievement of the gratuitous act. Think of the ways in which we admire the touch of the golfer as they weight their stroke to coincide with the topography of the putting green surface; the strength of the gymnast as they move gracefully in and out of the crucifix position on the rings; the subtlety of the badminton player who alters their wrist to contact the shuttlecock earlier in order to deceive their opponent with a drop shot instead of a high clear to the back court that was feinted; and so on. Second, there is a sense in which the act is ritualistic (this is of course not new, several authors have talked about non-necessitated action) but I think that this feature in some sense belies the gratuitous logic. This is part of Sansone's (1988) slightly incredible but original thesis that sport is the ritual sacrifice of energy. For while we may trace back the proto-movement vocabulary in running, jumping, throwing and so on to paleolithic hunters, and while their history is importantly tied to functional activities such as hunting, we need some explanation as to why (when rendered unnecessary to survival) these forms became celebrated in agonal contexts. It is not accidental that the ancient Greek word 'agon' meaning contest or struggle is the etymological root of agony and that sports are often called agonistic after Caillois (1955).

In contests we struggle variously to overcome nature, or others, and always the self, in myriad ways. And this is my third point: the gratuitous acts are in some way agonal in a socially structured way. I do not mean this in the sense that sports are necessarily competitive; that competition is *the* defining element of sport. What I mean, rather, is that sports engage their participants in a conversation with the past and the present whereby they strive towards standards, both technical and ethical, of past, current and future. This requires acknowledgement of the social and historical dimensions of their logic that is irreducible. I shall attempt to develop this notion in Chapter 3 but for the moment I wish merely to acknowledge that the forms of movement canonised in sports are part of a vocabulary that were born of very different motives where efficiency and necessity drove the honing of embodied capacities such as speed, strength and stamina, along with associated skills and strategic thinking (and maybe even proto-virtues such as bravery or daring).

Conclusion

I have tried in this chapter to sketch an account of sport that is sufficiently open but also sufficiently familiar with the family of activities that go by that name in schools and stadia, as well as in the media reporting of such. For my purposes, what typically allows us to recognise a sport is the arrangement of many of the following features: sports are activities characterised by a gratuitous logic involving, centrally, physical skills, and agonal qualities to which both technical and ethical standards pertain that are ritually derived. And I shall develop this account further, emphasising a particular account of the virtue-ethical nature of sports, in Chapter 4. For now I am content to note that the debates over whether certain characteristics are necessary and sufficient, or whether certain features are ineliminably bound to the concept itself or the social and economic climate are themselves part of a broader terrain of contested philosophies of sport. While there is no original exemplar of sport, we can see its genesis in play, historically developed into the variety of forms that the activity can take and for which no final or determinate shape can ever be captured once and for all in a definition; there is a certain openness to the concept that precludes such finality. Nonetheless, the account of conceptual characteristics sketched above resists its characterisation as either relativistic or essentialist and provides sufficient grounding of the concept of sport for me to embark on an ethical exploration of its nature and significance.

2   Sports, persons and sportspersonship

As a matter of grammar, the terms 'sportsman' and 'sportswoman' are genus of the species 'sportsperson'. As a matter of linguistic politics, 'sportsperson' is the gender neutral term to designate anyone who plays sport, despite the tendency of coaches and journalists alike in using the grammatically correct masculine designation for the collective noun. The term 'sportsperson' is, I suggest, deceptively simple. We use it all too unproblematically. Sports sociologists often peddle talk of 'sporting bodies' and sports psychologists often refer to 'sporting minds'. At one level it is neither difficult to understand nor complain about their language. On another this body–mind bifurcation, despite its long and reputable history in Western philosophy, is deeply regrettable. It clearly reduces the complex wholes that are persons into separable elements and does this in such a fashion, as Marx noted so well, of leaving minds to dominate dumb muscle.

I want in this chapter to uncover some of that undesirable philosophical history and refocus our attention from *sports*persons to sports*persons*. I do not wish to commit the fallacy of composition by simply bringing together the meanings of the two separable terms and then adding them to get to a composite meaning. Nevertheless, coming to an appreciation of a richer sense of the term 'sportsperson' requires an analysis of the complex concept of personhood and its ethical significance, not least of all for sport.

To do that I shall attempt to articulate the importance of persons as animals of a particular kind: with the capacity to interpret themselves and what matters to them, in part, out of their emotional life. This will set the ground of much of the later chapters that deal with specific virtues and their emotional content.

Persons as self-interpreting animals

Before diving deep into treacherous metaphysical waters, where sportsmen and women have often metaphorically drowned, I offer the following caveat. Given that this is not a project solely in philosophical anthropology there will be no substantive discussion concerning the possibility and/or nature of non-human persons. It may well be the case that aliens, machines and monkeys may come to be regarded as persons, but these issues do not affect, in any substantive way, the concern of this book.[1] Though the idea of men and women competing with machines is not a new one it is not one I wish to delve into here though I will have something to say of the promises and perils of biotechnology in sport in the final chapter.[2] Second, it should be noted that the substantive account I am going to develop is clearly not value neutral. The idea that such important questions about person could generate entirely uncommitted answers is something of a non-starter.

The account of personhood developed here draws initially upon parts of Charles Taylor's work in philosophical anthropology.[3] After a critical and selective appraisal of his work on personhood an account will be developed towards an inherently social and ethical account of sports and sportspersons enabled to live full and valuable lives in and through sports thus conceived.

Taylor argued that a person's self-interpretations and the experience of them are partly constitutive of the sorts of beings that persons are. Briefly put, this means that our self-understanding cannot be considered as an epiphenomenon. Instead this capacity is placed at the heart of our conception of what it is to be a person. His argument can be summarised in five propositions:

1   some of our emotions involve import-ascriptions;
2   some of these imports are subject-referring;
3   that our subject-referring feelings are the basis of our understanding of what it is to be human;
4   that those feelings are constituted by the articulations we come to accept of them; and
5   that these articulations, which we can think of as interpretations require language.[4]

It is necessary to examine each of these claims in some detail.

First, it is commonly held that the feelings, emotions and desires that are experienced are essentially related to certain objects. When someone is frightened, they are frightened of some thing, or some person or situation, that scares them; they experience shame when they are confronted by a situation that makes explicit the breaking of a confidence, and so on. But this characterisation of our experiences becomes difficult in the face of examples where an experience is not related to a specific object. It is not that there is *no* object in respect of which persons are, for example, anxious, it is rather that their unfocused anxiety is in relation to something that they cannot articulate fully. That is to say, there is a felt absence of an object; a gap where something ought to be. Furthermore, this inability to focus is part of the experience of the situation. The person must, of course, have some apprehension of threat or possible impending harm, it is just that they cannot articulate what it is in respect of. In consequence, then, one speaks more accurately of desires, motivations and feelings involving a sense of our situation rather than in terms of an essential relation to an object.

When, for example, someone says they are disgraced, elated, ashamed or humiliated they are clearly moved in certain ways. These adjectives describe what Taylor calls an 'import'. To make an import ascription is to say that in some way a thing can be relevant, i.e. of importance, to the desires, aspirations, feelings or purposes of a human being. Put succinctly, an import ascription is a property of some thing or situation that is a matter of non-indifference to a given person. In identifying this relevance or import, one depicts what it is in that situation that gives the grounds for those feelings, desires or motivations. It is this that enables us to recognise an emotion as one of shame, or fear, or pride. In such situations it is not the case that one is simply stating (in other terms) that a given feeling is experienced in a certain situation; it is much stronger than that. It is the point of our experiencing *that* feeling in *this* situation. The idea of an import is that there are certain standards within our sense of a given situation that relate to the feeling in a manner that constitutes it. That is to say, the emotion is internally related to the situation. This position has elsewhere been called a 'judgmental' view of emotion (Solomon, 1976). To experience an emotion is in part to have made a judgement about ourselves and the world.

Of course, one could imagine situations where the motivation for action could be conceived of in an experience-independent way. One can think of reflex actions; shuddering at someone scratching a blackboard or pulling away from a hot iron. The important point is, however, that where the situation calls for an import ascription it cannot be done without reference to the experiencing subject. Second, one might ask who, or what, could interpret the significance and sophistication of these import ascriptions? It appears that such imports could only be meaningful to a being who could be the subject of such (emotional) meanings, since they could only be explicated by and to such beings. Terms such as 'dignity' or 'shame' only have sense in a world in which there are beings who can experience its import. But there is a categorical difference between, for example, concepts such as 'shame' and 'pain'. The feeling of being ashamed, of doing something that failed to live up to the standard of the coach, or a parent or community, could be experienced by a being who could make sense of it.[5] By contrast, experiencing pain may go on independently of the awareness of its potential import. This is not to say that experiencing fear or pain is necessarily pre-linguistic – we need to teach infants not to put their hands in the fire after all. When we try to get to the ethical and emotional significance of more sophisticated notions such as guilt or shame and suffering (as I shall do in Chapters 8, 9 and 10) this sort of explanation is found wanting. Taylor refers to those properties whereby the import must in part refer to an experiencing subject as 'subject-referring'. This then explains claims (1) and (2) of the argument; some imports are experience dependent and subject referring.

The third stage of the argument focuses on the idea that by exploring our subject-referring emotions, our sense of shame, dignity, joy, remorse and the like, an insight into the life of such a subject qua person may be gained. Some of our seemingly immediate desires and feelings are 'partially constituted by a skein of subject-referring imports' (C. Taylor, 1985a: 60) that offer potential insights into our lives as subjects; what is of value, what matters to us. Our awareness of these things is central to us as reflexive animals. This point is pregnant with possibilities for virtue ethics and highlights the kind of critical reflection for sportspersons that the label "dumb jock" denies. I spend considerable time and attention in Part II of the book attempting to articulate the contents of this critical reflection in the virtues and vices of sports and related practices such as coaching and sports medicine.

Fourth, the issue of imports and their attribution is closely associated to arguments concerning the nature of feeling and reason.[6] Taylor argues that there is no such thing as brute data where feelings are concerned for they are always mediated by our consciousness. And the interpretation is part of the feeling (C. Taylor, 1985a: 60):

> [T]he feeling is what it is in virtue of the sense of the situation it incorporates. But a given sense may presuppose a certain level of articulacy, that the subject understand certain terms or distinctions. For example, a feeling cannot be one of remorse unless there is a sense of having done wrong. Some understanding of right/wrong is built into remorse to its attributing the import that it does.

Here one can say that the negative normativity is conceptually central of the notion of remorse. It is not as if one experiences X or Y feelings upon which is layered later the judgement that one had done wrong. If someone did not understand that they had done something wrong how could they be said (or indeed expected) to be remorseful? Or, put another way, if they failed to grasp that a subject must be a wrong-doer prior to feeling remorse it could be said that they have failed to understand what the concept 'remorse' meant and would be unable to attribute it to other cases. In short, they would be unable to follow the rule.

Feelings, therefore, incorporate an articulation of a given situation and, as has been argued, may sometimes be incomplete. One is thus enabled to attach import to them; if they were inarticulable this would not be possible.[7] These feelings attribute imports that open up the domain of what it is to be a person. The imports give a form to what matters to creatures such as ourselves. In offering a characterisation of our feelings and desires, therefore, questions are raised concerning adequacy, appropriateness, completeness and distortion: 'whether we have properly explicated what the feeling gives us a sense of' (C. Taylor, 1985a: 64).

Where subject-referring imports are concerned the articulation of these emotions must be self-validating. This is the fourth claim: feelings are bound up with the process of articulation. This is of course precisely the problematic junction of mind and matter and its relationship is notoriously difficult to articulate. What has been typical of Western thought however is a division of labour where rationality is assigned to an executive role over the body – here in the form of felt emotions. But to set out feeling and reason in this fashion is highly questionable, even if the idea does have a long and respectable history. Setting them out in the fashion of employer/employed is, as Midgley points out, hopelessly crude.[8]

Finally, the idea of articulation brings with it questions concerning the role of language. Taylor's strong claim is that our emotions open us up to the possibility of the good life; the ability to make discriminations, entertain desires and pursue goals. These fine discriminations among our mental states are only made possible because they can be articulated through language. These discriminations are referred to as 'strong evaluations' (C. Taylor, 1985a: 16).[9] Unlike weak evaluations, which merely consider whether some action will be a successful means to some desired end state, strong evaluation is of a different character. Some acts are considered to be good or bad, desirable or undesirable, and articulate it accordingly as praiseworthy or blameworthy. These evaluations consider the motivations for the action, which are laudable or repugnant. That is to say, qualitative discriminations are made among motivations, and they arise, so to speak, out of our feelings, emotions and aspirations. To make a strong evaluation is to render articulate the import to which the feeling relates. Our revulsion at an act of cheating is only possible when we are aware of the import of moral baseness.[10] Taylor summarises:

> This drawing a moral map of the subject is an intrinsic part of [. . .] discerning the good or higher life, or the shape of our aspirations, or the shape of our life as a subject. It involves entering the problematic area of our self-understanding and self-interpretation.
>
> (C. Taylor, 1985a: 68)

These strong evaluations attach to us in a very important sense. Thus, Taylor writes: 'Our identity is therefore defined by certain evaluations which are inseparable from ourselves as agents. Shorn of these we would cease to be ourselves' (C. Taylor, 1985a: 34).

The way in which the good life is related to our self-understanding (and hence the notion of language) can be represented thus; the subject-referring imports that are attributed to persons are shaped by the agent's interpretation of them. This in turn is shaped by the language through which he or she learns to express such ideas. Therefore language shapes these emotions.[11] It needs to be noted that, as was argued above in point (1), it is only subject-referring import attributes that are of concern here. Thus fear, shame, remorse and the like are considered but *not* the feelings that are experienced when, for example, someone runs their fingernails down the blackboard or someone pulling their hand from the hot saucepan. Such pains are language-independent and there is no difficulty imagining non-human agents performing them. However, as agents articulate the import in a situation, the emotions change as they become increasingly aware of themselves and their situation. This, or at least a very close relation of this idea, is sometimes known as the hermeneutical circle: what is understood is inevitably coloured by an agent's preconceptions and those preconceptions are in turn modified by what the agent comes to understand. Persons, therefore, characterise things differently; language transforms their experiences and the way they characterise these experiences. From this there is no turning back.[12] Only a language animal could have a person's emotions and thus entertain strong evaluations that come to frame a vision of the good life and an orientation to it.

In summary, it might be said that human language and linguistically constituted emotions are the prerequisite of qualitative discriminations that constitute any vision of the good life. It is not simply the means by which the question of what constitutes the good life is answered. The attempted definition of what matters to persons, their interpretations, are an ongoing affair that is part of why subjects such as ourselves are called persons:

> The paradox of human emotions is that although only an articulated emotional life is properly human, all our articulations are open to challenge from our inarticulate sense of what is important, that is, we recognize that they ought to be faithful articulations of something of which we have only fragmentary intimations. If one focuses only on the first point, one can believe that human beings are formed arbitrarily by the language they have accepted. If one focuses only on the second, one can think that we ought to be able to isolate scientifically the uninterpreted basis of human emotion that all these languages are about. But neither of these is true. There is no human emotion which is not embodied in an interpretive language; and yet all interpretations can be judged more or less inadequate, more or less distortive. What a given human life is an interpretation of cannot exist uninterpreted; for a human emotion is only what is refracted as in human language.
>
> (C. Taylor, 1985a: 75)

Thus far the idea of subject-referring imports has been discussed and a little has been said about the way in which these come to be shaped by the language one comes to deploy. The notions of emotions, feelings, aspirations and self-understanding were placed at the centre of the account as was the ability to discriminate qualitatively between them. It was also intimated that there was some direct relation between these two ideas and the opening up of a vision of the good life. Strong evaluations are not fleeting acts like deciding to buy this packet of sweets rather than that because one has, at that moment, a taste for sugar rather than bran. Rather, they are closely related to styles of action and, indeed, of life. By strong evaluation persons shape their commitments and thus reinforce ideas about the sort of person they are or the sort of person they wish to become.

Persons, minds and bodies

Central to Taylor's task in articulating his conception of person is to distinguish it from another conception that is inspired by the seventeenth-century, epistemologically grounded notion of the subject derivative of Descartes whose celebrated phrase '*cogito ergo sum*' supposedly captures our essential nature: persons are conscious beings. But consciousness on the Cartesian conception refers only to the capacity to frame representations of things, such as understanding complex cause–effect relationships or forming strategic action over time. According to Taylor this view of persons fails to attend adequately to the nature of agency. If persons are to be characterised by their performances in framing representations of things then this leaves us with the problem of relating the performances of physical objects to consciousness. Taylor's conception of person, in contrast, focuses on the nature of agency. Rather than identifying agents by their performances, what is crucial to personal agency is that things can matter; can possess significance. This means that we can, and of course do, attribute purposes, desires, motivations, preferences and aversions to agents in a strong, original sense. Importantly, it must be noted that the capacity to frame representations is not rejected. It is simply that our notion of consciousness is impoverished if we see it only as the capacity to frame representations. It is for this reason that I find repugnant the seemingly constant references by sports commentators to consistent sports performers via machinistic metaphors. One might ask probing questions as to the role of sports scientists, here, in their aim to continually push forward the frontiers of performance. Hoberman remarks pointedly:

> Sport science does not physically hybridize humans and machines; as of today there is no sportive equivalent to Dr. Frankenstein's monster. Instead sport science treats the human organism as though it were a machine, or as though it ought to be a machine. This technologized human organism comprises of both mind and body, for which there are distinct sets of strategies, in my view is a streamlined and decomplexified image of the human being.
>
> (Hoberman, 1988: 323)

The machine metaphor is inappropriate but it is easily adopted when persons become thought of as simply the centres from which representations are framed and strategic action formed. What is wrong with this picture is the palpable fact that things just do not matter to machines in the strong and original sense in which they do to humans. It is precisely because they do matter to humans that we engage wholeheartedly in such activities (as both spectator and participant) as sports. And it is in this point that our joy and fascination with them reside. Mary Midgley's (1974) remarks are apposite here. In attempting to articulate what is meant by a game (i.e. why we call games 'games') she brings into question one of the chief shibboleths regarding games and their supposed non-seriousness. She points out that when people say things such as 'Relax man, calm down, remember it's only a game' (Midgley, 1974: 237) we need to consider the motives the person has for playing in the first place, for they will be crucial to our understanding of their actions. Now the first point, of course, is that there is no machine analogue possible here. Second, this is the sort of remark that I sometimes make when playing rugby or soccer at the weekend in the seventh team or whatever. I have no great desires to push my playing limits any further than they are currently at and so my motivations may be, one might say, weak. I enjoy the social aspect of meeting with friends, the exposition of (albeit limited) skill, the aerobic and anaerobic workout, the competitive and fair striving for victory and so on. But my allegiance to neither game is total or totalising. I enjoy a whole range of ludic activities and often for similar though differing reasons. If a team-mate says to me 'calm down – it's only a game' when I start to question the referee's parentage the force of his point is palpably clear: 'get a grip', 'take a reality check', 'sort out your priorities' and so on. Imagine saying the same thing to Paula Radcliffe toiling in the Athens heat of the 2004 Olympics marathon as the pre-race favourite broke down at the roadside, outside of medal contention with perhaps her last realistic chance of a Gold medal gone and with world titles and a world record as scant consolation in her eyes.[13] Many British readers will also call to mind the famous photograph of a weeping 'Gazza' (Paul Gascoigne) during the semi-final of the 1990 Football World Cup after he had just been cautioned and *ipso facto* precluded from playing in the final of the competition.[14] Football is his game but the mention of non-seriousness in this context would be bizarre. Whether apocryphal or not, the legendary Liverpool football manager Bill Shankly is alleged to have said: 'Some people talk about football as if it were life or death itself, but it's much more serious than that.' What is typically called the ethos of games (though some philosophers have referred to this as the institution of games[15]) captures the way in which each ought to be played but it also responds to ritualised and historical practices. What is acceptable by way of conduct in rugby or ice hockey is scarcely appropriate in softball or cricket. But we do not even need to cross game types to find this particularity; nowhere near the same level of physical contact and aggression is allowed in soccer in the United States by comparison with Northern Europe. Games thus become important vehicles for certain forms of expression, central among which are emotional.

The sorts of emotions experienced in game playing give us further reason to distance persons from machines and non-human animals. In considering further the idea of agency we find that non-human agents do not have open to them the rich and varied emotional life that human agents who are also persons do. Notions such as praise, blame, shame, dignity, moral goodness and evil have no analogue in the non-human animal world, 'when we consider these human emotions, we can see that the ends which make up a human life are *sui generis*' (C. Taylor, 1985a: 102).

Such emotions as characteristic of humans are, of course, *not* divorced from matters of consciousness (or to use the familiar terminology, reason). Indeed, these emotions are only available to linguistic animals since they require the marking of distinctions either by the formulation of language or some expressive ceremonial that would have higher prerequisite demands than could be fulfilled by non-human agents. The problems of morality, so it seems, can only arise for us through the medium of a language.

By way of summary, then, the first conception of a person bases itself on the power to plan and it is this ability that I have to respect. In contrast, Taylor's preferred conception sees as problematic the notion of agency and human ends. Therefore, agents are centres of significance; beings for whom things matter. This is what enables them to have their point of view on the world. Persons, as opposed to other agents, have qualitatively different concerns. Taylor summarises thus:

> Consciousness is indeed essential to us. But this cannot be understood simply as the power to frame representations, but also what enables us to be open to these human concerns. Our consciousness is somehow constitutive of these matters of significance, and does not just enable us to depict them. This supports a quite different reading of the essentially personal capacities. The essence of evaluation no longer consists in assessment in the light of fixed goals, but also and even more in the sensitivity to certain standards, those involved in peculiarly human goals . . . The centre of gravity thus shifts in our interpretation of the personal capacities. The centre is no longer the power to plan, but rather the openness to matters of certain significance. This is now what is essential to personal agency.
>
> (C. Taylor, 1985a: 104–5)

Finally, in recognising this ability to focus on the significance things can have for us and our ability to apprehend and transform them through language, new areas are opened up for the characterisation of morality above and beyond the path to rights duties and obligations that are often thought to be at the heart of personhood.

Sports, persons and play

It might reasonably be objected at this point that the account offered is only one (albeit large) step in the right direction. What are often thought of as the mindless bodies of sportspersons, or captured in machine metaphors, is wildly wrong. Two particular objections might be made: first, is it true that language plays so dominant a role in the identity of persons seeking to live good lives; and, second, what has happened to that aspect of sports that is both visceral and visible? In emphasising the emotions and their linguistic/judgemental features I seem to have lost sight of the essentially corporeal nature of human persons. Of course it could be said that we feel our emotions and embodiment is a precondition of this: they are not merely cognitive judgements. This much must be conceded. But it is not enough.

One reason why we cannot simply disestablish sports, why they are central to our lives, is that they draw from the wellspring of play and that is not something we can do without. As human persons we are inherently embodied animals. And animals play. Indeed, as Huizinga (1970) noted, play is older than culture itself.

More than that, Huizinga tells us that play adorns culture. A considerable body of opinion in anthropology is inclined to support his conjecture. Sutton-Smith (1974/1981) notes the following cross-cultural generalizations. First, play and games playing are functionally related to culture and are not trivial, essential or random. This generalization provides support for the positions of both proponents and sceptics of play. Sceptics of play may draw attention to the fact that two major studies support the idea that play is not always and everywhere to be found in abundance in the early years of childhood. Sutton-Smith cites the work of Whiting (1963) in agrarian cultures in Kenya and Feitelson[16] in carpet-weaving cultures in the Middle East, which suggests that where children are vital links in a fragile economic framework there will be little scope for play. The important feature, however, is not necessarily the pre-industrial nature of the society (there are extensive records of Aboriginal play) but the direct and immediate economic necessities of the situation that require children to be initiated into adult, work-like activities. Supporters of play, on the other hand, will point to the fact that forms of play are neither trivial nor randomly occurring in cultures. The differences of the structure of play relative to its function within that culture is interesting too. It is suggested that Aboriginal play involves exploration and testing that would immediately be valuable in a functional sense to inhabitants of that culture, whereas in symbolic and achievement-oriented cultures most play involves make-believe and contest. Second, Sutton-Smith notes that persons in more complex cultures (howsoever defined) not only play more complex games but also play a greater variety of them. A point very much like this is capture in Rawls "Aristotelian Principle":

> [O]ther things equal, human beings enjoy the exercise of their realized capacities (their innate or trained abilities), and this enjoyment increases the more the capacity is realized, or the greater its complexity. The intuitive idea here is that human beings take more pleasure in doing something the more they become proficient at it, and of two activities they do equally well, they prefer the one calling on larger and more intricate and subtle discriminations.
>
> (Rawls, 1972: 435)

This point bears directly on the appreciation of Western sports, which form the bulk of my examples in this book. And it follows directly from the idea of a gratuitous logic that we entertain in sports so that the challenge they offer us is neither too simple nor too difficult. Nor should it be too open to chance or luck, but tied closely to merit and thereby encapsulating the idea of responsibility.

Third, and closely related to the above, there are structural relationships between games playing and patterns of association within a culture. Strategy is linked with obedience, training and the complexity of the social systems; chance is linked with responsibility, divination, nomadic habits and economic uncertainty; physical skill is linked with the tropics and hunting; central person games are linked with independence, training and marriage. What these generalizations alert us to is the hazardous enterprise of conceptualizing play in a manner that is insensitive to rich contextual factors.

The forms that sports take bear relationality to our particular animal nature, which is tied to some basic biological facts as well as the anthropological ones noted above. It is tied to the basic motor actions: running, throwing, jumping, gliding, catching, striking and so on. Although sports give form to play, they are dependent on it. And these forms are themselves dependent on our typically bi-pedal nature, forward looking eyes, sideways ears, developed central nervous system and so much more.[17] All these valuable remarks about the ubiquity of play remind us that our nature is as rational animals. When we remember this we can avoid the lopsided evaluation and exaltation of rationality.

Is there still, however, a rationalist predilection in the concept of strong evaluation? The weak and strong evaluators are set out thus: weak evaluators can only reason between means to ends: which is the most efficient, the quickest, and the most productive. It is this capacity that is often called technical or instrumental rationality or means–ends reasoning according to the discipline in which the form of thought is being presented. By contrast, strong evaluation entails the contrasting of worth among our chosen means and ends: actions, choices, habits, predilections and values. The contrast is an important and a seductive one. And Taylor gives a rich account of how we come to better understand ourselves and our place in the world both by emotion and reason that are well ordered. But a nagging doubt remains: need this capacity be so strongly linked to articulacy?

Sports journalists often mock the "dumb jock" who apparently fails to account for the excellence of their performances; the well-timed run for home by the middle distance runner; the perceptive interception of the handball player; the fake pass by the quarterback; the deft flick of the striker who lifts the ball or puck over the advancing goalkeeper. They exhibit in their action performances to be marvelled at yet seem incapable of articulating the 'why' of the action in the post-contest interview. Now this may not trouble so many philosophers beyond the sphere of sport, but in ethics can we cauterise morality from the inarticulate – those who cannot specify the 'why' of their actions of benevolence, or courage, or indeed love? This leads Flanagan (1991), among others, to question the role of articulation as basis of the distinction between strong and weak evaluation and hence of non-persons. It seems to render problematic the knowing of the body that phenomenologists have often talked of: the non-linguistic acquaintance with things and persons that seems important to us. On Taylor's account, the concept of personhood seems to be loaded with a weight it cannot bear.

We can begin to explore this intuitive response in relation to Frankfurt's (1988) work on personhood and the structure of the will. Taylor follows Frankfurt's lead by developing the distinction between first and second order desires. Frankfurt notes that we not only desire certain things (let's say a beer) but we can also have desires of a second order that relate to the first (let's say the desire not to give into my desire and instead get on with some writing). So the distinction is in the hierarchy of desires, where the latter have an executive function over the former. Imagine the following sporting scenario. Anyone who has played basketball, or football, or hockey has engaged in what physiologists characterise as a multiple sprint activity. And those with the experience of these activities will know the dreaded devil lactic acid. This is the necessary by-product of anaerobiosis. In lay language, this means the energy system(s) that deliver(s) quick bursts of energy of approximately 40–50 seconds. The first 10 seconds or so are delivered by the breakdown of phosphocreatine, which is limited in supply but which, luckily, has no nasty side effects. One simply runs out of energy stores that can contribute to short duration intense activity. The demand of energy may not abate though and the body draws unconsciously upon stores of glycogen (from carbohydrates), which produces lactic acid that inhibits muscular contraction and can range from the mildly irritating to the excruciating. So the first few sprints – with a little recovery time – go well but as we increase frequency, duration, repetition, our legs feel like they are wading through treacle, our calf muscles turn into knotted sinews, the legs and lungs feel like they will burst, the sickening dryness at the back of the throat reaches the front and (to anyone who has done multiple 400m training), wretching soon follows.

It is easy to think of this intense physical performance as merely that: 'physical' or worse 'mindless'. Yet short of hypnotic training, this is a grossly inadequate description. Each step of the way is mindful even though we need not think of the reflection in action as intellectual. Consider an attenuated catalogue of judgements that inform my emotionally laden experiences as I run: how quick should I go in the first repetitions?; do I burst into or ease into it?; can I keep up with my superior running partner?; will I try to establish my preferred tempo in the first set?; will I save myself for the latter?; how full is my foot plant?; am I running too much on the outside of my feet and reducing power output?; am I relaxed in my neck and shoulders and allowing for the smooth transition of power from the arms and torso?; is my stride shortening as the lactic acid bites into my thighs?; will I stick to the schedule and do my full sets of ten repetitions or will I steer clear of the final repetition like a coward? If anyone thinks of the performance of the training schedule as mindless or machinistic they are clearly mistaken. Yet the catalogue of interior dialogue I have included is multi-faceted and heterogeneous.

Applying Frankfurt's analysis one can readily find oneself questioning one's commitment to the training plan. Sure I had the first order desire to complete the $3 \times 3 \times 400$m session but can I really face the last set? My legs feel like they will knot up in cramp and my lungs feel like they are outside of my body.[18] Sooner rather than later the second order desire to give up early overtakes the first order desire to complete the session and supplants itself with a desire not to have the desire to complete it (which itself driven by guilt may be overtaken by a third order and so on) until such time as I act to end the series. This is all straightforward enough. But does the account of weak evaluation exhaust the description?

Taylor's account analogously distinguishes between levels of evaluation. Both may decry the moral status of the mere wanton: the one who cannot regulate their desires but must give into them or bow to their superior weight over an inferior or diminished will. On Taylor's account, the weak evaluator is the one who can only come to consider the technical merits of different courses of action, from the person proper: one capable of determining between the ignoble and the noble; the admirable and the contemptible; the fat ego from the generous soul. Of my thin catalogue of some phenomenological aspects of 400m training, only once have I asked the kind of question that looks like contrastive, strong, evaluation. How will I conceive of myself if I give up? Ought I interpret my actions as cowardice or prudence? How will I understand the emotional flurry inside my suffering body and soul? Recognition of this categorical distinction certainly seems to take us into a conceptual terrain beyond Frankfurt's framework.

To see whether the distinction holds up in relation to difficult cases, consider another example. Elite sport is often said to be young man's/woman's game. This is a fact saturated with ethical import with respect to the vulnerability of those with less developed modes of self-critique and reflection. As a top level swimmer, teenagers are often expected to train twice a day for five or six days of the week; one can easily imagine their devising training strategies that combine water and land-based regimes. Maybe the coach scours recent physiological research to most effectively combine training modes, muscle recovery times, co-ordinate their peaks and troughs in training intensity to match the yearly competitions cycle and so on. They present the plan to the swimmer who may (or more likely, may not) evaluate the new plan. The ends of athletic excellence – that which above all the elite athlete properly desires – are assumed and what are contrasted are the most effective means. Such a person is already disciplined and focused. They are scarcely wantons: incapable of controlling their desires. But their conception of the ends aimed at may have been arrived at (to use Bertrand Russell's beautiful phrase) without the consent of their deliberate reason. Many elite swimmers have been training since the age of 5 or 6 and the source of their self-esteem and even identity is often deeply interwoven with their athletic status. Few may be able to conceive of themselves outside of the role of swimmer. In this role-immersion, to invent a term of art, they are incapable under Taylor's account of strong evaluation. When, then, they are confronted with new techniques for performance enhancement they are limited in their evaluative capacities to considerations of effectiveness: how quickly will my performance gains arrive?; how long will they last?; with how much effort?; with what health side effects, if any?; is there a positive outcome from risk or cost–benefit analysis? The strong evaluator asks themselves: is this technique ethically defensible?; even if it is, is it admirable?; is it the action of one who is worthy of esteem and respect?; does it represent an unfair advantage?; would my parents and those whose values I aspire to think it wise or foolish?; would I be proud to win on the basis of the type of preparation it allows me?; will I feel guilty if I use it?; would I be ashamed if it became public knowledge?; and so on. I have set out the weak from the strong evaluator in stark terms; it is fairer, however, to recognise that the weak and strong evaluator categories as housing persons of varying depth and breadth (Flanagan, 1991).[19] Yet these latter questions certainly seem to take us to the heart of sports when they are engaged in and envisaged as ethically significant practices for persons. I will elaborate this conception in the chapter that follows, but although I have now cast off the misperception of the mere physicality or animality (so to speak) of sportspersons, I appear to have reinforced the cognitive or judgemental aspect of sports engagement as ethically significant. This requires further comment.

Taylor's thesis demands that persons and their identity are bound up in strong evaluation. Flanagan (1990) among others argues that this is, to use a sporting metaphor, setting the bar too high. How many human agents will satisfy this strong demand ethically to evaluate the means and ends of their actions, character, choices, habits, reflections in the course of planning and enacting their life plans? Should we deny the descriptor of the 400m athlete 'sportsperson' on the grounds he or she cannot evaluate him or herself ethically in the dominant social sphere of his life? It is certainly counter-intuitive to consider those who are not deep in the required sense somehow not persons given that we typically think that those belonging to that category enjoy widespread rights and are obliged to respect equally widespread duties too. Flanagan's less linguistic thesis coheres in large parts with key features of Taylor's account. He agrees that the persons must be created in intersubjective contexts, that they must be self-comprehending and that this must have normative force. Flanagan insists, however, that the capacity for comprehending normativity is not merely to be found in developed linguistic competence but in the activities of living, which may admit of dim and inchoate self-awareness. In the last two points we see a subtle shift away from Taylor's linguistic abilities to comprehend the way in which emotions open persons' conceptions of the good life. He argues that persons can satisfy these conditions without being obliged to reach the heights of Taylor's strong evaluation. He summarises thus:

> If firm, self-respecting identity is possible for persons who are both inarticulate and (let us suppose) unaware of contrastive possibilities, and if

both these things are necessary for strong evaluation then it follows that strong evaluation is not a necessary foundation and indispensable font of identity and motivation.

(Flanagan, 1990: 47)

He goes on to critique the demands of articulacy in Taylor by arguing that although it is necessary for strong evaluation it is not sufficient since one can very well imagine weak evaluators who are articulate just as we can imagine strong evaluators who are capricious or vicious. To be fair to Taylor, Flanagan's alternative proposal is somewhat sketchy. He tentatively proposes an alternative anthropological scheme whereby persons that are 'relatively impoverished linguistically' (1990: 52) can develop means of self-comprehension. This might comprise normative feedback by gesture, body language, feelings of co-ordination and integration and so on. Oddly enough, Flanagan chooses an example, rather than a sustained argument to push his point home and it is taken from sports (or as is typical in US English, 'athletics'):

> Great athletes often cannot coach, because they cannot say how they do what they do. It is not that they linguistically know how they do what they do but simply cannot get at the module that contains the relevant linguistic description. Often, if they were not coached in certain ways, there was never cause to linguistically formulate the relevant skills. But surely what such athletes are able to do involves highly developed know-how, reflexive comprehension and self-control.

(Flanagan, 1990: 53)

I want largely to agree with Flanagan here but correct his perception in two ways. The first is a problem with generalisation. It is a mistake made too often that people generalise about the conditions and character of sports in ways that lump all the activities in one category. For analytical purposes we can do this. In ethical evaluation it is at best infelicitous. For the cultures and subcultures of sport, their ethos(es) so to speak, are highly particular. The variation is not merely between sports but among them. Ice hockey in Sweden is played, coached and observed according to social rules notably different from those of the USA and Canada where not infrequently naked violence can be a key variable in the determination of victories. But the differentia are not merely geo-cultural. Contrast elite women's football (soccer) with its male counterpart in Western Europe at least. Note how skill is more pervasive and power and aggression less dominant. Mountaineers and orienteers often attract sportspersons from middle-class backgrounds. Competitive boxers (by which I exclude health clubs and their sanitised 'boxercise' conceptions) are typically drawn from the most disadvantaged of our societies while polo players are drawn from the social elite of the world who have more in common with their economic equals than almost any of their national brothers and sisters. Equally Nilsson (1993) argues that there are different perceptions of the good player and the good game in the eyes of rather young players. So my point here is that to imagine that there were some particular coaching style (linguistically driven or otherwise) is to make a weak empirical claim. Sometimes coaches will use demonstrations with no language, at other times they will provide lots of information, sometimes verbal, sometimes visual, sometimes aural, and so on. Much will depend not merely upon the coach's education but their sport, the age of the population, their skill levels, their experience of the game, their own abilities and disabilities, the preferences of their learning styles and so on.[20] I shall say a lot more about the significance of these facts in the chapters that follow and a little more after the final critical point. Flanagan's analogy is a weak one for the similarities between linguistic and motor-skill (henceforth motoric) are somewhat strained. One might argue that what disabled these would-be coaches was their inarticulacy, but one might just as easily argue that their ability had been such that they rarely experienced clumsiness, lack of balance or co-ordination in skill acquisitions. Equally, they may never have experienced what their charges were feeling in acute and distressing self-awareness at the all-too-public display of their ineptitude: embarrassment, ignominy, even humiliation. Equally, they might never have felt the contempt being signalled by the ex-great athlete significantly in their own career. All these things, and many more, might explain the deficiency of the would-be coaches and what really let them down was a distinct lack of empathy, not diminished articulacy.

I am not trying to deny here Flanagan's excellent point that Taylor has overstated the role that articulacy plays in the assignation of personhood,[21] or the construction of our identities of those struggling to conceive of and enact the living of good lives. My point is simply that (1) the apparent inarticulacy of certain performers and coaches may be a more heterogeneous phenomenon than he conceives of it; and (2) there seems to be something awry in *his* example of motoric learning as an analogy for moral development.[22]

Another of Flanagan's examples is that of peasants in Tolstoy's writings. The idea of simple peasants leading good but unreflective lives seems at least a logical possibility. Mackinnon (1999) challenges this example by pointing out the seduction of a simple life lived close to nature, free from the stresses of complex modern life. Nonetheless, she argues that this freedom has its price: '[T]hese peasants cannot understand themselves and the kinds of beings they are in ways which more consciously self-interpreting beings can. They cannot lead fully human lives. They cannot be fully autonomous agents' (1999: 88–9).

I have some sympathy with this view. There is something ethically significant missing in the lives of those whose critical self-awareness is attenuated. There is something absent that demands a mode of response that is neither nostalgia nor pity. To be sure pre-articulate choices and responses in and to the world can be made, but only in response to a limited mode of being. Living in complex, multilayered societies the spaces for these agents is limited as are the possibilities of their flourishing therein. For my purposes at least, the ethical character of strong evaluation opens up the possibility of a greater scope of good living. Of course spelling out what this demands requires a full account of practical reasoning the like of which is not possible here. For our purposes relate to developing a richer sense of sportsperson than the mere descriptor: those who play sports. And there is no denying the inarticulacy of so many who play sports excellently.

For the sake of clarity I will offer a brief summary before passing on to the notion of sportspersonship. Taylor seems to set the bar too high in arguing that strong evaluation is necessary for his conception of personhood and identity. Flanagan seems to lower it perhaps too generously to include those agents with 'dim and inchoate' (1990: 44) self-awareness. There is something to be admired though in the capacity for deeper, contrastive, evaluation that resonates with our emotional responses and vocabularies that open up the possibility of good living which is undeniable. It can set an ideal for those who love sport to develop something a little deeper, ethically admirable and more meaningful to the self-striving to attain excellence in sports and that will lead us a good way down the path to articulacy. As Mackinnon puts it:

> While it need not be denied that some good behaviours that contribute to an agents' well-being are pre-articulate, the more self-conscious and articulate an agent is about the kinds of choices she is making and the kinds of lives she admires, the more fulfilling and meaningful she will find her life. If excellence in practical reasoning underpins the best kinds of choices humans can make in the questions to lead good human lives, and if this kind of reasoning requires agents to recognize ends as more or less worthy for humans, as more or less suited to human nature, then we would expect humans to have to be cognisant about human nature and the fittingness of human ends. It is difficult to see how this would be possible without the kind of conceptual richness made possible by linguistic categories.
>
> (Mackinnon, 1999: 89)

Yet in conclusion she echoes a point made by Flanagan about the insufficiency of the strong evaluators' capacity to lead full and valuable lives:

> A richer vocabulary increases the chances of identifying optimal choices, but it does not ensure it. Being articulate about one's options will not, on its own, guarantee that the right kinds of choices will be recognised or made.
>
> (Mackinnon, 1999: 90)

What does assure that the right kinds of choices are made, other things being equal, is a good character and nothing less than that. How this is formed is necessarily a developmental story about emulation, habit, initiation, instruction and so on: in short the virtue-ethical position I wish to develop in this book.

Sportspersonship is not simply *a* virtue

I openly confess to the reader that it seems to have taken an age to get to this point. What then is the picture of a sportsperson I wish to commend? Having said that I wanted to avoid the fallacy of composition, simply adding the concepts of sports to persons,[23] I want also to avoid the idea of sportspersonship being thought of as a single virtue; a mistake made by psychologists and philosophers alike.[24]

Before offering an account of 'sportspersonship' it is necessary to ask the questions: 'what use is the concept of sportspersonship for?'; 'why do we need a concept such as sportspersonship?'; and 'what role does the concept play in our playing, spectating and teaching of sports?'. Given the account of sports in the previous chapter, it seems reasonable to say that the answers to these questions will be made in the context of certain standards of athletic excellence in persons striving mutually for exclusive goals by admirable standards of conduct and character. With the devotion to the *telos* or ends of sports being so focused we understand the temptations to behave in ways that might be described as moral minimalism. Such engagement with the practices of sport, as we shall consider them in the next chapter, ought to aim above mere rule keeping in order to satisfy the proper motives for engagement. In this context, sportspersonship is an ideal: a set of standards, without precise specification in the modes of attainment, that might be aimed for so that they elicit and ramify the best in our conduct and character as persons in the strong sense that I have developed, via Taylor and Flanagan above.

What are the contours of this conception of 'sportspersonship'? I want to say that sportspersonship is exemplified by the athlete, player, contestant, who is able to act in ways that either are (1) the effects of strong evaluation; or (2) illustrative of the product of strong evaluation. I have expressed it in this manner in order that I do not make sportspersonship *necessarily* a hostage to developed ethical articulacy though clearly that is the more mature reflection of sportspersonship. Expressing it in this manner leaves open the possibility of the assignation of sportspersonship to young children who have been properly habituated in the best standards of human excellence in their sports, or indeed those who lack moral maturity but are nonetheless uncritically reflective but good, or even those incapable of self-critical reflection, or with severely diminished capacities for self-critical awareness, are nonetheless good. In 2006 I spent a short sabbatical at the Norwegian University of Sport Sciences. During my stay my host invited me to an international competition-festival (Ridderenet) for disability skiers at Beitostolen in the West of Norway. I found myself lost in admiration (among a welter of other emotions) for those from the entire spectrum of disability who simply flew down mountains and across terrains with courage and élan assisted by the athletic elite of the University's students. Of course, that admiration is itself a strong evaluation. It was a recognition that here was a sporting community richly deserving of respect and support. Many of the skiers were amputees, blind, deaf or suffering from other debilitating conditions. They represent an alternative to the paradigmatic sports communities we typically think of and those which sports philosophers write about.

In the welter of emotional experience during that visit, I learnt later that part of my emotional response was untoward. I certainly pitied the athletes who were, by virtue of their impairments, forced to struggle with everyday acts (such as getting out of their wheelchair or mobility apparatuses), putting on equipment and clothing, holding equipment with a difficulty that able-bodied persons have, for the most part, no inkling of. In discussion with disability sport colleagues later I was instructed as to the inappropriateness of that emotion since it implied a wrongly privileged position of myself as able-bodied. Here then, the emotions are educated by better judgements and the subsequent experience was patterned both in feeling and perception as well as cognitive judgement. Yet it is for such people that Flanagan's critique may well prove to be auspicious in a way that he had not intended. Might not sports communities for the severely disabled be offended by the failure to incorporate them into the categories (sports)persons? It is absolutely clear that they are capable of sportspersonship – that they may have appreciated, recognised, taken on board the exemplars of courageous, honest, tenacious competitors and imitated their conduct so as to make it their own. I want to say then that strong evaluation is still a valuable heuristic tool for sports ethics despite the dominance of linguistic articulacy in Taylor's earlier writing if we allow it to depict an ideal to which all can and should strive in their pursuit of athletic excellence.

I shall now offer a paradigmatic example of what I consider sportspersonship. When Australia play England at cricket in the traditional 5-day contest format, they play for a symbolic urn referred to as The Ashes. The name refers to the ashes of the burnt bails of wood which sit on top of the stumps of wickets that the batsmen defend against the bowlers. Upon losing their first series of matches ("tests") against Australia in 1882, the Ashes – symbolically the remains of English cricket – were presented to Australia and became the unofficial trophy for all ensuing tests. The rivalry between the two teams is the stuff of legend and in recent years the Australians have been so dominant that many tests have been rather one-sided affairs. In the 2005 Ashes series of five tests, Australia beat England easily in the first test but were on the receiving end of a rejuvenated England in the second. Going into the final day the Australians had only two wickets remaining (two batsmen to be got out) and were nearly 100 runs behind. After losing their last recognised batsman, Australia were left with two batters attempting to score around 60 runs: an all but impossible situation for what are really specialist bowlers (ie pitchers). Little by little, however (and by luck and guts as much as technique or skill), they kept scoring runs. One of them, Brett Lee, was repeatedly struck by the ball travelling from England's lead bowler at around 80–90 miles per hour. With only three runs to win, the other batsman Kasprowicz was caught out and all hell broke loose around the Edgbaston ground. English relief-fuelled jubilation was tangible as players jumped for joy, hugged each other, screamed, and so on. Nevertheless, the most poignant picture in all the papers had escaped the TV crew though not the photo-journalists. Amid the mayhem, England's man of the match, Andrew Flintoff, had gone to console Lee whom he had struck so many times with sickening blows. Both were crouched on their haunches, heads bent toward each other in mutual recognition of suffering and success. To have borne in mind the suffering of his competitor in such a way, while all around were losing their heads, speaks volumes for the ethical capacity of Flintoff to rise above the egoistic triumphalism of the masses and show what really counted. Flintoff's actions displayed a range of virtues including empathy and fairness, and dominant among those virtues was the rare one of compassion. This was as forceful an example of the capacity of strong evaluation one could wish for – acting for the sake of the fine and noble as Aristotle would have put it. And it stands out in the minds of many as the defining picture of that great summer of cricket.

(Sports) persons and the scope of (sports) ethics

Throughout this chapter I have drawn heavily from the resources of Charles Taylor's writings. His general standpoint in ethics in many ways coheres largely with that of Alisdair MacIntyre whose work in moral philosophy has influenced sports philosophers widely and will be the object of critical discussion in the next chapter on sport as a social practice. The third philosopher I wish to draw into the debate is Bernard Williams. While many and various aspects of their philosophical thinking separate these celebrated figures in philosophy, I draw upon them as sources since their philosophical concerns go well beyond the avoidable battles of twentieth-century philosophy, which was often concerned exclusively with the articulation of the meanings of concepts. Of course no philosopher worth their salt is unconcerned with conceptual clarity. But there is much more to philosophy and especially philosophical ethics, in and out of sports talk, than the elaboration of concepts such as cheating, deception, doping, fairness and fair play, promising, rules and rule-following. Despite the valuable task of enunciating the various and sometimes competing concepts and conceptions, the primary task for applied philosophers will be to move people in the world to conceive of the good and to act in accordance with it. That means, very often, getting off and well clear of the fence of mere clarification.

MacIntyre, Taylor and Williams are prominent among the philosophers who have attempted to chart the moral topography of contemporary Western culture. Some commonality can be found in their insistence that morality and moral theory is incomplete if it focuses solely on the nature of our obligations. And just as mainstream philosophical thinking in ethics had followed the linguistic turn and reified a special moral language, so too sports philosophers had largely focused on their counterparts in sports. Like others, this triumvirate has decried the manner in which much contemporary moral philosophy in the Anglo-American tradition has narrowly conceived its direction, importance and responsibility. Modern moral philosophy for at least two hundred years had tended to focus on what it is right to do rather than what it is good to be. This focus either led philosophers to rule that the currency of moral thought was moral action whether this was inspired by a recognition of one's rational moral duties or the moral imperative to maximise happiness in the world. As with many dualisms this simple dichotomy between moral action and moral being, what it is right to do or good to be, is somewhat misleading.

Many accounts of personhood are woven into an account of morality in the language of rules as duties or obligations or some other principle such as the maximisation of good consequences. In discussing the nature of morality many philosophers have adopted the stance that acting morally is related to certain principles about what we should and should not do that could be universalised, that is, to be done by all people in all places at all times where the situation was appropriately similar. They have argued, in a manner characteristic of the time that acting morally requires sticking to principles rather than responding to moods and feelings. This axis between universalised moral demands and rationality is one that will be the object of considerable discussion when I try to articulate a virtue-ethical account of sports and sportspersons in later chapters. For the moment I want to signal the sources of discontent in writers such as MacIntyre, Taylor and Williams.

Williams, against the grain of universalistic moral demands, argued that obligations ought to be viewed as merely one type of ethical consideration among others. MacIntyre, following Aristotle's lead, argues that we should return to the ethical ideal of living well as opposed to acting right. Both offer an account of the good life and of moral philosophy which was greater in scope than the 'peculiar institution' of morality. This moral language was cauterised from daily living: *moral* rules became rather special rules. Their properties could be teased out with linguistic care: they were universal in scope, impartial in application, and prescriptive or action guiding in nature. People in all walks of life became familiar in conversation with the idea that somehow *moral* decisions are categorically superior to, more important than and more demanding of, other kinds of decisions. A dominant belief was that how one should conduct oneself generally and how one should *morally* conduct oneself were somehow separate. Morality had a special and overriding 'demandingness' in contrast to other practical reasons encountered in the course of living. It is no accident that Williams began his powerful book *Ethics and the Limits of Philosophy* with the words Plato recalls of Socrates: it is no trivial matter how one is to live their life. This is no simple project of ethical nostalgia, but a complex attempt to widen the focus of ethics, and to understand the life of moral agents that are persons, to a wider vocabulary of living well.

Taylor too addresses himself to the question 'what is it that makes life worth living?' He outlines a cluster of notions that are central to ethical life: the respect for life, integrity, well-being and the flourishing of others. These concerns, indeed Taylor calls them 'demands' (1989: 4), are so deep-rooted that one could be forgiven for considering them instinctual. Examples of such demands might, specifically, be the compunction to inflict death or injury on others as well as the inclination to help those in injury or danger. Culture helps define 'relevant' other demands but not the basic reaction itself. Even if the notions of duty, obligation and rights were constitutive of morality then we must also recognise that there are other demands upon us that bring in strong evaluations that are also of central concern to us:

> These are questions about how I am going to live my life which touch on the issue of what kind of life is worth living, or what kind of life would fulfil the promise implicit in my particular talents, or the demands of someone with my endowment, or of what constitutes a rich, meaningful life.
>
> (Taylor, 1989: 14)

More precisely, Taylor articulates three axes for moral thinking in its most general sense: (1) our sense of respect for and obligation to others; (2) our understanding of what makes life full; and (3) the range of notions concerned with dignity (Taylor, 1989: 15).

In an important qualification, Taylor states that the meaning of 'respect' in (1) is not the usual respect for rights but rather the respect we have for someone we look up to or admire such as is affirmed when we say that someone 'has our respect'. Taylor demarcates this special sense by calling it 'attitudinal'. Similarly, he refers to as 'attitudinal' the notion of dignity in (3) whereby it represents our sense of ourselves commanding the above sense of respect.

Setting these axes in the contexts of sports ethics it seems fair to say that the majority of writings have thus far followed the dominant traditions of modern moral philosophy as deontology (duty ethics) or consequentalism (usually some form of utilitarianism). A considerable body of knowledge on rule-keeping and rule-breaking emerged for example in early debates about formalism within games (Leamon, 1988; Lehman, 1981) and more recently with respect to moral realism and the moral authority of the rules within sports (Dixon, 2003; McFee, 2003b; Morgan, 2004; Roberts, 1998; Russell, 1999, 2004; Simon, 2000, 2004a, 2004b[25]). The classic statement of a strict deontological sports ethics duties of sports contestants and coaches alike is in Fraleigh (1984) while other authors focus on issues of justice and (in)equality (especially Loland, 2002). Occasionally a representative of utilitarianism has promoted that particular moral rationalism to problems such as cheating, doping, and the morality of sports technology (most notably Tamburrini, 2000, 2006). Less frequently has there been any extended and systematic treatment of sports ethics within the second axis (with the exception of Arnold, 1994; Gibson, 1993; Reid, 2002).

Conclusion

The questions that turn around the meanings our life can possess, fragmented and conflicting as they are, are the very stuff of persons. I have followed Charles Taylor here in arguing that a capacity to evaluate among our goals and the means by which we pursue them is definitive of persons. This sets the bar rather high with respect to personhood, namely foetuses or those with severe intellectual disabilities. I am aware that his account is not without its regrettable consequences. The consequences of the account, however, are nowhere near as corrosive in the vast majority of adult populations who at least attempt to conceive of their activities and goals in a critical way. And this is the manner in which I wish to promote the proper understanding of sportspersonship.

It is the case that in 'all' times there has been a framework regardless of how poorly articulated it has been, that enabled people to define the demands by which their lives are judged as less or more full. These pictures, or 'narratives' as MacIntyre calls them, are never so dominant that they can command universal assent. Moreover, he has forcefully argued that modernity is characterised partly by the fragmentation of competing traditions. His argument rests upon a proper recognition of the practices, goods and virtues to be found in historically formed social traditions. Into this idea the account of sportspersonship I have developed here is to be insinuated. To be a sportsperson, in the normative sense that I have struggled to articulate, is to engage wholeheartedly with the actions of sport as one's own, at first by training and emulation and then by critical reflection until the choices one makes are fully one's own and no longer in need of constant intentionality. To this idea, instantiated in sports, I now turn.

3 Sports as practices

In the previous chapters I have sketched an initial account of sport and presented a critical account of personhood that will serve as the foundation of the argument that good sports and sportspersons are to be conceived in virtue-ethical terms. The basis of the explicitly ethical conception of sports I want now to develop is based on another philosopher who has attacked the modern liberal worldview: Alasdair MacIntyre. Like Taylor, he is uncomfortable being labelled a communitarian but many of his writings sit comfortably under that banner. Discussion of MacIntyre's arguments surrounding his notions of 'practices', 'institutions,' and 'virtues' have been taken up by many philosophers of sport[1] who have used them to articulate the inherently ethical nature of sports and their apparent recent decline. While I am persuaded by much that is central to MacIntyre's brilliant analysis of morals in modernity, I argue that applying his general account to the particular case of modern sports is not without difficulty.

The chapter is based around four such difficulties (1) the clarity of the distinction between practices and institutions and the methodological limits of his analysis; (2) the manner in which the individual is transposed to the social; (3) the apparent reductivism of his account of virtues and their function in practices; and finally (4) the characterisation of internality and externality of goods to practices. This will pave the way for a critical discussion of particular vices and virtues in sports in Part II of the book.

After MacIntyre: sports as practices

One of the chief reasons for the influence MacIntyre's account has had over the philosophy of sport, I suggest, is due to the sterility of analytical accounts of sports with respect to their ethical nature. It would, however, be futile to offer an extended description of MacIntyre's position as set out in his classic *After Virtue* (1986) since critical commentaries of the work are now legion. I therefore offer only the briefest of overviews sufficient for the purpose at hand before illuminating some difficulties for philosophers of sport wishing to utilise his account. And I attempt in the remainder of the book to make good on some of these criticisms by developing an account that builds upon them.

In his rejection of modern morality with its individualism, fragmented incoherence and interminable disagreements of modern societies, MacIntyre sets out by contrast the richness and coherence of conceptions of ethics in Ancient Greece, notably those found in the works of Aristotle. The picture of the good life MacIntyre focuses on is one lived in accordance with virtue against a background of a proper nature of 'man' [*sic*]. The virtues are excellences that enable us to achieve our goal (*telos*) of flourishing and are also an ingredient of the attainment of that goal at the same time. What MacIntyre attempts to supply is a revised Aristotelianism with its focus on a narrative self, situated in place and time, who is possessed of a core of virtues that are acquired, displayed and produced in a variety of shared social practices that are themselves constitutive of broader cultural traditions.

With something approaching litigious precision, MacIntyre sets out his account of practices and their internal goods in the following way. A practice is defined as:

> Any coherent and complex socially established co-operative human activity through which goods internal to that form of activity are realised in the course of trying to achieve those standards of excellence which are appropriate to, and partially definitive of, that form of activity, with the result that human powers to achieve excellence and human conceptions of the ends and goods involved are systematically extended.
>
> (MacIntyre, 1985: 187)

While the account is far from easy at first sight, in his examples of what are and are not practices, MacIntyre brings further light and shows the ready application of the idea to modern living. MacIntyre first distinguishes between technical skills and the institutions that give them their context and allow us to make sense of them. Tic-tac-toe (hopscotch) is not a practice in this sense nor is the throwing or catching of a football. The game of football, however, is. Similarly bricklaying is not a practice, but architecture is. Other examples of practices are arts, games, sciences, and the making and sustaining of family life. In his later book, *Whose Justice, Which Rationality* (1998), MacIntyre offers a more variegated list, the elements of which he argues are the sites of the production in which human excellences are instantiated:

> [W]arfare and combat, seamanship, athletic and gymnastic activity; epic, lyric and dramatic poetry; farming both arable and the management of animals; rhetoric and the making and sustaining of the communities of kinship and the household and later of the city-state. To this list architecture, sculpture and painting were to be added, as were the intellectual enquiries of mathematics, philosophy and theology.
>
> (MacIntyre, 1998: 30)

None of these practices can be reduced to the various skills that are required to exemplify and sustain them without remainder. Nor can they simply be thought of as the institutions that give rise to them. Football/soccer cannot be reduced to its technical skills or the various clubs and administrative structures, though these are important in our understanding of, and successful participation in, football/soccer as a practice.

The notion of goods internal to a practice is central to MacIntyre's account. What they are, in Brown's words, is far from easy to say. Indeed Brown (1991) goes as far as to comment that his account of internal goods is almost hopelessly vague.[2] They are most readily comprehended by distinguishing them from those goods that are external. MacIntyre considers the example of teaching an intelligent young child how to play chess. The child is motivated to learn the game only in so far as he or she is offered a given amount of candy to play, and even more upon winning, a game. When candy is the primary motivation, the child has every reason to cheat and no reason not to cheat since the game is irrelevant (or at the very least secondary) in his or her motivational hierarchy. Over time, however, the child may come to recognise and value the achievement of a certain kind of analytical skill, strategic imagination, competitive intensity and so forth. These are internal goods and are specific to the practice of chess. MacIntyre then holds that if the child cheats after recognising these internal goods, this will not constitute defeating the tutor but his or herself. This example is supposed to show that there are goods that are externally or contingently related to the practice of chess, and, alternatively, that there are those goods that are internal to that practice. It is fairly clear here that the candy is an external good in MacIntyre's example. In other areas of life, power, prestige, status or wealth are external goods. These goods can, by definition, be isolated and achieved by alternative means that are not exclusively tied to engagement in a particular practice. External goods stand, therefore, in an instrumental relation to practices. Where external goods are the locus of value and motivation for the practitioner, it should be noted that they may be brought about by a variety of means that are more or less successful in that task. This explains the disinterestedness with which some approach practices; only as a means to secure external goods. On the other hand, there are goods internal to (or inherent within) a practice that cannot be had except by engagement in that practice. These goods can only be gained by first-hand experience of them in the relevant practice, and those who lack this experience are not competent to judge those practices.

With the game of chess, MacIntyre says that the internal goods cannot be had except by playing chess or 'some other game of that specific kind', but it is not clear just what this latitude opens up. In what follows this point will briefly be addressed. Perhaps this exclusivity is in any case a little too strong. Many philosophers may find more defensible the idea that Stout suggests, against MacIntyre's scepticism, that the requisite experience and competence to judge a practice, and therefore its internal goods, may come second-hand 'through a skilful reporter's thick descriptions' (Stout, 1988: 267).

More convincing is the idea that these goods can only be specified in the language of such practices and through examples of them. Brown captures this point well:

> One of the good things to be achieved by participating in a practice is the development of human capacities in the manner dictated by a given practice, its goals, skills, styles and procedures insofar as they promote the flourishing of human powers and potential.
>
> (Brown, 1991: 73)

When we move on to consider the relationship between institutions and practices we find an apparent paradox. For not only is it the case that the respective institutions are corruptive of their practices, they are also essential to them. Thus:

> Institutions are characteristically and necessarily concerned with what I have called external goods. They are involved in acquiring money and other material goods; they are structured in terms of power and status, and they distribute money and power and status as rewards. Nor could they do otherwise if they are to sustain not only themselves, but also the practices of which they are the bearers. For no practices can survive any length of time unsustained by institutions. Indeed so intimate is the relationship of practices to institution – and consequently of the goods external to the goods internal to the practice in question – that institutions and practices characteristically form a single causal order in which the ideals and the creativity of the practice are always vulnerable to the acquisitiveness of the institutions, in which the co-operative care for common goods of the practice is always vulnerable to the competitiveness of the institution. In this context the essential function of the virtues is clear. Without them, without justice, courage and truthfulness, practices could not resist the corrupting power of institutions.
>
> (MacIntyre, 1985: 194)

There are several points of importance here that will form the substance of what follows. In the first instance, the celebrated distinction between practices and institution, though intimate,[3] is one that allows MacIntyre to celebrate the characteristic features of the former while deriding particular corruptive influences upon them by the latter in the context of 'contemporary emotivist cultures' as he calls them.[4] MacIntyre's selective emphasis upon the deleterious effects of the latter are worthy of note, as is the sharpness with which the further distinction between internal and external goods is drawn and the respective virtues and vices that enable the agent to secure them. First, however, I wish to discuss one of the ramifications of MacIntyre's communitarian stance and the manner in which it operates in relation to the notion of internal goods in sporting practices.

Practices and virtues: personal and/or social

MacIntyre sets store by three virtues to ward off the corruptive influences of institutions: justice, courage and honesty. It has been suggested that his justification for this lies in the essentially social nature of these virtues.[5] This coheres with MacIntyre's moral, social and political polemic against liberal individualism. By locating the virtues in practices in which social co-operation is essential, the virtues become irreducibly social. Seung (1991) argued that by restricting his conception of a practice to the domain of social co-operation, MacIntyre excluded from consideration those activities that do not require social co-operation. It would follow, then, that mountain climbing would be a practice if performed co-operatively but not if performed individually. This interpretation misconstrues MacIntyre's position. He is nowhere so exclusive about practices. Indeed, his historical layering of practices allows precisely for such cases. Here individuals toil only in apparent isolation. Alternatively, they may be viewed as participants who co-operate over time in a tradition according to the canons developed over time between other participants. This would apply just as much to Van Gogh developing postimpressionism in seeming isolation at Arles as it would to a mountain climber attempting some new technique while on an ascent of Mount Everest. Their activities may only be understood in the light of the ongoing practice. To label them 'individual activities' as Seung does (1991: 207–8) is to ignore the purpose of MacIntyre's third tier of practices, which requires that the understanding of (practitioners') actions ought not to be wrenched from their social and historical context. Such a move, dubbed the 'ontogenetic fallacy' by Gellner (1967: 53), misses the mark somewhat as a criticism of MacIntyre's thesis.

What can be rescued from this line of criticism is the idea that MacIntyre's emphasis on the social aspects of virtues and practices effectively obscures the notion of personal achievement. While it is true that rules and standards structure the public nature of the achievements and set goals for future practitioners, they also attach to the individual in a strong and important way. MacIntyre argued that external goods are characteristically someone's property or possession. They are exclusive such that, for example, your having X denies my having it. Now although internal goods may be the object of competition, it is characteristic of their achievement that the good of the whole community of practitioners is advanced. He cites as an exemplar W. G. Grace who advanced the art of batting in cricket. As with the example above, however, the achievement attaches to the individual in a strong and original way. Though other practitioners are indebted to these individuals and may emulate their achievements, they are not esteemed in the same way. Those who have broken new ground are thereby rewarded and esteemed. Athletes remember, with propriety, the fact that Dick Fosbury introduced the 'flop' to the world of track and field. They will not know, nor ought they to, that you or I acquired the skill and displayed it with considerably more modest competence. After the 1974 Football (Soccer) World Cup every school boy was imitating the Cruyff turn where the ball was played behind the non-playing leg of the player in possession so as to put off-balance the defender. Yet their achievement of this technical trick is of course secondary to its progenitor. In a similar vein, Geoff Hurst is written deep into English football folklore by scoring a hat-trick in the 1966 World Cup final, and Martina Navratilova is credited with raising women's tennis to new heights of athleticism and competitive intensity. It is true that the whole community has been advanced by their achievements but not in the manner in which the individual is heralded. In one of the earliest texts in the sociology of sport, Inglis entitles a chapter 'The name of the game' with insight 'The memory of a people – now let us praise famous men [*sic*]'. It is the celebration of such people that correspondingly is the celebration of the practice. MacIntyre recognises this point at the level of tradition while failing to acknowledge the disjunction between the individual and the practice. Inglis writes with insight:

> Sporting photographs are like the snapshots of a national photograph album. They bring back memories of what has been lost, and is irrecoverable. And just because it is irrecoverable, the men and women who stir up those lost hopes become special heroes, whose like we shall not look upon again. So it is forever that old men forever tell young boys, "You ought to have seen Victor Trumper or Bobby Jones."
>
> A queer use of "ought really"; the young boys could hardly have seen Victor Trumper or Bobby Jones. Yet the young boys in their turn will say the same sort of thing when they themselves become old men, and the young boys of the future will shuffle their feet, and yawn inwardly, and wonder when the old men will fall silent. This is how society makes its history. How its imagination continues and makes a tradition: an assembly of names and occasions, great victories and defeats, of ways of seeing and celebrating these things.
>
> (Inglis, 1977: 5)

The function of such stories and their relationship to the sustaining of practices through narrative raises important questions in relation to practices generally and sporting practices specifically. More will be said of the nature of rewards and their relation to the goods of practices below. Yet before moving on we should note that the idea of rewards, remembered and venerated in such narratives, is neither as pernicious nor as contemporary as MacIntyre appears to suggest. As was noted earlier, it is not the case that MacIntyre's monsters of modernity have brought about a new (over-)emphasis on rewards to the detriment of practices. There is ample evidence of such customs from Ancient Greece onwards (Kyle, 2007). In this historical vein, Santayana, writing at the end of the nineteenth century, concurred with the view that sports have their own integrity that can be diminished with emphasis on external goods, yet he reminds us:

> Athletic sports are not children's games; they are public spectacles. . . . Spectators are indispensable, since without them the victory, which should be the only reward, would lose half its power. For as Pindar, who knew, tells us:
>   Success
>   Is half the prize, the other half renown.
>   Who achieves both, he hath the perfect crown.
>
> (Santayana, 1894: 185)

It is clear that, in relation to their celebrative character, sports (especially elite sports) are public affairs, while performances still flow from, and are properly regarded as, the products of the exercise of individual agency. The just distribution of such rewards depends precisely upon this recognition. It would be wrong, however, to focus on elite sport only, for to do so might reinforce the framing of success, reward or the achievement of goods in sport at that level and in so doing over-emphasise the public aspect of achievement. On a larger scale, there is a real danger of losing sight of the personal dimension in adopting or employing uncritically MacIntyre's conception of practices in the contexts of sports. I am suggesting that sporting heroes do exist and ought still to be celebrated. Though it is often the case that those who are called 'sporting heroes' are mere celebrities whose fame and/or notoriety rests upon reasons other than desert; it is still the case that we may properly celebrate individual excellence within a particular practice without slipping into romantic individualism. Without the context that makes meaningful their excellence of course, they cannot be so understood. Such an account need not be a new one. Homer's *Iliad* is just such an account of heroes within tightly knit communities with shared evaluations as to the good life and its constituents. But the notion of local heroes, even in modernity, is not unheard of. From any objective standpoint it may well be inconsequential that the standards of a practice are advanced by any particular person. But from the personal viewpoint it is not.

When MacIntyre uses examples such as W. G. Grace and Turner he is talking of performances at the outer edges of practices. And this emphasis is not only apparent in *After Virtue* but also in his later *Whose Justice, Which Rationality* where, in properly recognising the subordinacy of novices or initiates in a practice to those more authoritative therein, he writes:

> The concept of the best, of the perfected, provides each of these forms of activity with the good toward which those who participate in it move. What directs them toward that goal is both the history of successive attempts to transcend the limitations of the best achievement in that

particular area so far and the acknowledgement of certain achievements as permanently defining aspects of the perfection toward which that particular form of activity is directed. Those achievements are assigned a canonical status within the practice of each type of activity. Learning what they teach is central to apprenticeship in each particular form of activity.

(1998: 31)

While I am in agreement with the general point being made here, a corrective needs to be made about this emphasis. Most persons engage in practices at the humdrum level of mediocrity against this absolute standard of excellence. Few will ever become a Beethoven or a Pelé; 'ordinary mortals' very often do not possess the potential in terms of natural capacities, tendencies or capabilities to justify the pursuit of a single calling to such absolute excellence. Nonetheless, anyone can pursue excellence in various activities where this is interpreted in relation to their own particular circumstances: their own previous best performances, or comparisons among standards of contemporaries in terms of age, body composition, years of training or education, and so on. Here the individual may make advances that are utterly unimportant to the practice as a whole but that are of enormous personal significance. Nowhere is this more the case than with beginners whose abilities may, at the initial stages, increase rapidly in range and sophistication. Yet MacIntyre's over-emphasis on the public or the social nature of recognition and inclusive achievement in practices stands in need of a counter-balance of the phenomenological character of achievement.

The British philosopher of education, Ray Elliot, once gave a beautiful account of the phenomenological character of initiation and personal development within a practice (that could as easily be applied to any of MacIntyre's post-Homeric practices whether athletics or mathematics) which is richly suggestive:

[A] child at school finds a subject attractive, takes delight in it, and begins to look forward to the lessons in which it is taught. The subject seems to welcome his [sic] attention, his work pleases his teacher, and he comes to think of himself as "good at" the subject. It becomes "his subject." During its lessons time passes with a strange swiftness. He believes it to be "better" than other subjects, and is prepared to give up other pleasures because absorption in his subject pleases him still more. Perhaps he develops a passion for it, and begrudges time spent on anything else. In due course it dawns on the student that his enthusiastic interest in his subject is not enough. There are standards which have to be met, and to meet them he has to develop skills and abilities which he did not originally associate with his subject. He also has to do a good deal of work which seems to be commonly like drudgery. Pleasures do not come easily now, but he finds fulfilment in trying to satisfy the demands his subject makes upon him. He has become devoted to its disciplines and feels at times that he has been enlisted in its service.

(Elliot, 1974: 6)

There is every reason to believe that this account of initiation is precisely what MacIntyre was driving towards both in terms of the non-egoistic engagement with practices and a non-hedonistic account of the way in which success in practices enriches our lives. Moreover, it gives a corrective to the exemplars whose achievements are to be understood as belonging to the practice as a whole. Now it might be argued that this stress on the quasi-individual character of achievement highlighted by Elliot, along with esteem that attaches to the absolutely excellent practitioners, is antithetical to MacIntyre's overall project. It would appear to be an attempt to incorporate a quasi-individualistic ethos into the broader communitarian worldview. To this the response must be that there are communitarians and there are communitarians. MacIntyre is never as staunch as Sandel (1982), who in his earlier writings appears to transpose the individual entirely to the social so that the individual appears to be no more than the nexus of situated narratives.[6] Yet by arguing for the objective status of internal goods, against the idea that they can also be felt- satisfactions of a personal kind, MacIntyre effectively closes the door on the personal dimension. He is so concerned to eschew subjectivism that he rides roughshod over the phenomenological aspects of internal goods as experienced by the agent.

The distinction between practices and institutions and its methodological status

A central motivating factor behind the virtues MacIntyre wishes to attribute to his practitioners and their relationship to those practices is something more deep than what is typified in the phrase 'the three minute culture'.[7] He expresses distaste for the acquisitiveness and fleeting disengagement that is often thought to be a defining characteristic of liberal capitalism in late modernity. A significant partner in the establishment of such a shallow culture is the rise of institutions that treat the ends that practices embody with indifference, ignore the authority invested in them over time, and usurp them with mere subjective preferences represented by the economic demand of a not necessarily educated, but consuming, public. Examples of such sporting corruption are legion. Athletes who competed in the marathon in the Seoul and Barcelona Olympics were told to their dismay that they would be competing in the noon-day sun. This posed a serious threat to their health. The apparent justification for such a potential hazard was the maximization of media revenue; a consideration external to the logic of the practice.[8] Likewise, professional tennis players have regularly complained at being forced to compete in the New York Tennis Open tournament in the twilight hours under floodlights with the incessant noise of John F. Kennedy airport traffic overhead. While undermining the players' attempt to personify the best of their abilities such a move made more random the outcomes of contests that more properly should be settled by the defining excellences of the activity: skill, strength, speed, co-ordination of hand and eye, anticipation of one's opponent's actions and so forth – not the ability to see the ball under floodlit conditions or to concentrate on one's game through the noise of peak flying times from the nearby New York airport.

Despite acknowledging the supportive role that institutions play in organising, regulating and promoting practices, MacIntyre emphatically wrote of the institutions' corruptive powers and emphasised the fact that the practice is always vulnerable to the acquisitiveness of the institution. It is to save practices from such perversion that the nature and functions of the virtues are located, by contrast, in practices. He reinforces this view by setting out institutions as the agencies that organise and distribute external goods or rewards, such as power, wealth and status, while passing over their supportive role. Arnold (1992, 1994), Brown (1991) and Schneider and Butcher (1993, 1994) do not equivocate on this matter. Morgan (1994)[9] has given an extended and less one-sided treatment of the institutions related to sport, though he is no less scathing in his criticism.

If practices are coherent and complex forms of socially established co-operative activities, and institutions are the mechanisms through which external goods are distributed, where do we place sportspersons, coaches, officials, parents of young sports players and so forth? Imagine a scenario at the end of a successful season of Little League baseball. There is of course an annual meeting to celebrate the team's successes, to thank the parents who faithfully drove the kids around to the various venues, encouraged them to perform to (and often beyond) the best of their abilities, maybe even to playfully admonish those who too often abused the umpires. Here the team committee functions precisely like an institution in MacIntyre's sense by distributing external rewards such as medals, trophies, acclamations, maybe even monetary or token rewards. But given that the self-same people may have been the guardians of various traditions upheld in the club, given that they too are the initiates and initiators to the various skills, strategies and standards of excellence and modes of conduct as are characteristics of all that is good in the activity, they appear to be part of the practice also. The lack of clarity of the distinction once pushed shows a certain ambiguity. Perhaps it is the case that they can at one time be a member of both the practice and the institution.

It should be clear that such ambiguities, as are present on the borderline, scarcely undermine the entire MacIntyrean position. A distinction need not be watertight to be valuable. It does raise, however, some questions about the 'empirical content' of the thesis. While it is clear that, in sports at least, when MacIntyre talks of the institution, we unproblematically instantiate the idea with names such as the IAAF (International Amateur Athletics Federation), the IOC (International Olympic Committee), the

FIFA (Fédération Internationale de Football Association), the NBA (National Basketball Association), and so on. It is easy to see how the distinction operates. Lower down the order things are less clear.

Morgan, in his characterisation of the relationship in a sporting context, is more careful than other philosophers of sports have been. He takes time, even though he focuses on large-scale organisations, to adumbrate the varieties of functions of institutions from distributing external goods to the nurturing, regulating, normalising and legitimating of various aspects of the practice. Like MacIntyre, however, it is not long before Morgan moves to strong critique. The main target for his detailed and penetrating analysis is the fact that institutions necessarily operate in the economic marketplace with an unsophisticated and inadequate qualitative vocabulary that is inimical to the practice. Morgan approvingly quotes Nozick to the effect that money is not 'a vehicle for nuanced expression' (Morgan,1994: 143) and that the institution, in Walzer's phrase, issues 'scandalous couplings between people and goods' (Morgan, 1994: 141).

There are two respects in which this interpretation is selective. Following Lasch, Morgan argues that (1) there is a specific historical juncture (the late 1940s and 1950s) where we can mark out the importantly deleterious effects of sports' institutionalisation; and (2) contemporary institutions have wrought new havoc to the internal logic of practices by attempting to replace them with their own institutional logic. At the heart of this critique are the notions of corruption and distortion – the notion that institutions have moved well beyond their functions of nurturing practices by de-emphasising the internal goods of practices via the domination of goods external to the practice. Morgan quotes Walzer effectively: 'To convert one good into another, when there is no intrinsic connection is to invade the sphere' (Morgan,1994: 146).

First, then, we must ask the question, 'Why select this historical juncture?' Would not a cursory glance at Greek and Roman sports (or any other epoch for that matter) offer us a not dissimilar picture of the usurpation of the internal goods of sports by external goods wielded by the institution?[10] Similarly, as MacIntyre wrote: 'Where the notion of engagement in a practice was once socially central, the notion of aesthetic consumption now is, at least for the majority' (1985: 228). MacIntyre offers no evidence for his claim; given the fact that his examples of practices are so varied, perhaps he could not. In our specific case, it is not clear if such a shift has ever taken place because it is not known what levels and kinds of performer–spectator relationship have existed hitherto. With elite sport, however, by definition it will be representation of specialist labour, and it might not be unreasonable to expect the same for any elite instrumental practice that is wedded to economic consumption. Furthermore, while it is of course true analytically that there is no logically necessary connection between sports and external goods by definition (that is to say if they were not extrinsic why should we call them 'external' goods?), we can at least meaningfully ask when sports were ever present without their existence. This relates strongly to whether we use the distinction between practices and institutions as descriptive or merely heuristic. Just to be clear, though, I am not denying the corruptive influences of external goods promoted and distributed by institutions. It is just that it is not clear how we are to conceive of them on strictly MacIntyrean lines. A much better case seems to be articulated by Walsh and Giulianotti when they argue that there is a need to identify the point at which the institutional commodification of sports becomes pathological. They write:

> Commodification is ethically undesirable when it leads to an elimination or significant limitation of the epistemic space available for the pursuit of non-commercial internal goals that supervene on sport and which are an essential element of the moral value that sports generate.
>
> (Walsh and Giulianotti, 2007: 63)

Secondly just as examples of usurpation are legion, so too are examples in which the institution has chided players, coaches and spectators alike for poor ethical standards in their chosen activities. Most recently the Tour De France, one of the greatest spectacles in all sports, has thrown up precisely such a case. The event, organised since 1903, is a monumental challenge of human (some would say "superhuman") capabilities. Cyclists travel over 3000km during 22 days of relentless back-to-back competition. Of course the reputation of the Tour has been sullied by year upon year exposure of doping-related offences to the point that the general public is entirely sceptical as to there being honest winners. Recently Barne Riis, the winner from 1996, bowed to pressure and confessed (as several of his team mates had done earlier) to taking banned stimulants during the race. One of his colleagues proclaimed that he took amphetamines only when it was strictly necessary to help him recover and get through the next day's cycling – which was just about every day! So guilt-ridden indeed has Riis felt that he says he left his famous winner's yellow jersey in a plastic bag in his house. Many commentators have argued in the past that the world body for the sport, the International Cycling Union (UCI), is partly to blame since it turned a blind eye for so many years to the systematic approach to doping that was endemic in the sport. Doping in professional cycling was an open secret.

Whether motivated for reasons of a financial kind, or for the love of their sport (or most likely for both, but in that order) the UCI enacted, with the support of the French legislature, tougher measures to catch and sanction doping cheats. The race in 2007 saw the expulsion of not one yellow jersey rider, but two. On the 24 July the Russian cyclist Alexandr Vinokourov tested positive for blood doping having performed a near miraculous comeback from a previous days exhausted and below par performance. The pattern followed that of Floyd Landis last year whose dramatic recovery between stages had first raised eyebrows and then headlines. The very next day, however, Danish cyclist Michael Rasmussen was expelled for violating internal "whereabouts" rules of his team by missing two random tests. These out-of-season tests are thought to be essential to catch doping cheats in their out-of-competition training cycles where they can enhance their physical capacities with illicit substances or procedures while not under the watchful eye of doping agencies. Rasmussen claimed to be in Mexico visiting relatives when it turns out that a journalist had in fact seen him training in Italy. All this might seem an unacceptable case of guilty until proven innocent until one thinks of the veritable litany of doping offences that have surrounded the Tour in the recent past. Mistrust, it seems, begets itself.

As if this were not enough, on 20 September 2007 there was confirmation of the fact that last year's disgraced winner Floyd Landis had his challenge to the efficacy of the doping results rebutted and now finds his claim to fame has transformed from being winner of the Tour to first winner to lose the much coveted title.

It is not a coincidence that the leading team, Channel Discovery, who has won the Tour team event for eight of the last nine years, has been forced to disband because it cannot find sufficient sponsorship. Here it seems we have the clearest of examples of the paradoxical influence of corruption/support by a sporting institution.

What is unclear throughout the text of *After Virtue* is just how the distinction between a practice and its simultaneously supporting/corrupting institution is to be interpreted. This problem may well be paradigmatic of certain methodological queries about MacIntyre's conception of philosophy itself. Having charted MacIntyre's long-standing commitment to ethical theory and practice with one eye on both historical and sociological factors, one might ask whether his distinction between practices and institutions (indeed any part of his critique and positive thesis) is best to be seen as either a (quasi) factual account of contemporary ethical life or a heuristic philosophical device. It is worth quoting MacIntyre at length for the purpose of accurate exposition:

> It is Ferguson's type of sociology which is the empirical counterpart of the conceptual account of the virtues which I have given, a sociology which aspires to lay bare the empirical, causal connection between virtues, practices and institutions. For this kind of conceptual account has strong empirical implications; it provides an explanatory scheme which can be tested in particular cases. Moreover, my thesis has empirical content in another way; it does entail that without the virtues there could be a recognition only of what I have called external goods and not at all of internal goods in the context of practices. And in any society which recognized only external goods competitiveness would be the dominant and even exclusive feature. We have a brilliant portrait of such a society in Hobbes's account of the state of nature; and Professor Turnbull's report of the fate of the Ik suggest that social reality does in the most horrifying way confirm both my thesis and Hobbes's.
>
> (MacIntyre, 1985: 195–6)

Of course one of the great problems of skating the thin line between proto-description and ideal typical analysis is the selectivity of social facts marshalled in favour of one's adopted position. MacIntyre is acutely aware of this. Midgley (1983) gives short shrift to Turnbull's interpretation of the Ik's unfortunate state. The Ik are a desperately unfortunate tribe who have lost their traditional hunting and gathering grounds after the redrawing of political frontiers. In consequence, the tribe are literally starving and the traditional culture is effectively disintegrated. They act toward each other in horrific brutality. This does not prove, as Turnbull asserts, that society is some kind of luxury to be dispensed with since the Ik are (just) coping without it. Midgley (1983: 299–300) argued that social animals such as humans cannot live a life that they are fitted for without particular forms of society. She writes:

> Turnbull found little or no altruism among the Ik, which is not surprising when you consider that they have already been in their present desperate situation for quite long enough to ensure a steady selection of those interested solely in surviving. They are a dying society. But what does it mean to suggest that everything else in their lives was a luxury? Is the idea that only extreme situations are real and serious? If so, most of life is unreal: what sort of unreality is this?
>
> (Midgley, 1983: 300)

It may well be the case that in any society that recognises only external goods, competitiveness may become the dominant factor. But citing the Ik as confirmation of MacIntyre's thesis is question-begging to say the least. In what sense can we still describe this poor unfortunate existence as a 'society'? In what sense do they 'recognise' external goods? The verb seems wholly out of place when it appears there are virtually no goods of any sort on offer; one can scarcely choose (recognise) options (goods) not on offer. Such are the problems of selectivity when philosophy meets social description. Now the point at hand is whether the distinction is supposed to be accurate description or heuristic device. More specifically, it would be helpful to unpack precisely what MacIntyre means by the term "empirical content", since it is far from clear. Morgan (1994: 128–75) adopts the latter stance. Indeed the point may be viewed as the central and strongest stance in his excellent book. He charges the 'Leftists' with failing to offer a description of sporting practices aside from their institutional character. The logic of the critique is precisely what the anti-emotivist moral philosopher Kovesi (1972), among others, offers: no evaluation without description. One can only proceed to evaluate a given object or activity when one has offered a description of its proper nature. Whether such latitude should be given, however, is another matter.

The problems, as with any institution that seeks to preserve a practice and its tradition, are twofold: what criteria are chosen to justify changes that will benefit the practice while at the same time preserving its integrity, and who will decide them? Perhaps, the general problems here are conceptual: how should we understand the notion 'integrity' in instances such as these and what virtues are to be developed in our practice communities if that integrity is to be maintained?[11] I want to suggest a vague and very probably unsatisfactory answer to this question after addressing the notion of the virtues within MacIntyre's account of practices with specific reference to sport.

The nature and function of the virtues

I want now to draw attention to the manner in which MacIntyre sets his account of virtues to work in his overall thesis about the role and importance of practices. This is separable from the issue of whether it is the only true, or merely the best, definition of a virtue for it is clear that there are many and competing definitions of virtue. MacIntyre sets a first, partial and tentative definition of a virtue thus:

> A virtue is an acquired human quality the possession and exercise of which tends to enable us to achieve those goods which are internal to practices and the lack of which effectively prevents us from achieving any such goods. . . . For it is not difficult to show for a whole range of key virtues that without them the goods internal to practices are barred to us, but not just barred to us generally, but barred in a very particular way.
>
> (MacIntyre, 1985: 191)

I want partly to stall a discussion of the relationship between the virtues and the different types of goods until I have discussed more fully the nature, range and functions of the virtues. What is noteworthy here, however, is that MacIntyre's subtle three-tiered thesis of the virtues is incomplete without reference to practices, the narrative unity of a human life and authority of tradition:

> I have suggested so far that unless there is a *telos* which transcends the limited goods of practices by constituting the good of a whole human life, the good of a human life conceived as a unity, it will both be the case that a certain subversive arbitrariness will invade the moral life and that we shall be unable to specify the context of certain virtues adequately. These two considerations are reinforced by a third: there is at least one virtue recognised by the tradition which cannot be specified at all except with reference to the wholeness of human life – the virtue of integrity or constancy. "Purity of heart" said Kirkegaard, "is to will one thing." This notion of singleness of purpose in a whole life can have no application unless that of a whole life does.
>
> (MacIntyre, 1985: 203)

I shall not enter into a discussion of the notion of the narrative unity of a whole human life here. Brown (1991) gives that dimension of MacIntyre's thesis an interesting application elsewhere. Furthermore, problems concerning the relationship between practices and who is to contribute to the maintenance of their integrity were discussed in the last section. In the penultimate section I shall deal briefly with the notion of integrity or purity in respect of the narrative unity of a human life and internal goods. It is commonplace to note the conservative strand in MacIntyre's thought whereby he invests the *de jure* authority of what is to count as purity or integrity within the tradition and those who are already committed to its constitutive practices. This notion of internality prioritised over externality runs right through MacIntyre's whole account and is closely related to the means–ends relation characterised by modern morality.

MacIntyre points out that it is a feature of modern theories of morality and reason that means and ends be clearly distinguished. But MacIntyre's theory of the virtues is one that denies such a classification. His virtue-based theory of the good is one in which 'being a causal condition of the good does not rule out being constitutive of it' (Taylor, 1989: 25). For MacIntyre the virtues are functionally valuable; they help us to secure internal goods, and without them we simply cannot attain them. But the relationship is not one of simple means and ends. The term 'virtue', as Taylor points out, can refer to two kinds of qualities: either facets of the good life or properties that have the effect of bringing about and preserving the good life. What is central to Aristotelian ethics, and which MacIntyre re-invigorates, is the notion that the latter class also forms part of the former. The virtues are not only constituents of the good life but also the means by which it is secured and maintained. The distinction between internal and external means must be drawn, MacIntyre argues, if we are to understand what Aristotle intended.

The virtues, then, stand in an internal relation to practices, the narrative unity of a human life and the concept of a tradition. They can be interpreted as goods-securing and practice/tradition-sustaining, as most philosophers of sport have interpreted them. It is interesting that few have noted their crucial role as institutional correctives. They may function both within the practice and/or inside the institutions. While quick to applaud sports as potentially valuable sites for the cultivation of virtue, it is easy to ignore (1) the fact that, as MacIntyre notes, where the virtues flourish so too may the vices, and (2) that sports administrators need no less to ally themselves to the practice, and just as any other persons must seek the good life no less through their employment in institutions as in their leisure time. Virtues are needed more than ever to stall their wayward and acquisitive nature. Is it that institutions, because of their logic, can never be co-operative enterprises? Can we not conceive, for example, of sports administration as a practice with its own excellences, or would that undermine the whole point of applying the distinction between the institutions and practices of sports?

But there is another dimension in MacIntyre's account of the virtues that is important to note. Pincoffs (1986) argued that several of the most notable moral philosophers, including MacIntyre, have been involved in a form of reductivism. The purported reductivism has taken more than one shape. On the one hand there are philosophers such as Kant and Mill who have celebrated single virtues such as conscientiousness and benevolence, respectively. Then there are cardinal virtues of courage, honesty, justice and temperance, which the Church fathers accepted and to which Aquinas added three theological virtues (faith, hope and love). To avoid this reductivism Pincoffs generated a list of the moral and non-moral virtues. Like MacIntyre, he locates the virtues in a functional setting but not the setting of practices that MacIntyre does. Instead he argued that virtues are dispositional qualities of persons that give us reasons for our preference or avoidance of them. He describes the virtues as the natural language of categories in terms of which we justify our choice, not of acts or lifestyles but of persons.[12] Whether or not we accept this picture of the virtues, what is more important is that it will generate a more heterogeneous account of the virtues than MacIntyre offered us:

> If we understand virtues and vices as dispositional properties that provide grounds for preference or avoidance of persons, the list will be indefinitely long, and it will be functionally various. There can be many different sorts of reason for preference [...] and a definition of virtue that picks out one or a very few dispositions as constituting the whole of virtue must shoulder the burden of showing that it is not unjustifiably reductive.
>
> (Pincoffs, 1986: 82)

Pincoffs set out two broad classes of virtues that are instrumental and non-instrumental. The former is subdivided into aesthetic, meliorating and moral, while the latter is divided into agent and group instrumental virtues. MacIntyre's analysis, Pincoffs argued, has an uncomfortably reductivist appearance in the sense that he limits his list of virtues to those that stand in a particular relationship to the internal goods of practices. There is another sense in which MacIntyre's account appears reductivist that is not mentioned by Pincoffs. Without the virtues of courage, honesty and justice, the practices could not resist the corrupting influences of the institutions. MacIntyre, however, does not state that the virtues are only gained in and through practices (1985: 187, 201) nor that these are the only three that secure internal goods, sustain the practice, and deter its institutional corruption. Though he does say that they are necessary, he does not commit himself to the view that they are sufficient (1985: 191–2). Nevertheless, his consistent emphasis upon the location of the virtues within practices and his exemplification of only those three at least give grounds for interpreting him as involved in an apparent double reduction.

Why is this long excursion into the location of the virtues, their nature, functions and extent important for philosophers of sport? There are several answers to this question. First, if the virtues are not merely exhibited in practices, how should we view those people who engage in activities on the borders of sporting practices such as weight training, keep fit, aerobics and step classes. While these sports-related activities are not practices in the MacIntyrean sense, they often engage many of the embodied dispositions that we value in sports and may contribute to what may be called an 'athletic way of life' or perhaps, in a phrase that has been barbarously abused by a range of ideological forces, a 'healthy lifestyle'. It seems clear that they require similar commitments and dedication even if the range of internal goods they encapsulate is somewhat etiolated. Second, we may come to evaluate more even-handedly the role of institutions, which, like practices, require of their members a whole range of virtues in order for their nurturing and distributive functions to be carried out effectively and morally so that practices flourish.[13] Third, there is much mileage in the notion of considering a virtue to be the basis of evaluating persons, and it is, I surmise, at the heart of the discussion of sportsmen and sportswomen as role models. It has often been said of sports and their excellent practitioners that we esteem them as ideals; they offer us pictures of what we may become if we immerse ourselves in the practice and become committed to the socially and historically embedded achievements they instantiate. Finally, most philosophers of sport have taken MacIntyre literally on the exultation of justice, courage and honesty as the primary virtues required by and developed in sport. To be sure these are three of the four cardinal virtues (temperance notwithstanding) and it may be the case that justice, courage and honesty are our best travelling companions in that quest for narrative unity in our lives. But sports are after all highly instrumental endeavours and the range of virtues they encapsulate, like any other instrumental practice, is much richer than this. Sports exalt instrumental action. Indeed we invent sports and games for their 'gratuitous difficulties', as Lasch (1979: 181) put it, in order to devise arenas for instrumentality (or purposive action as Best (1978) put it), albeit of a non-utilitarian kind.

Pincoffs (1986) listed the following agent instrumental virtues: alertness, carefulness, cool-headedness, courage, determination, energy, persistence, prudence and resourcefulness. It would not be difficult to contextualise each of the virtues in a sporting context. For example, what sports coach would not desire that his or her athletes were cool-headed in moments of intense pressure and would never give up until the final whistle was blown. By contrast, who would favour as team-mates the arrogant, callow, docile, fickle or merely selfish? This is not to say that in any and all circumstances, each of the agent instrumental virtues would apply but that in situations where instrumental action is required specifically, those virtues become prominent.

In his briefer list of group instrumental virtues, Pincoffs (1986) listed co-operativeness, practical wisdom and the virtues of followers and leaders. The list is not conclusive and consideration of specific practices may illuminate other, more fruitful, additions. Moreover, to think in that direction might well lead us to ask why some virtues are categorised as they are. I will offer only brief comments regarding this point in the following section.

Before turning to that discussion, and by way of linking themes, we should consider a remark made by Pincoffs (1986) that remains undeveloped. One of the strengths and, paradoxically, one of its weaknesses is the great generality of MacIntyre's application of the notion of practices, which are everywhere around us (law, education, medicine, sports, the arts, and so forth). And while it is certainly true that practices require the exercise of virtues to secure their internal goods and also for their continuance, we need not only ask, as we have already, precisely which virtues are required but also what sort of practice is it in relation to which the virtues are functional. Yet it is worth noting with Pincoffs that, given his fairly broad definition, there appear to be practices in which the external goods appear to be a 'kind of barbarian intrusion', whereas there are others in which the internal goods 'are at least arguably secondary to those gained from the consequences of successfully engaging in it' (1986: 97). Part of the problem of ascertaining whether such intrusions are, as it were, 'barbaric' rests upon a further discussion of what is to count as internal to practices.

Internality and externality re-examined

Much of MacIntyre's thesis, by his own admission, trades upon the idea of internal and external goods. And this distinction is not without its problems. Earlier I argued how the notion of internality should be interpreted partly as the felt-satisfactions of personal achievement derived from various performances. This accords with the idea that intrinsic value is subject-dependent. MacIntyre, however, wanted the notion of internality to have objective status, in the sense that the internal goods exist independent of any particular subject (i.e. person). The chess-playing example is supposed to secure this by the objective or public demarcation of goods that are internal and external to the practice. The selective example, however, wins the point without requiring vigorous defence. To be sure, his candy-seeking child exemplifies an instance in which the subject is motivated by something external to the practice. The child is extrinsically motivated; their reasons for playing are derived from the candy and not the chess. Here the means are neutral to securing the valued ends.

Not all relationships between goods are so straightforward. One can imagine the child playing chess for enjoyment, not because it is simply one means among many of being entertained, but because it is the exercise of their capabilities in that discipline that they desire. Furthermore, chess may well be the activity in which they are known by others to excel and is so esteemed. It is not only for the internal goods they seek to play the game but also for the external goods that they may, otherwise, be unable to secure. The playing of chess is, then, not merely instrumental to their securing entertainment, it is itself a specification of the very thing that is sought.[14] MacIntyre recognised the existence of such a relationship as we have seen but failed, implicitly or explicitly, to apply it in this manner. Because MacIntyre wanted to specify the internal goods as objective characteristics of the practice, he failed to apply the notion of internal means to those instances in which the personal satisfactions and their attendant motivations mean that a given activity is a valued (by a particular subject) and valuable (independent of my particular subject) means to securing external goods. Relying on the traditional vocabulary of intrinsic and extrinsic valuing is unhelpful here and to convey more clearly the subtlety and complexity of the activity and/or the attitudinal stance of the person, I shall use the term 'relational value' or 'relational valuing' to cover these ranges of meaning.

Certain activities may fulfil several aims for the participant at one and the same time and may be open to even greater variation in description. This is one aspect of those activities that prevents their complete explanation in simple means–ends terms. The individual's aims in playing sports (catharsis, esteem, fun, health, social affiliation and so on), may be sought through other activities if they are isolated into atomistic entities. It may be the case that one participates in a given practice because, empirically speaking, one could nowhere else secure that particular range of goods in that particular manner. For instance, MacIntyre argued that strategic imagination and competitive intensity are goods internal to the practice of chess and that internal goods can be sought only within their respective practices. He wrote: 'There are goods internal to the practice of chess which cannot be had in any way but by playing chess or some other game of that specific kind' (1985: 188). It could be argued, however, that strategic imagination might be developed in activities such as war, and competitive intensity might be promoted at least as well through sales marketing. Neither of these are what might be described reasonably as 'games of that specific kind'. Moreover, the development of strategic imagination and competitive intensity may be no part of my motivation to play chess but may be the consequence of my playing. How are these aims to be reconciled? Which refer to internal and which to external goods? And if no one actually valued such things as competitive intensity and strategic imagination, would this make them internal goods?

Philosophers have sometimes argued that some goods are valued in their own right, irrespective of consequences, and that others are valued exclusively for their consequences.[15] It seems difficult to cash out these two extremes. What would an activity look like that was valued for its internal goods but produced no valuable consequences? What sort of activity could yield valuable consequences but was, itself, of no value? Where the value of an activity is situated between these polar extremes it is often overlooked. These goods are, as Plato called them, 'mixed goods' (1974: 102–4), which he conceived to be the highest category of good. The motivation for considering mixed goods as higher lies in the fact that all actions have consequences even if those consequences are not the prime feature in the motivational hierarchy of the agent. For an agent to conceive of an activity in its wholeness is to include both its internal features and the direct consequences it produces as a product of that participation.

Chess is an example, like all sophisticated games, which belongs to the category of mixed goods; it is of relational value and may be valued thus. It can be valued for its own sake due to its internal features as one project among many to which persons become committed. At the same time, it may bring about external goods such as prestige, esteem among contemporaries, or wealth. Further, these external goods (if this is indeed what they are) also contribute significantly towards the living of valuable lives. Finally, there are those activities that have been called relationally valuable because they have internal goods and are at the same time specifically valuable ways of achieving (what have otherwise been called) external goods. One ought not ignore the consequences a practice may bring just because those goods might be secured alternatively. We should avoid the 'isolationism' entailed in considering activities apart from their direct consequences and consequences apart from the activity that wrought them. This enables us to see that if a good is valuable for its internal features and for the consequences it secures then it may be seen to confer greater benefit than that which is 'simply' valued for its own sake and that which is valued merely for its consequences. Yet ought sporting practices be offered as exemplars of activities that may be valued relationally as mixed goods? Part of the problem here is that MacIntyre is not prepared to concede the relationship between the participant who is at one and the same time fully committed to the practice (1) for both the internal goods that are intrinsically rewarding and (2) for the value of his or her commitments to the athletic form of life and the external rewards that he or she can only gain from that particular practice. From the first-person perspective, this or that practice need not be a neutral means to the securing of external goods. Even in his second edition of *After Virtue*, MacIntyre ran roughshod over this distinction in his negative evaluation of a 'grandmaster' in chess by describing an altogether different example. Instead of describing the example previously mentioned, he went back to the clean cut internal/external (pure/impure) characterisation of his earlier chess example. He asks us to consider the great chess grandmaster who cares only about winning. MacIntyre asserts that such a player

> could have achieved precisely the same good, that of winning and its contingent rewards, in any other field in which there is competition and there are victors, had he been able to achieve a comparable level of skill in those fields.
>
> (MacIntyre, 1985: 274)

There are two points to make here. First, reducing sophisticated practices to a single feature (their competitive logic) is spurious since the ranges of goods they encapsulate go far beyond the truism that practices with competitive logic will throw up winners and losers. Second, MacIntyre, in order to give force to his remark, begs two empirical questions: Could that person with particular capacities, potentialities, and environmental situation have achieved 'precisely the same good' elsewhere?; and are these goods really so practice-neutral? Is winning in chess really the same as winning in football or winning a violin competition or presenting the most cogent argument in a philosophical debate?

An answer to this question is closely related to the very question with which the previous section was concluded. Does the focus on external goods represent a barbarian intrusion in or of the practice? It seems reasonable to argue that there will be no satisfactory universal answer to that question, not even for the category of sports. While it is clear that the range of practices to which MacIntyre alludes are sufficiently diverse to warrant diverse answers it is less than clear that it ought to spawn such diversity within a single category such as sports. If business and the making of war (perhaps even politics) are to be seen as practices then it would seem peculiar to use MacIntyre's list of external goods as indeed external. The making of money in business, or so it seems at least, is a partially definitive internal good. Likewise, the ascertaining of power is to the excellent politician as esteem is to the excellent academic.

Part of the question of whether, say, the payment to professional sportspersons is the importing of an external logic rests upon the manner in which MacIntyre has drawn the distinction between internal and external goods. This same terminological distinction has been differently characterised by John Kekes[16] who broadly agreed with MacIntyre that 'internal goods are the satisfactions involved in the successful exercise of some of our dispositions in the context of a way of life to which we have committed ourselves'. But Kekes set out a different interpretation of external goods and their relationship to practices and persons as they are recast as 'satisfactions involved in possessing the means to their exercise and in receiving various forms of recognition for doing well' (1989: 187).

One may anticipate that a MacIntyrean might have little difficulty with the idea of external goods as forms of recognition (this is the point argued in earlier that elite sports are partially related to 'esteem' when justly conferred in an internal, not external relation) but might still want to dispute the propriety of receiving external forms of recognition that are inimical to the internal logic of the practice. What they could further argue, as Morgan has done so thoroughly, is that the sporting institutions have typically executed their distributive duties unjustly. While this may be the case, it does not force us to abandon Kekes' position.

It is the source of this reinterpretation, and the position against which it sets itself, that is most interesting. There seems to be implicit in MacIntyre's work (and hence in Arnold (1992, 1994), Brown (1991), Schneider and Butcher (1993, 1994) and Morgan (1994) by implication) the notion that the goods of our lives ought properly flow from the successful exercise of our own agency and not from considerations that we have not merited. This is one of the points at which MacIntyre sets himself against Nozick (1974) and Rawls

(1972). Kekes traces this line of argument to Socrates' position that the good man [sic] cannot be harmed since those harms and injustices the world heaps upon us may not be of our making and that the goodness of good lives depends upon what we do and not what is done to us. Kekes sharply criticised this conception of the purity or integrity of a practice since it falsely presupposed that 'moral purity requires turning inward, working for one's salvation while ignoring as much as possible the soiling, corrupting influence of the world' (1989: 188).

By contrast Taylor, in tracing the historical landmarks of moral sources, discusses the turn to 'inwardness' in his remarks on Plato. In using the language of 'inside/outside' he remarks:

> Thus if we think of the external as the realm of action in the polis, and the internal as that of the soul's disposition, then we could express the doctrine of the hegemony of reason in contrast to that of glorious action as an exaltation of the internal over the external.
>
> (Taylor, 1989: 120)

Taylor argues that this is the central point of Plato's *Republic*, that irrespective of external success the truly wise person will live a life of virtue irrespective of the pains he or she suffers for it. This is the crucial turn inward to reason as Taylor sees it and is related to the myth for example of Gyges' ring which I will discuss in relation to doping and its attendant vices in sport. What is more interesting perhaps for present purposes is that 'an ethic of reason and reflection gains dominance over one of action and glory' (Taylor, 1989: 117). This is exalted in Homeric times as celebrative of the physical and moral prowess of the warrior-cum-sporting ethic.[17] This difference of view was one of the reasons why I laboured over the issues of articulacy and critical self-awareness in the good life in the previous chapter.

The disdain that MacIntyre appears to reserve for external goods in contrast to internal goods may well be the product of a latent evaluation; practices would be pure but for the corrupting institutions they are vulnerable to.[18] But to think in terms of mixed goods may allow us to defuse at least part of the normative cutting edge of this distinction.

Internal goods are the products of my own agency justly conferred since no one can deny that my securing them was primarily my responsibility with the obvious caveats regarding the importance of persons of standing and authority in the practice to whom I submit my skills and judgements. So when I feel the delight at getting a back somersault just right, the feeling of exhilaration at achieving significant vertical elevation, allowing time for a tight tuck and patient, controlled, opening to landing, I feel (commensurate with that display of relative excellence) a partially defining good of gymnastics; I deserve it and no one may deprive me of it. External goods, however, require individual effort neither as a necessary nor sufficient condition. Status, prestige or wealth may always be accorded to those undeserving of it through the caprice of the institution just as the deserving may not be so rewarded upon such contingency.

It is important to be clear of what does not follow from this. It does not follow from this that external goods are necessarily randomly conferred; just as it does not follow that internal goods are solely the product of the successful exercise of some of our dispositions within a sporting form of life. When the institution conducts its distributional role properly it will be neither fortuitous nor incidental. Likewise it might be said that securing internal goods is not entirely due to one's own merit since, as Peter Singer[19] argued, we deserve no merit for coming up trumps in the genetic lottery. In a sporting context the acclaimed Scandinavian physiologist Per Åstrand (Åstrand and Rodahl, 1986) once said that if one wishes to maximise his or her chances of becoming an Olympic champion, one must be selective in choosing one's parents. While such successful choosing may not be a sufficient condition of securing the internal goods of sporting practice it may well be necessary.

The emphasis present in Kekes and absent in MacIntyre is the awareness that external goods such as esteem, security, status and respect can be valued intrinsically as public recognitions, when properly conferred, that our achievements are valued:

> They are intrinsically satisfying in two ways. First, as justly earned rewards they are public confirmations that we are doing well at our ways of life. . . . And second, external goods are intrinsically good also as specific contents that forms of appreciation have. They confer privilege because their recipients receive a greater share of scarce good than others. If the system of distribution is just and if the goods received enhance the enjoyment of their lives without injuring others, then there is nothing objectionable about such privilege.
>
> (Kekes, 1989: 192)

What this implies for practices such as sport is that the presence of external goods as rewards for achievement is not inherently bad except that their corrupt and distorted systems of distribution make them so. Of course paying a sports coach much more than the nation's prime minister or president is absurd. To be sure, external goods are competitive; we cannot all have as much as the other, but this scarcity points to them as rewards. Internal goods may be had by us all to the same degree, ability, motivation and context, notwithstanding. They are shared, social or public goods in this sense, but this does not exclude them from being private, felt satisfactions, as MacIntyre seemed to imply. Although offering public forms of recognition for sporting excellence does not seem inherently bad, I am uncertain as to how far this latitude should be extended. I have argued that at least some of the things that MacIntyre has called external goods appear not to be a barbarian intrusion in sport, at least not elite sport. I have mentioned, albeit briefly, that monetary rewards have been with us so long that they are only by heuristic analysis distinguishable from elite sport and that esteem is tied to the internal logic of practices such as sport since they are public celebrations of ludic capacities.

I am unclear whether the philosophers of sport who have utilised MacIntyre's thesis want to take his *Weltanschauung* on wholesale. His idea that the good life takes the shape of a narrative quest seeking itself, the good life always requiring and displaying the virtues in practices, is both challenging and noble. I am, however, less certain about the underlying picture of purity it seems to incorporate. I am happier with the following notion:

> The ultimate test of the goodness of our lives is whether they involve lasting possession of external and internal goods and whether the satisfactions derived from their possession outweigh, in quantity and quality, such hardship and suffering as we experience.
>
> (Kekes, 1989: 202)

This proper balancing of internal and external goods gained from our engagement in shared practices such as sport depends of course on their existence as the morally situated endeavours that MacIntyre so eloquently described. But their purity or integrity must be actively supported not merely by the practice and its best practitioners but also by those committed in other ways to the practice or institution. Given that sports, at least elite sports, have been historically, though contingently, associated with some external rewards, it seems preposterous that we abuse them so thoroughly. Even MacIntyre accedes to the necessity of their presence. And given that public recognition, in at least some forms, is central to the celebrative character of sport, we should perhaps focus more on the kinds of hierarchically organised moral perspectives in order to sustain the practices in the best kinds of ways we can. Of course, anyone who thinks only of external goods abuses the practices that afford them; and a life lived only in their pursuit will be shallow and meaningless. Because practices offer us the variety of goods that sports do and a range of public recognitions for our relative excellence in them, in proper part and justly conferred, we have all the more reason to value them. This will not be done by denying the place of external goods in those practices and in our lives but by ensuring their subordination to our prior commitments to the internal goods but by keeping them in their place.

Conclusion

I have attempted in this chapter to develop a minor though critical revision of MacIntyre's account of institutions, practices, virtues and their relationships in order to make better senses of the ethics of sports. I have tried to show that the generality of his application opens MacIntyre up to the charge that his ideological commitments focus on the shared social aspect of goods, practices and virtues to the detriment of the individual counterparts therein.

Furthermore, the diversity of applications to which MacIntyre puts the idea of a practice to work, glosses over what appears to be salient differences between practices and therefore the virtues that sustain them and preserve their integrity. I presented a less reductionist account of the virtues which hopefully displayed greater phenomenological fidelity than is suggested by MacIntyre. Finally, this move towards greater complexity was made manifest when considering the relationship between the practitioners, the practices and the goods, both definitive of and secured by the practice. I have retained MacIntyre's overarching framework while attempting to rework, in small and specific areas, some limited ideas in order for that framework more successfully to catch the nature of sports as practices. In the following chapters I hope to illuminate a broader range of vices and virtues that are to be found widely in sport and which cash out the value of the reductionist account originally given by MacIntyre and adopted widely in the philosophy of sport.

4 Sport and ethical development

Introduction

In the previous chapters I have begun to build a case for a particular vision of the ethical status and potential of sports. Of course, the arguments over whether sports build or merely reveal character is probably as old as sport itself. The aim of this chapter is to further develop an account of the moral educational potential of sports from a virtue-ethical perspective. While this may seem straightforward enough, it is not. In recent years social scientific research has denied the possibility of ethical development in sport. Indeed, it has typically argued that sport arrests development at an egoistic stage.

In an attempt to better understand the problem, certain philosophers (see Carr, 1998; Gough, 1998) have attempted to undercut the validity of that research and have argued for the impossibility *in principle* of any kind of science of ethical development. While I am in substantial agreement with these philosophers, my position here is more open to the aims of the dominant psychological approaches to moral education (which is necessarily conceived of as narrower than ethical development as I shall discuss later) in sport, and I attempt to bring out certain aspects of agreement that might be reached by philosophers and psychologists in their attempt to explore this contested and important matter. Of course, the translation of theoretical frameworks and conceptual revisions is a hazardous affair. I am mindful of the particular pitfalls of operationalisation when researchers attempt to go out into the field and assess carefully a range of controversial and complex issues such as are involved in the moral dimensions of sporting participation and performance. This chapter attempts to critique both the theoretical assumptions of that social scientific research and its methodologies and to consider more carefully the museums of normalcy as they have been called,[1] where sports may significantly build, shape, test and challenge the virtuous sportsperson.

Moral personality and the emergence of the moral development tradition

In current psychological research into sport and morality, cognitive developmentalism has been the dominant theoretical approach. To understand this dominance it is necessary to appreciate how early researches into the psychology of moral development, notably Jean Piaget, Lawrence Kohlberg and Norma Haan committed themselves to various theoretical positions regarding human agency and morality itself. Subsequent research design and analysis in sports that denies the moral educational potential of sports is a hostage to these commitments, which I criticize and reject in this chapter.

Although moral philosophising in the West has been with us since the Ancient Greeks, empirical moral psychology has twentieth-century roots. Hartshorne and May (1928) were the first to investigate the link between personality traits and moral action. They compared hundreds of children's behaviour in certain contexts with their self-attribution of moral traits including dishonesty and deceit. In keeping with the dominant behaviourist Zeitgeist, their findings pointed towards situational factors rather than personality traits of the children as the primary causal explanation for behaviour. These early findings raised a number of questions about the existence of moral character and personality, and more specifically about which psychological theories, concepts and methods have the most heuristic force and predictive potential. In particular, the 'thought–action' problem highlighted by Hartshorne and May, the unreliable relations between what people believe to be right and what in fact they do, is a ubiquitous and perplexing conundrum for moral psychology and undermines much research in the area of moral psychology in sport. In his account of *akrasia* or weakness of the will we find that Aristotle had already said much about that particular problem but in that positivistic time in the history of psychology, philosophizing was pejoratively thought to be beyond the realm of fact and thus epistemologically unreliable.

In his important book in moral psychology, Flanagan (1991) argues that Hartshorne and May's results are mistakenly taken as evidence against the existence of moral personality seen as a collection of traits. It would follow then that their critique need not consign the virtue-ethical account of character to the pre-scientific dustbin. Rather than abandon the idea of moral traits altogether, Flanagan (1991: 291) argued that the results can be read as evidence for the existence of traits 'albeit not traits of unrestricted globality or totally context – independent ones'. Reports, therefore, of the death of traits was premature. Rather, it is a particular conception of a character trait – the idea that it was a simple disposition enacted every time a person found himself or herself in a given situation – that should be rejected. The development of a more sophisticated account of moral traits and their role in moral character is the appropriate response to this research, and other studies such as Stanley Milgram's (1964) (in)famous research into obedience to perceived authority, which lends weight to the plasticity – though not complete malleability – of moral character and traits.[2] What is important to recognise in the non-trait globality issue from the perspective of current sport-related research, is the primary influence of Hartshorne and May's studies on alternative theoretical and methodological foci.

Piaget (1932) later conducted extensive studies focused on moral aspects of children's interactions. Describing himself as a genetic epistemologist he was interested in the growth of knowledge or cognition and conceptions of ethics based solely upon powers of reason. In keeping with the times he largely ignored the development of emotion that was thought to be antithetical both to reason and ethics. Piaget believed that rationality was the normative end point of cognitive development because rationality itself was the primary adaptive capacity of human agency. He argued that the development of human rational powers occurred in stages, each of which represented a particular logical-cognitive structure. The stages were progressive; each subsequent stage accommodated its predecessor in a more complex cognitive structure. The development of cognitive powers was therefore linear and unidirectional. His studies of morality, groundbreaking as they were, are necessarily a hostage to a narrowly focused conception of human rationality. As a hostage to the spirit of the then 'new' scientific age he wrote:

> Readers will find in this book no direct analysis of child morality as it is practiced in home and school life or in children's societies. It is the moral judgment that we propose to investigate, not moral behaviour or sentiments.
>
> (Piaget, 1932: 8)

Piaget makes it clear that his interest is narrowly focused on the moral judgement – its structure and form – since it is this that is a scientific indicator of the child's stage of development. The focus takes explanatory priority over affective and behavioural considerations. Although Piaget explicitly denies the reduction of moral development to the development of moral judgement, there has been a de facto reduction of moral development to the development of moral cognition (moral judgement) in subsequent moral psychology. I will argue in subsequent chapters that this posture has important consequences for the consideration of the role of emotions in ethics generally, and sports ethics specifically (see Chapters 7, 8 and 9 in particular).

Another important feature of Piaget's groundbreaking work was the introduction of explicit normative criteria for the stages of cognitive and, therefore, moral development. The child's development is seen in the adaptation to the natural and social environment. The development of moral judgement, therefore, is an adaptation to the moral world. Given Piaget's elevation of rationality, it is no surprise to philosophers that Kant's moral theory provides the normative criteria to evaluate these moral judgements. Kant also provides the conception of the moral world in the Piagetian scheme of thought. 'All morality', he wrote 'consists in a system of rules, and the essence of morality is to be sought for in the respect which the individual acquires for these rules' (Piaget, 1932: 9).

In order to study the moral development of the child Piaget focused on their understanding of rules in games. Notwithstanding methodological criticism, Piaget concluded that there were two stages to the development of the child's understanding of the obligatory (i.e. prescriptive) nature of rules. The first is a heteronymous understanding of morally right action wherein the child believes that it is subject to an external law that ought universally to be followed. The second stage is characterised by an autonomous understanding of the obligatory nature of rules. Following Kant, rules are obligatory if they are the result of rational deliberation. All moral rules, being at the same time rational rules, have such weight as they compel all rational beings to comply with them. It is worth reiterating that Piaget did not study rule–compliance, but rather examined the ways in which children understood the rules. The form of the judgement, whether it is heteronymous or autonomous, is more important than the content. Two children may follow the same rule thus visibly performing the same behaviour, yet only one may have a proper understanding of the rules' obligatory requirement. Only the latter may be said to be acting autonomously and therefore morally. The context and the content of moral rules, therefore, became largely unimportant for his project compared to the understanding of the source and grounds of legitimate obligation. In light of these factors Piaget's work marks the beginning of the methodological focus on what people *say* rather than what people *do* that came to dominate much moral psychology in general and the moral psychology of sport in particular.

The most important development after Piaget was the work of Kohlberg (1981) who embraced his central theoretical commitments, and constructed a more complex six-stage developmental sequence. His research design utilised a dilemma-based questionnaire to gather data on moral reasoning and judgement. Crucially he argued that people reason consistently according to their stage of moral development. This element of consistency of moral agency went some way to countering the situationism suggested by Hartshorne and May's (1928) studies. Although sharing significant common ground, Kohlberg made significant philosophical and psychological revisions to Piaget's work. First, he further embraced Kantian moral theory and argued that the moral world was governed by universal moral principles. Kohlberg (1981) believed that 'justice' was the overarching moral principle and the end point of moral development, or 'moral maturity', which itself was characterised by consistent judgements that embodied this principle. Second, departing from Piaget, he explicitly advocated the causal role that cognition played in moral agency and action. So although cognition, and its embodiment in judgement remains central, Kohlberg believed that moral cognition and moral action are more or less synonymous.[3] He argued that mature moral character was unified and consistent just as the rules in a moral theory. In its ideal form moral reasoning (and therefore moral action) is always in accordance with principles of justice. This rationalist picture of morality, driven very much by both Ancient Greek (Plato) and modern European (Kant) thought, holds that those who know the good choose the good. Therefore, those who are said truly to know the right thing to do will always act correspondingly. The guiding belief here then is one of a normative account of morality grounded in rational and universal moral principles. The impartial application of principles, not the plasticity of situations, should dictate moral action, which can be assessed through the reasoned judgements of agents.

Within this theorised picture of morality, moral judgements based on moral rules ought to be consistent and not contextually variable. The right thing to do is always the right thing to do; the wrong thing to do is always the wrong thing to do. The fact that other features of the situation (oneself, one's close relations or one's friends) might find their way into some children's reasoning was a sign of moral immaturity since these features necessarily compromise the impartial character of morality. Based upon such apparently secure foundations children can therefore be classified and ranked according to the stage of their moral maturity; their ability to reason about the right thing to do – which follow moral rules that were universal in scope, prescriptive in nature and impartial in application.

Kohlberg's theory is reductive in a number of problematic ways. First, (im)moral action is reduced to (un)principled action, and moral agency or moral character is reduced to a mature grasp of moral duty.[4] The emotions and other character traits are devoid of intrinsic moral worth. They are morally significant only in so far as they function in the impartial application of universal moral principles. Critics of Kohlberg's theory are legion[5] despite the continued propagation of his theory and method in education and sport research. Gilligan (1982) objected to the reduction of moral concerns to those of justice. Kohlbergian findings typically evaluated girls and women on a lower level than boys and men who reasoned more impartially. Gilligan argued convincingly that this picture of the moral reasoner as an independent rational chooser ignored the complex of rationality and affect in our estimations of moral judgements. She argued that moral concepts such as care, which was set aside because of its emotional character, might be equally important in evaluating moral maturity.

From a psychological perspective, the main weakness of Kohlberg's theory is the extent to which moral maturity is predictive of action across different settings. Paradoxically, situation, or context variation, was the very criticism aimed at Hartshorne and May (1928) and the very issue his theory aimed to avoid. Kohlberg (1984) himself recognised this problem and argued that people did not always take responsibility for moral action even though they might know what ought to be done. Moreover, he also thought that the prevailing moral atmosphere of the context might inhibit moral reasoning (Power *et al.*, 1989). Flanagan (1991) argued that a defence of Hartshorne and May's (1928) findings could be constructed on similar grounds.

In light of some of the problems with the theory, a former research collaborator of Kohlberg, Norma Haan developed an important revision to the Kohlbergian tradition that attempted to move away from his rationalistic preconceptions both of human agency and morality. Haan (1978) argued that morality was not to be narrowly characterised as a set of universal principles but rather a socially constructed set of norms, values, rules and solutions that could not be exclusively deduced from the principle of justice. Rather they must be constructed in a process called 'moral dialogue'. Moral dialogues, according to Haan, can result in moral balance and/or moral truth. The former refers to a mutually acceptable agreement in dialogue. The latter, moral truth, refers to solutions achieved under the procedural conditions of fairness. Moral truth is most likely to occur, therefore, in dialogues between those most capable of fair negotiation, or in dialogues heavily influenced by those who possess such egalitarian instincts. Haan assesses the maturity of moral agents based on the legitimacy of their strategies in moral dialogue. Most importantly, she proposes five stages that although similar to Kohlberg's do *not* represent a linear developmental sequence but rather provide normative criteria for evaluating the quality of moral interaction.

Haan partly avoids the 'thought–action' problem by observing moral interaction rather than merely evaluating moral judgements. Scores are then assigned to individuals based on the conduct of the subjects observed. This combination of a humanistic conception of morality and the observation of *actual* behaviour is supposed to deliver greater ecological validity. Some of the purported methodological advantage is lost, however, because the moral dialogues are constructed role-play situations that are themselves artificially constructed.

That factors extraneous to a person's cognitive capacities often influence the way one behaves may not come as a great surprise to those of a less cognitive persuasion. In addition to her important advances in methodology and operationalisation of the concept of morality, Haan looks to the psychoanalytic concept of ego-processing to explain these inter-test inconsistencies in moral action. Many children and adults as they play sport know that breaking the rules is wrong, they simply fail to carry that understanding through to action for a variety of personal (e.g. contingent self-worth (Duda, 2001; Duda and Hall, 2001), egoism, the untrammelled desire to win) and environmental (e.g. the motivational climate (Duda, 2001; Roberts, 2001), coach-induced norms (Stornes, 2001)) reasons. Haan argues that consistent moral engagement requires that a person remains 'coping'. A person who is coping remains in control of thought and action. If a person is suffering stress in the situation and fails to cope effectively, or employs defending processes, inconsistent moral action is likely to ensue (Roth and Cohen, 1986; Weinberger *et al.*, 1979). Although Haan refers to the importance of coping processes, her perspective does not readily account for spontaneous, or 'heat of the moment', rule violations.

What most of us know through our own experience in and out of sport is, as I noted earlier, the phenomena Aristotle called *akrasia*: the weakness of the will. We do not always and everywhere exhibit the consistency of belief and action that a moral theory – when conceived of as a scientific theory – exhibits. Thus in Haan's scheme there is an expectation that systematic discrepancies will sometimes occur among the moral levels that people use when they think about what a hypothetical person should do, what they should do, and when they act. Further, it is assumed that these discrepancies will not only be associated with people's moral capacity but also with their more general ability to cope with the complexity, intensity and content of particular situations (Haan, 1975). Having charted the normative development of the cognitive-moral developmental psychology we are now in a position to critically situate our evaluation of more recent psychological research, which is particularly damning of the ethics of sports.

Sport psychological and ethical development

Early studies of morality in sport seemingly confirmed what Kohlberg himself wrestled with, namely that moral judgements were contextually sensitive and that the 'moral atmosphere' of given contexts had a role to play (Power *et al.*, 1989). Bredemeier and Shields (1984a) found that individual moral judgement gravitated towards the prevailing level of moral judgement in the researched context. They introduced the term 'game frame' to refer to the particular 'atmosphere' of sports contests. In philosophical literatures this concept is often referred to as the 'ethos of sports'.[6] Sports contests are widely taken to be rule-governed instrumental activities hived off from other aspects of life by their peculiar gratuitous logic and their temporal and spatial boundaries. As such participants are characteristically instrumentally orientated. Bredemeier and Shields (1984a) suggest that this collective instrumental orientation or the 'game frame' is usually detrimental to what they call "optimal moral functioning".[7] It frequently promotes and rewards moral judgements of a lesser maturity than one might expect to find in non-athletic situations. Bredemeier and Shields (1986a) argued that 'game reasoning' is characteristically egocentric and suggested that the structure of competitive games locate moral responsibility with the official or the rules consequently encouraging the abdication of responsibility by the competitors. Moral autonomy under such a conception cannot be attained and this results in retardation of moral growth it is said. More recent studies, for example Guivernau and Duda (2002), provide further empirical support for the important influence of the 'moral atmosphere' of sports activities. Moreover, they found that the players' beliefs regarding their team, coaches and parents significantly shaped the moral atmosphere. Moral atmosphere (as perceived to be manifested on the team and at home) predicted self-reported moral behaviour of individuals.

Irrespective of gender, or the particular scenario involved, the athletes perceived the coach as the most influential figure. Of course, in Greek ethics the

idea of the *phronimos* (the wise practical chooser) is an important consideration in our considerations of role modelling and the selection of the right sorts
of persons we choose to emulate when we reflect on difficult choices. I will
develop the salience of this point with regard to both critical habituation and
role modelling below. Another closely related and significant early finding
was that moral reasoning correlated significantly with other moral indica-
tors. Bredemeier and Shields (1984b) found a significant inverse relationship
between high moral reasoning scores and aggression.[8] Bredemeier (1994)
argued that moral reasoning is predictive of both aggressive and assertive tendencies in sport. In addition Bredemeier (1985) found an inverse relationship
between the numbers of potentially injurious acts respondents found
acceptable, and their level of moral maturity. These findings offer empirical
endorsement of the Kohlbergian belief that moral reasoning is a significant
determinant of moral action.

This sustained research programme also proposed that other important
factors demanded consideration. Consequently, a model of moral action
(Shields and Bredemeier, 1995) and a measure of "moral functioning"
(Stephens *et al.*, 1997) that integrate their main conclusions were formulated.[9] Informed by Piaget (1932), Kohlberg (1981, 1984) and Haan (1978,
1983), and their own discoveries (Bredemeier and Shields, 1984a, 1984b,
1986a, 1986b), Bredemeier (1985, 1994), Bredemeier *et al.* (1986, 1987),
Shields *et al.* (1995), and other research, Duda *et al.* (1991), their model
represents a more complex and holistic account of moral agency or moral
functioning.

Drawing on Rest (1984) they argued that moral action is rooted
not just through judgement but also through additional processes central
to the foundation of their model of moral action. The first process is
interpretative consisting in the identification and recognition of situational
cues. The second process consists in the making of a moral judgement,
which coheres with Kohlberg's account. The third process is the choice of
a value that will guide moral action. The final process is the actual implementation of action (irrespective of the action chosen). In a further development they offer a brief account of the virtues that might operationalise
their model.

At first sight, the model distances itself from the excessive reductionism of
Kohlberg's original formula. The model describes moral agents as more than
just stage-specific moral reasoners recognising that values, attitudes, beliefs
and motivational orientation are important constituents of moral agency.
The import of the additional processes, however, gives rise to some related
problems. For Kohlberg, moral maturity was considered significantly, if not
exclusively, to be predictive of moral action on Socratic lines: 'who knows the
good chooses the good'. Yet folk psychology and common sense tell us that
those who know the good also need to interpret well, choose the right value
and implement appropriate action in conjunction with formulating a mature
moral judgement.

The recognition that "moral functioning" involves more than moral reasoning is borne out in the sports psychology literature. The construct that has received the most recent attention is that of achievement-goals. In sport in particular, research suggests that an over-emphasis on winning, conceived as concerns relating to the demonstration of superiority, leads to poor "moral functioning".[10]

Notwithstanding the complexity of Shields and Bredemeier's model and the subsequent attempts to investigate the value-dominance problem for athletes, two problems persist. First, the methods only measure cognitive components of morality: what people say rather than what people do is what counts. This problem is rooted in the belief that moral behaviour is intentional and that intention must be characterised, and driven by, appropriate moral motives. Moral motives cannot be seen or inferred; they must therefore be accessed in speech acts:[11]

> One difficulty with direct behavioural observation, however, is that the meaning of specific behaviors is never transparent and the researcher who observes a behavior must invariably interpret the meaning of that behavior if the observation is to be meaningful.
> (Stephens *et al.*, 1997: 374)

Within this research programme, then, researchers must therefore interrogate the motivating values and principles in order to make a judgement about the moral status vis à vis their reflective values or moral maturity. A morally praiseworthy action in this scheme requires that the intentions and motives behind it are themselves morally praiseworthy.[12] Still, as I will argue below, the model remains at best a thin account of how (sports)persons come to act qua moral agents. Although the idea of moral functioning is an expanded one, it lacks what we consider to be a substantive account of the qualities (and their development), above and beyond moral reasoning, that a person requires to function. Moral rules still dominate the picture, but are supplanted by certain virtues that are highly selective, and without an extensive rationale.[13]

In a gesture towards virtue ethics Shields and Bredemeier (1995) briefly present four qualities of character, or virtues, that are important for the model. They define character as 'the possession of those personal qualities or virtues that facilitate the consistent display of moral action' (Shields and Bredemeier, 1995: 193). Like MacIntyre they too opt for a reduced catalogue of virtues but, it seems, for very different reasons. It seems to me that their catalogue is driven by operational expediency. The four virtues, considered sufficient for this task, in Bredemeier and Shields' model are (1) compassion; (2) fairness; (3) sportspersonship; and (4) integrity.

Each of these virtues supports an allegedly specific component of the model of moral action. First, compassion, they argue, facilitates interpretation of the situation in order to decide upon a course of moral action. Second, having interpreted a situation compassionately, fairness facilitates the right judgement and, third, sportspersonship facilitates choosing values. Finally, the virtue of integrity is necessary to facilitate implementation of action. The four virtues selected appear, however, to raise more questions than they answer. Why should compassion merely drive interpretation and not action? Why could a perception of the fair thing to do not move us straight to action? We should keep in mind the most significant lesson of Kohlberg's research programme, from a meta-ethical viewpoint, that sometimes compassion and fairness clash violently. As was argued in Chapter 2, sportspersonship is not a singular virtue but rather an internally complex amalgam of values, attitudes and beliefs that hang together in a more or less loose way. In the same vein we can ask whether integrity is a singular virtue or does it suffuse all other virtues in order that the moral agent comes to the right choice? This, in particular, is a classic problem in Aristotelian and Platonic scholarship. Is virtue one or many? Do the virtues combine to form a mutually supportive network in an integrated character or are they at times in conflict? Rorty (1988: 314–29) offers an elaboration of this thorny issue and a proposed resolution (I subscribe to) in favour of a conflict-model where the more-or-less integrated character seeks to hold itself together while always in tension. Two points need to be made here. First, one could not reasonably expect a group of psychological researchers to have final answers to problems that have dogged moral philosophers since Plato. The desirability of multi-disciplinary scholarship (between philosophy and the social sciences) should be clear. Second, meta-ethical questions are present from the start in all such research whether they are theoretically (e.g. philosophical and/or grounded in a conceptualisation of moral motivation or moral functioning) or empirically (i.e. data) driven. A point of the deepest import attaches to whether indeed morality is to be seen as a quasi-scientific theory of rules and axioms or whether it is both more piecemeal and conflict-ridden from the beginning. While I favour the latter position, time and space do not permit an elaboration of such.[14]

A further and more general criticism attaches to their conception not of individual virtues per se but of the idea of virtue in itself. In the model, virtues, following Erikson (1964), are described as strengths that animate moral ideals. This picture of virtue is found most famously in the writings of Immanuel Kant, whom many consider to be the founding father of modern deontological (duty theory) ethics that have underwritten most modern moral developmentalism.[15] For Kant, the virtues are subordinate to the concept of duty and were important only in so far as they facilitated the exercise of duty. The virtues are defined primarily, therefore, in terms of their executive function, which in this case is the achievement of mature and consistent moral action. The deontological commitment to rationally grounded moral principles, initially taken by Piaget (1932) and adopted by Kohlberg (1981) and Haan (1978), remains a cornerstone of Shields and Bredemeier's (1995) model. The adjective 'moral' is exclusive and is reserved for the cognitive capacities of the agent, namely their moral reasoning ability. As for Kant, other capacities are only moral in an instrumental sense if they are exercised in the service, and facilitate the achievement, of an a priori standard of morality. Concepts such as care, consequence, courage and duty must play a role in any adequate moral theory. The precise shape that they play must be subject to coherence of course. One cannot just add and stir components. As Hampshire remarks:

> Ways of life are sharply coherent and have their own unity in the trained dispositions that support them, and in the manners and observances and prescriptions which as children we are taught to see as normal. [. . .] At some time we may be introduced to a museum of normalcies which have accumulated in history. But still we cannot pick and choose bits of one picture to put besides bits of another: the coherence of the pictures comes from their distinct histories: this may be called the no shopping principle.
>
> (Hampshire, 1983: 148)

There are a number of reasons why Bredemeier and Shields' model is problematic. Before proceeding to the critique of the model it is important to stress again that their model represents an important advance of previous research attempting to accommodate a more complex and multi-dimensional model of moral action than had been present in previous research. Part of my critique rests upon theoretical controversies in moral philosophy that do not appear in the operation of the model while others pertain to the robustness of individual stages of the model, or furthermore to the internal coherence of those features.

The ongoing debate between various forms of virtue or (agent) centred ethics, and rule (or act) centred ethics is clearly important in the evaluation of the model. Shields and Bredemeier's model seems to be a psychological hybrid that attempts to draw on the strengths of both camps. The firm footing that deontology boasts gives the model a universalist flavour. From virtue ethics comes the ability to explain contextual variation and a sense of embodied agency. In one sense the model is a concerted attempt to rectify a particular criticism made of Kohlberg's work concerning its inflation of the cognitive capacities of reasoning. Flanagan (1991) argues that any moral theory must be more than an abstract philosophical or psychological model and must adhere to a principle of minimal psychological realism. It must be 'possible, or perceived to be possible, for creatures like us' (Flanagan, 1991: 32).

Although there are some reservations about the normative commitments and the methodological strategy of much of the psychological research, what emerges is a body of empirical evidence that points towards a more complex picture of moral development and education. The Piaget/Kohlbergian account of development prioritised the reorganisation and increasing adaptation of cognitive capacities. Cognitive dissonance or disequilibria drives development. The primary goal of the educator is to provide the stimulus, the disequilibria, that necessitate the reorganisation and adaptation of perception, emotion and judgement. Given that empirical research in sport undermines the exclusively cognitive antecedents of moral functioning, a different account of moral education is also required. Evidence suggests that the moral atmosphere is a strong mediating factor, and the influence of the coach, as a 'moral exemplar' seems crucial.[16] Moral education should therefore take into account the moral climate of sport, particularly the example set by the coach, if the moral behaviour of individuals in sport is to improve. The qualities at which education aims must also be wider in scope than the exclusively cognitive capacities that Piaget and Kohlberg focused upon. Haan's (1978) ego-processes, and Shields and Bredemeier's (1995) four virtues, point towards the need for a more expansive focus. Although I welcome a move towards concepts of virtue and character, a more faithful approach is required. I shall now consider the contours of an Aristotelian account that is also developmental in character, yet gives a greater emphasis on the emotions, a more considered view of deliberation, and exults the necessary non-cognitively saturated account of moral training that is the basis of praiseworthy conduct and character.

Back to Aristotle: character, emotion and judgement

Baechler (1992) describes how, nearly 30 years ago, the Académie Française (French Academy) ceased the performance of its annual ritual wherein one of its established members gave a public lecture on virtue. It was indeed a sign of the times. On the one hand, as we have observed above, the scientific academy had apparently debunked its folk psychology. While on the other, as Baechler observed, the 1960s were in full swing and the idea that good and bad could not be objective but were rather relative to each and every culture became ever more fashionable. Both trends worked against the middle, each assaulting the very idea of virtue. One group of scholars (usually sociologists and historians) thought it too fixed and insufficiently attentive to cultural differences, the other (usually psychologists) thought it too loose and yearned for a scientifically valid measure based on a single more concrete concept: justice.

In contrast to the moral reasoning model of Kohlberg, the Aristotelian model appears antiquated to psychologists. To social scientists and historians, Aristotelian thought represents a 'brave' leap back to antiquity an inappropriate and ill-considered revival. What merits might there still be in a scheme of Aristotelian moral development? Recently, and perhaps especially in applied ethics, there has been a move back towards a virtue-theoretical approach to moral philosophical thinking and practice inspired by (though not hostage to) the seminal work by Alasdair MacIntyre whose ideas were presented and, to a limited extent, revised in the previous chapter. Agreeing largely with this Aristotelian scheme of thought and living which celebrated the virtues as essential travelling companions in our search for a good life, I now turn to the idea of what a theory of ethical development, inspired by Aristotle, might look like in the contexts of sport.

In the first instance we should say that an Aristotelian theory of ethical development would be aretaic. This concept derives from the ancient Greek word *Arēte* (usually translated as 'virtue' but denoting any form of personal excellence and not merely those that are widely recognised as moral). So an aretaic conception of ethics focuses first and foremost on excellent character; on being a certain kind of person. This picture is essentially distinct from the deontological picture of the rational moral agent disposed to follow certain kinds of rules and performing correspondingly obligatory acts. This focus is often captured in ethics in the idea that virtue ethics is more concerned with being rather than doing, with goodness rather than simply rightness. The right kind of person (i.e. a good one, a virtuous one) is one who does the right thing, for the right reason, at the right time, feeling the right way about it as they do it. Having said that explanatory primacy must go to personal character rather than rules, we must acknowledge the situated nature of character, of vices as well as virtues.[17]

Kohlberg's famous jibe, that the problem with aretaic ethics was that everyone had his or her own bag of virtues, contains an important criticism despite its rhetorical style. The kinds of persons that are celebrated as paradigms of human excellence do change somewhat over time and between cultures. It does not follow, however, that goodness is merely a hostage to relativism. There are certain human excellences that span time and place. As we saw, MacIntyre cites justice, courage and honesty as key among the virtues of any civilised community. And in addition to that we might also cite respectfulness, responsibility, integrity and a host of others, some of which I explore in the following chapters. Are humans not all better for these traits as opposed to disrespectfulness, irresponsibility and wantonness? Of course, precisely which actions these virtues issue in, and when, will be a thorny problem. But that does not mean we should throw the baby out with the bath water.

If we agree then upon the importance of character, some other things will follow. First, we should eschew simple reductionism for the reasons set out in the previous chapter. Whether in philosophical accounts such as MacIntyre's or psychological ones such as Bredemeier and Shields', we must be careful to give robust psychological accounts of human being and action so that our experiments into sports ethics are not predicated upon diaphanous apparitions, thinly operationalised human agency, in order merely to facilitate empirical research.[18] Second, as noted above, we have to acknowledge the important contribution of context, for as Rorty observes, 'community is the context of character' (1988: 324) and MacIntyre's practice-communities thesis is a robust articulation of such a context, even if it is not the only one. A recognition of context-sensitivity is one place where Bredemeier and Shields have notably made ground in describing the role and influence of the moral atmosphere of sports and how these alter according to age, gender, playing level, sport-type and so on.

One of the ways in which our accounts of action in sport can become more ethically robust is by attending to the tripartite account offered by Aristotle.

Action typically issues from relatively settled dispositions to see, feel and think, and is the product of our habituation. This requires an emphasis on the concept and importance of childhood learning, imitation, emulation and so on that is rather more powerful than is commonly acknowledged. This requires an examination of the patterns of normalcy as a complex of perception, emotion and deliberation. Of course, reasoning and judgement are critical to our moral development but crucially they will be a product of a habituation into modes of perception and feeling that are not simply precursors to, but rather constitutive of, mature moral action and reflection.

Thus, in the Golden Age, as Freud referred to it, 'hooked up securely to the sources of nourishment and comfort, the infant is indeed in a state of blissful totality' (Nussbaum, 2001: 185). Then, of course, the child is born into the world of objects and beings and things start to get more complex and confounding. Birth through infancy can be called the initial stage of Aristotelian moral development.[19] As Nussbaum (2001)[20] argues, psychoanalysts typically focus on the gratification of physical needs and basic desires while ignoring how the world is itself an object of interest and pleasure, fear and anxiety. Notwithstanding this, emotions and proto-cognitive mastery are there pretty much from the beginning. It is the centrality of these features of early experience that are frequently ignored or diminished in cognitivist accounts of moral development. It is as if childhood can be thought of as a necessary evil rather than a complex and emotionally charged view of the world. A crucial part of that world is the connectedness of the infant and the carer. It is precisely this essential connectedness that the Kohlbergian picture eschews in its desire to put an autonomous judger at the apex of moral development. And, it must be noted, this too is gendered from the beginning:

> Taught that dependence on the mother is bad and that maturity requires separation and self sufficiency, males frequently learn to have shame about their own human capacities for receptivity and play, whereas females are more likely to get the message from their parents that maturity involves a continued relation of interdependence, and that emotionally expressing need is appropriate.
>
> (Nussbaum, 2001: 219–20)[21]

Along with the growing awareness of language, the inchoate emotions emerge, and with them the growth of ethical sensibility, however limited throughout infancy. Even at this stage, there is means–ends reasoning related to wants and needs (ice cream is preferable to fruit) but also to relations (jealousy arises at the carer's attention to siblings; a sense of unfairness is felt when deprived of what was before given without qualification).

In the intermediate stage, habit formation is critical to the development of moral sense. Practice does not make perfect, as sports psychologists are fond of telling us. Rather, it makes things permanent, as Aristotle (1980) observed long before the psychologist's remark became a commonplace: 'It makes no small difference then, whether we form habits of one kind or of another from our very youth; it makes a very great difference, or rather *all* the difference' (Bk. II.I; 1103b22–5).

It is, therefore, the acquisition of good habits that we are crucially after in general and in particular in sport. The moral educational potential rests precariously on sports as a moral laboratory in which habituation can be first enlisted and only later reflected upon and, if necessary, problematised. In the intermediate stage the character is in transition. Children and youths learn to adopt attitudes less egoistically driven and come to care as well as to reason for others' interests and needs. But crucially it is also a time for the formation of reflexive emotional attitudes that are cognitively grounded. In this stage, moral emotions such as regret, shame and guilt, as well as pride and loyalty, come to be conceived of as appropriate responses to situations and acts. These are the fare of strong evaluation as I set it out in the context of sportspersonship in Chapter 2. Typically, these responses come to form patterns of more or less stable perception, emotion and deliberation. But they must be struck upon the right reasons of course. To act virtuously is indeed to act from a settled character that sees and feels and judges things properly.

Moral instruction, in its various forms, will be critical in this stage in addition to the more informal modes of learning. Two are particularly noteworthy. The first relates to the powerful though old-fashioned notion of a role model. In Aristotelian thought, understanding the right thing to do, feel and see is a product of our learning from wiser souls than ourselves:

> Actions, then, are called just and temperate when they are such as the just or the temperate man would do; but it is not the man who does these that is just and temperate, but the man who also does them *as* just and temperate men do. It is well said, then, that it is by doing just acts that the just man is produced, and by doing temperate acts the temperate man; without doing these no-one would have a prospect of becoming good.
>
> But most people do not do these, but take refuge in theory and think they are being philosophers and will become good in this way, behaving somewhat like patients who listen attentively to their doctors, but do none of the things they are ordered to do. As the latter will not be made well in body by such a course of treatment, the former will not be made well in soul by such a course of philosophy.
>
> (Bk. II.V; 1105–21)

Several points need to be made here. First, we must acknowledge the situatedness of Aristotelian thought. It is clear that the practices of Ancient Greece would be misogynistic by modern lights. As I noted in the methodological note in the introduction, a revival project is not needed. Indeed, Aristotle talks of the good and wise 'man' and often of the 'great-souled man' when he is referring to acts of manly courage and nobility. Of course, our interpretation needs to be revisionist in this regard. Nonetheless, this notion of habituated action is still apposite. Aristotle's beautiful remark that we will come to the palace of reason only through the courtyard of habit and tradition is well made. For in times of uncertainty, we literally act according to our early habituation and only thereafter according to our appreciation of what good people would do in such situations. This is how we learn to perceive the rule (how properly to proceed when faced with competing claims on our motivations) and to follow it with cognisance. Merely blind rule-following observance is in a clear sense not the same thing as following a rule wholeheartedly, where one's actions are predicated on a conception and dedication to do the right thing by being the right kind of person.[22] Nonetheless, this stage is characterised by uncertainty and unreliability. True, one comes to begin to resist one's motivations and values that belong to and persist from the earlier more egoistic stage, but developing mature reflexive attitudes and developing these self-critical attitudes in relation to their evolving value-scheme is still an undertaking in the process of becoming.

Character training[23] in the intermediate phase helps our evolving moral agent to reliably (re)produce the right acts at the right times while coming to feel appropriately about them. It is a mistake, however, to think of this habituation as mere rote learning in the way that early skill-psychologists believed. It is as if we need, in moral learning, to replace this arcane way of thinking with a more open-ended framework to understand and explain action. One learns the generalised responses and then one must refine them, becoming ever more sensible to the particularities of each situation.

This stage is often summed up by the phrase that one has learnt the 'that' of moral action. One appreciates that one must act according to the dictates of virtue. In order to fully mature, to reach the final stage of Aristotelian moral development, moral agents must also comprehend the 'why'. As Tobin puts it: 'Acquiring the why in ethics will help [those in the intermediate stage] to overcome the gaps, unclarities, and straightforward mistakes in his moral awareness' (1989: 203).

Fully, to act virtuously, which as always at the same time to act wisely, is a matter of hitting a mean between acts that are lacking in some regard, or excessive in others. It is here that Aristotle's celebrated 'Doctrine of the Mean' gives guidance as to how moral training and education, with appropriate exemplars, gives rise to our feeling, judging and acting virtuously. Here again we have a critical point of contrast with both Kohlbergian and Haanian thinking.

On the one hand, doing the right thing and being the right kind of person in a Kantian-inspired Kohlbergian scheme is about deducing action-guiding conclusions from general principles. On a Haanian scheme it is about coming to uncoerced and fair agreements that we can simply be comfortable with. So the operationalisations of these ideas in sports psychology has meant one of two problematic methodological and theoretical paths are followed. First, we can use a universal measure of morality (as in Kohlberg's universal principle of reasoned justice) and then we see the extent to which our sportspersons can approximate it in action. Or alternatively (in Haanian fashion) we measure the extent to which the moral balance that has been struck between competitors' clashes of interests (I want to win. OK, so too do you) has been fairly made. There are correspondingly two points of theoretical contrast I wish to make here. On the one hand one can come to fair agreements that are not ethically defensible. It seems in professional North American ice hockey that 'everyone' agrees to be violent. No problem of unfairness there then. Equally, for the Kohlbergians, there is no appreciation that ethics is *to a certain extent* situational. And the appreciation of this point – that morality is not some special sphere of universal obligations but a matter of trying to live good lives – is central to the Aristotelian scheme I am trying to develop in this book. In our guidance as moral educators whether as coaches, parents or pedagogues we must hit the mean between vices of cowardice (a deficiency) and rashness (an excess) if we are to act courageously in the face of danger or things that we are properly afraid of. Consider those who over-conform to violent norms of sports sub-cultures (Coakley, 2001). This is not courage as a virtue, but rashness, a failure to see what dangers are properly to be faced; failure emotionally to attach significance to the respect owed to the health and well-being of an opponent. As Sherman (1989: 35) puts it:

> Action which hits the mean is directed towards the right persons, for the right reasons, on the right occasions, and in the right manner. The overwhelming sense is that virtue must fit the case. But, as Aristotle insists above, the formula of the mean itself seems to offer little concrete guidance.

This last point, that ethical perception, affection and decision are open-ended is critical to the final stage of moral development. We can only go so far in our moral training in sports as elsewhere. There will be no formulaic application of principles that are necessarily to be adapted to circumstance and context. This philosophical point, crucially, must be amplified by political strictures. Which of us will operate in Kohlberg's level six or Haan's level five? Which of us will be the perfect practical and moral reasoners? None of us that are human, that much is for sure. While the final stage is what we aim for, we commonly fail and we can do so just as easily by failures of perception (or moral blindness we might say), of emotion (we become unfeeling automata, conditioned to blot out our affectivity) or of judgement (we simply apply the rule wrongly, select an inappropriate value) and of course we may do all things right, but fail to move ourselves to action in one or all of these ways.

Thus, after good and critical habituation, there will always be the matter of institutionally and politically creating the strong and supportive structures that will incentivise and punish those whose perception is blinded, whose affections have withered under the calluses of indifference and whose reasoning has been thwarted by continued and robotic observance to their tribal attachments whether as team or school or college or nation.

Conclusion

In this chapter I have tried to show how a critical appreciation of the historical and theoretical antecedents of moral philosophy and moral psychology place us in a stronger position to present a critique of current sports psychological research into the ethics of sporting participation and performance. It has enabled us to reach back to a richer tradition of moral thought, itself arising from a competitive social culture, that offers a better 'museum of normalcy' from which to situate moral character and conduct in sport.

Whether such a scheme can offer anything that would yield a moral barometer with which to test the atmosphere of sport is yet to be revealed. While Carr (1998) and Gough (1998) argue that it cannot do this in principle, I prefer to leave the door ajar. What Carr and Gough properly object to, and what I have illustrated and amplified here, is that a positivistic science in the area of ethics is a logical non-starter. Science proceeds by observation and experiment. And as I have argued, our observations of sports ethics are already saturated with normative commitments in the concepts of 'duty', 'respect', 'rule-following', 'virtue' and so on. Second, any empirical research in these fields must itself make theoretical assumptions about the very nature of morality, which is then presented as the standard against which behaviours are described and evaluated. What I do know is that moral learning, development and maturing can occur. I have attempted to set out a richer conceptual scheme in which to consider such learning and development. I have shown how that must take childhood patterns of perception, emotion and deliberation more seriously along with modes of increasingly critical habituation in a strongly supportive community. Whether this can yield anything approximating a scientific programme must itself be the object of further research. In developing a picture of particular vices and virtues in the following chapters I want to take seriously both MacIntyre and Rorty's view that community is the context of character and to situate the moral psychology of sportspersons within an aretaic scheme.

Part II
Vicious and virtuous sport

5 Codes of conduct and trustworthy coaches

Introduction

During the 1980s and 1990s considerable discussion was generated concerning the regulatory checks and balances for a number of occupations. Perhaps the key drivers for the development of social responsibility were the excesses of stock market traders or CEOs who toiled happily under the leitmotif 'greed is good', affording themselves huge financial salaries and bonuses unchecked by the market or their own corporate structures. What followed thereafter was the development of a serious debate about the loss of personal virtues such as responsibility and organisational values such as accountability and trust. This very general atmosphere was compounded in sports, at least in the UK, by two other factors. The first was a process of professionalisation where what had ruled in sport hitherto, whether in terms of administration or coaching, was distinctly unregulated. The voluntary nature of most sports labour (from youth sport and even up to national sports federations) seemed to lack structure, efficiency, accountability and control. Second, coupled with this awakening was a plethora of child abuse cases where the lack of organisational checks and balances allowed paedophiles to move freely within the structures of sports and similar youth movements under voluntary labour. The response both within and outside of sports was the development of rule-based codes of conduct. Into these codes of conduct can be read a moral conservatism; a flight back to the language of moral certainty, of duties, obligations, principles and rules. The task of how we should understand these codes of conduct and what may properly be expected of them in the context of sports coaching is explored in this chapter. In order to effect this task I set out a caricature of professionalism that is partly at odds with the rule-based conceptions of ethics and, utilising the concept of 'trust', I attempt to underwrite the notion of sports coach as professional.

Professions and professionals

The clergy, medicine and law are often referred to as the 'liberal professions'. They represent paradigmatic examples of professions in which persons ply their occupation's knowledge and skills in a very particular way. The list, though traditional, is somewhat incomplete and based upon historical contingencies that have much to do with the manner in which the labour employed in these spheres was monopolistically constructed. This feature was surely the motivation for George Bernard Shaw's quip that all professions are conspiracies against the laity. There is already, however, a significant literature in sports regarding the ideas of 'professional' and 'professionalism' though it is typically centred around the payment of athletes and the apparent contrast with the idea and ideal of amateurs and their motivational sets. I do not intend to review those arguments here[1] and instead focus on the idea of coaching as an emergent or aspiring profession. Instead, I take the spirit of Daryl Koehn's analysis of the liberal professions and situate it in the context of sports coaching.

Koehn argues that the concept of 'professional' is inherently normative since any attempt to describe the boundaries of the concept is at the same time to recommend a particular version of the powers of a person under that description. Koehn sets to ground the *moral* authority of professionals in contradistinction to two alternative models that are not uncommonly characteristic of relationships in sporting contexts: (1) the professional as expert; and (2) the professional as service-provider for fee. Neither of these conceptions, it is said, can underwrite the trust we place in professionals. Koehn draws upon Baier's work in feminist ethics to argue that trust is the heart and soul of professions and professionalism.[2] And it is in this vein that I want to recast the ways of working of sports coaches.

The notion of professional as possessor of expertise deals only with techniques or means and is not tied to proper ends among which is the client's good; in this conception the expert pursues their own private agenda which may or may not coincide with their client. The professional as service provider for fee is similarly untrustworthy. This contractual understanding of the relations between professional and client, although placing the client's agenda in the foreground, can serve to obscure the proper end of the profession. The caricature is the defence lawyer unconcerned with justice but hell-bent on achieving a result of not guilty for their client. The professional, placed in the service of the client, becomes little more than a (more or less expensively) hired hand.

Koehn begins her account by drawing upon interesting etymological support. The word 'profess' comes from the Greek verb *prophaino* meaning 'to declare publicly'. The Greek *prophaino* became the Latin *professio*, a term applied to the public statement made by persons who sought to accompany a position of public trust (Koehn, 1993: 59). Developing the idea of a public profession of trustworthiness, Koehn (1993) sets out seven conditions, which I elaborate in square brackets, that are intended to ground the moral authority of the professions and thus professionalism:

1   the professional must aim at the client's good [whose desires do not simply entail that good];

2   the professional must exhibit a willingness to act toward this aim;
3   such willingness to act thus must continue for as long as is necessary to reach a determination;
4   the professional must be competent [in the appropriate knowledge and skills];
5   the professional must be able to demand from the client [specific appropriate knowledge and performances];
6   the profession must be free to serve the client with discretion [which, as with (1) above, need not be consistent with their desires];
7   the professional must have a highly internalized sense of responsibility.

From these conditions, the grounds for trusting the professional are given moral authority the like of which enables a fairly open-ended definition that, at least on the face of it, does not disqualify sports coaching. As professionals, sports coaches aim towards the production of relative and absolute excellence of their performers; this is the proper end of sports and what is to be aimed for within the framework of the relevant practices. Moreover, the coaches have been initiated into a body of knowledge and skills in areas ranging from the physiology of conditioning, efficient techniques of skill acquisition, performance motivation, goal setting and so on. Further, and reciprocally, the coaches demand from their athletes appropriate performances. At least in most cases, the 'client' is not the master of the entire agenda. Finally, some authority, often paternalistic (with old and especially with young athletes), is invested in coaches whose powers are effected with discretion in a framework of responsibilities to self, performer and sport. Not in reference to sports, but applicable to them, Koehn summarises:

> A professional is an agent who freely makes a public promise to serve persons [. . .] who are distinguished by a specific desire for a particular good [. . .] and who have come into the presence of the professional with or on the expectation that the professional will promote that particular good. In other words, agents become professionals by virtue of what they profess or publicly proclaim before persons lacking particular goods.
>
> (Koehn, 1993: 59)

She later states that 'professionals must have some way of establishing that they are worthy of the client's continuing trust. Adherence to the professional pledge in each and every interaction with the client constitutes a solution to this problem' (1993: 68). The notion of a public pledge is one that finds no home in contemporary sporting practices just as medical professionals too have eschewed the Hippocratic Oath. But oaths there were in antiquity and were not merely sworn by the forerunners of medical physicians but sports coaches too.

Swearing public oaths in sports and medicine

In Ancient Greece the *gymnasiarchos*, literally the leader of the *gymnasion* or school, held official roles to oversee the tutelage of young educands (those to be educated) (Miller, 1991). The *gymnasiarchos* were responsible for the education of youths from 15–17 of wealthy families. Their training was not just in gymnastics as the name implies, but also in music, literature and philosophy. The *gymnasiarchos* not only supervised training, but also directed the activities of the pedagogues and even acted at times as their benefactor, and were empowered to make judgements where the law was unclear or unspecific (Harris, 2007). And, given the separate careers, so markedly different in public prestige and payment, the proximity between their oath and the Hippocratic Oath (fourth century BC) is quite striking. Although commonly and wrongly confused with the Latin dictum *primum non nocere* (first, do no harm), the oath to the Greek God Hippocrates runs as follows:

> I swear by Apollo the physician, by Asclepius, Hygeia, and Panacea, and I take to witness all the gods, all the goddesses, to keep according to my ability and my judgment, the following Oath.
>
> To consider dear to me as my parents him who taught me this art; to live in common with him and if necessary to share my goods with him; To look upon his children as my own brothers, to teach them this art if they so desire without fee or written promise; to impart to my sons and the sons of the master who taught me and the disciples who have enrolled themselves and have agreed to the rules of the profession, but to these alone the precepts and the instruction.
>
> I will prescribe regimens for the good of my patients according to my ability and my judgment and never do harm to anyone.
>
> To please no one will I prescribe a deadly drug nor give advice which may cause his death.
>
> Nor will I give a woman a pessary to procure abortion.
>
> But I will preserve the purity of my life and my art.
>
> I will not cut for stone, even for patients in whom the disease is manifest; I will leave this operation to be performed by practitioners, specialists in this art.
>
> In every house where I come I will enter only for the good of my patients, keeping myself far from all intentional ill-doing and all seduction and especially from the pleasures of love with women or with men, be they free or slaves.
>
> All that may come to my knowledge in the exercise of my profession or in daily commerce with men, which ought not to be spread abroad, I will keep secret and will never reveal.
>
> If I keep this oath faithfully, may I enjoy my life and practice my art, respected by all men and in all times; but if I swerve from it or violate it, may the reverse be my lot.

Not restricted to the avoidance of harming the patient the bar is set much higher. In pursuit of the goals of healthy living, the avoidance of the procurement of death whether by abortion or euthanasia, the physician publicly declares himself to a range of virtues such as his trustworthiness, the bindingness of his confidence to the patient, but also to the 'purity' of his profession. While no one knows for sure the precise historical origin of the oath it is thought to emerge around the fourth century BC.

While not quite as ancient we might think of the first sports code of conduct, the Beroia Law for the *gymnasiarchos* which dates back to the third century BC. One particularly noteworthy feature of the Law is the specificity of the behaviours that it demands, permits and proscribes and the penalties to be exacted upon their transgression. Modern codes might well learn from its precision irrespective of the fact that only fragments remain of it.

The Beroia Gymnasiarchy Law

No one under the age of thirty shall take off his clothes when the signal is lowered, unless the leader should give his permission. When the signal is raised, no one else shall do so, unless the leader should give his permission, and no one should anoint himself in another wrestling-ground in this city, and if he does, the gymnasiarch shall prevent him and fine him 50 drachmas.

All those who come to the gymnasium shall obey the person whom the gymnasiarch appoints as leader, as is prescribed by the gymnasiarch. The gymnasiarch will flog whoever does not obey (the leader) with a rod, and fine the others.

The ephebes and those who are under twenty-two years old shall practice javelin throwing and archery every day, when the boys have anointed themselves, and, equally they should do anything else that it appears necessary for them to learn.

Concerning the Boys

None of the young men may enter among the boys, nor talk to the boys, and if someone should do this, the gymnasiarch will fine him and prevent him from doing any of these things.

The physical trainers of the boys shall present themselves twice a day in the gymnasium, at hours that the gymnasiarch shall set, except in case of illness or some other trouble that compels it; otherwise, they shall report to the gymnasiarch.

If one of the physical trainers of the boys should neglect his duties, and not appear before the boys at the appointed hour, the gymnasiarch shall fine him five drachmas each day.

The gymnasiarch shall have the power to flog the boys and their paedagogoi who are disobedient, if they are not free, and to fine those who are.

He shall order the physical trainers of the boys to make an inspection of the boys three times a year, once every four months, and appoint judges for them, and crown the victor with an olive crown.

Those who may not participate in the Gymnasium

(A person) may not take off his clothes in the gymnasium if he is a slave, or a freedman, or the son of one of these, or *apalaistros*, or a prostitute, or works at a trade in the agora, or is drunk, or mad. If the gymnasiarch knowingly allows one of the people indicated above to anoint himself, or if someone has revealed and pointed this out, he will pay a fine of 1000 drachmas. To ensure that the fine will be paid, the person making the denunciation will give a written statement to the city auditors so that they will place his name with the city praktor. [If] they do not lodge his name, or the praktor does not act, they will also be fined the equal amount, and give a third of the sum to the person making the denunciation.

If the gymnasiarch has been written up unjustly, he shall respond within [t]en days, and be judged before the appropriate court.

Future gymnasiarchs shall prevent those who act against the law from anointing themselves. [If] they do not do this they will be subject to the same fines.

No one may verbally abuse the gymnasiarch in the gymnasium. If a person does, he will be fined 50 drachmas. If anyone should move to strike the gymnasiarch in the gymnasium, those present should prevent and not allow him to do so, and (the gymnasiarch) shall fine the person who sought to strike him 100 drachmas, and he shall be liable to prosecution according to the common laws. Any of those present who, although able, did not come to the aid of the gymnasiarch, shall be fined 50 drachmas.

> http: //www.umich.edu/~classics/programs/class/cc/372/B015.html;
> accessed 9.4.06

Now it might be said that the time when one might autocratically flog one's charges is long gone and good riddance. But this is not exactly true as Koukouris (2000) points out the practice is alive and "well" in rural Greece to this day. So perhaps we should not assume that democracies are respectful of basic human rights across Europe let alone the rest of the world (David, 2005). Moreover, having a rule and a fine to attach to those who verbally abuse sports coaches or commit acts of violence against them might well be worth reconsidering as would the idea of fining those who fail to prevent them from so doing.

In modern times it is simply presumed that the coach always acts in the interest of their performer and, indeed, of the sport. Where the paradigmatic professions have been thought to be related to essential social goods (justice, health and salvation) their import might be such that the public pledge was a strong normative lever. Sport seems by comparison to be trivial. Why would such a pledge be necessary? Well, the preparation of athletes must begin at a young age. Athletes stand before coaches in need of their sporting wisdom. It may be the case that to trust them requires not merely that they are, qua professional, virtuous but perhaps that they have been legitimised by the appropriate authority *and* are regulated in proper ways by that authority. It is in this lacuna then that codes of conduct in sport may find their *raison d'être*.

Codes of ethical and professional conduct

Why should professionals adopt a code of practice to govern their conduct? It is commonplace in moral philosophical circles at least, to search for authoritative support for ethical commitments in order to avoid caprice or arbitrariness. Likewise it is often thought that moral rules allow us to point up most clearly the clashes between permissible and impermissible conduct. We can still ask, though, why we need a *code* of rules to guide ethical conduct in professional life?

In answer to this question a number of reasons recommend themselves: first, they offer *apparent* clarity and simplicity in a confusing world; second, they set out standards and criteria to evaluate provision and expectation in relationships that are consistent over time; third, they offer a neutral framework for resolving conflict or ambiguity to those under the authority of the organisation; and fourth, in constraining certain actions they allow exclusion from that organisation anyone who will not conform to the code.[3] In short we might say that codes of conduct franchise 'blameability' and consequently 'punishability' to their respective organisations. The closeness of these ethical objectives to a legal mindset is apparent. 'Blame', as Williams reminds us, 'is the characteristic reaction of the morality system' (1985: 177); it invites us to think of the whole of ethical life in terms of a series of obligations of increasing power that must be met for fear of incurring blame and possible retribution.

Characteristic of these guides to professional conduct is the codification of a set of rules that describe, prescribe and, more commonly, proscribe the actions of professionals. The codes are a pastiche of eclectic ethical notions. But one particular portion of the picture dominates: a 'common sense' view of morality as a set of rules or principles that stops people from acting *purely* in the pursuit of their interests to the detriment of others. The sums of these rules or principles, both negative and positive, constitute the moral code enshrined in ideals, duties, rights and obligations. To what extent does this common sense picture recommend itself above others?

The sheer range of ethical theories in this pastiche makes the task of summarising difficult. In keeping with the brevity of this argument, albeit following many philosophers before, we may separate ethical theories into two categories: those that concern themselves with actions and those that concern themselves with agents, or, put another way, those that focus on what it is right to do and those that focus on what sort of agent it is good to be. In keeping with the above, I will eschew felicity for the sake of brevity and generalise further by naming them rule-based and virtue-based theories of ethics. I will now consider how these caricatured positions underwrite codes of conduct.

Rules, rule-following and rule-based ethical theories

My compass here is necessarily broad and the targets I aim at are less than well focused. The name 'rule-based ethical theories' is not intended to be definitive. Rather, what it captures is the fact that the ethical considerations that belong to a theory under this description are centred around considerations to do with actions that are governed by something like a set of rules that is designed to frustrate the worst of people's desires and that is grounded in reason (such that they have an authoritative voice). These were the moral foundations that bolstered social scientific research into sports and ethical development that I criticised in the previous chapter. In rule-based theories, being largely modern, there is no appeal to a deity; the rules are human constructions. Given that professionals are faced with problems of how to decide between competing courses of action in a way that is not merely capricious nor God-given, the rules are supposed to point us towards what any reasonable person would agree is right.

Perhaps the most well-known theories of right actions are deontological in character and the most celebrated of these belongs to Kant.[4] To act rightly is to refrain from things that can be known, before the fact, to be wrong. The rules are effectively negative, whether as constraints, proscriptions, prohibitions or norms. They prevent us from doing, with good conscience, things that are known before the fact to be wrong, irrespective of all consequences, including good ones. Characteristic of deontological theories is the prioritisation of the right over the good. The fact that my harming one person may save the lives of several others does not weigh with the strict deontologist; the rules guide my conduct that is good or bad *in itself*, and not in respect of other considerations. A deontologist writing a code of conduct would not be directly concerned with maximising happiness or minimising pain or indeed with any of the range of considerations that an emotivist, intuitionist or virtue-based theorist would necessarily appeal to. Instead what would inform the rules of conduct is the distinction between that which is and is not permissible. This distinction enables agents to perceive what is the right thing to do. Again, this may be stated negatively: I am obliged *not* to do that which is not permissible. This negative characterisation of morality is captured well in Mill's 'Essay on Liberty':

> Its ideal is negative rather than positive; passive rather than active; Innocence rather than Nobleness; Abstinence from evil, rather than the energetic Pursuit of the Good; in its precepts (as has been well said) "Thou shalt not" predominates unduly over "thou shalt".
>
> (Mill, 1859 cited in Mill, 1962: 177)

Deontological constraints are paradigmatic of such rules. Three considerations show their nature and structure.[5] First, though it is possible to formulate these rules or constraints positively (for example one might say 'never lie' can be translated into 'always tell the truth'), they are negatively formulated and there is neither entailment nor equivalence between them. Additionally, the rules are narrowly framed and directed. One is not permitted to act in ways that are wrong. Not only does this give them a form of specificity to the rule but it also puts into context the distinction between actions intended to bring about certain outcomes intentionally and those where, for example, bad outcomes result from foreseen and unforeseen consequences from our prima facie permissible action. For the deontologist writing or indeed enforcing a code of conduct, wrong action (rule-breaking) is necessarily intentional action.

In many ways the moral value of games and sports has resided in rather opaque accounts of rule-responsibility. It is thought that if we can develop children (or coaches for that matter) who follow the rules (moral and non-moral) then we will thereby develop moral maturity (or professional conduct). But all this is still a far cry from the idea of a moral *code*, a systematised set of principles, not merely aggregated and ultimately reducible to one. Thus we often find reductions from many rules to the 'Golden Rule', and this is instanced in more than one type of ethico-religious system and, perhaps, most famously in philosophical terms by Kant's Categorical Imperative 'act so as to treat rational beings always as ends and never as means only'.[6] Yet the elegance of Kant's formulation of moral actions motivated by impartial duty with universality of application under the assent of practical reason is not mirrored in codes of conduct. Where Kant attempted to achieve a non-conflicting order of moral principles (notwithstanding the distinction between perfect duties that oblige to all rational beings to act in specific ways that observe the rights of all rational beings, and imperfect duties that are not categorical but are selective and do not have corresponding rights), codes of conduct tend to be more eclectic. They have maintained, perhaps implicitly, the idea that rule-responsibility is at the heart of ethical conduct.

From here it is a short step to the assertion that the heart of the rule-based ethics, especially deontological ones, is negative; moral behaviour consists in the avoidance of wrong acts.[7] This is one reason why codes of conduct are framed explicitly or implicitly in rule-like ways but also because of their legalistic nature and the blameability they offer. Where there are rules we should be able to distinguish right from wrongdoing and wrongdoers.

There are, however, weaknesses in this way of thinking. I shall take, for the purpose of exposition, merely one principle from the code of conduct of the most important coaching organisation in the United Kingdom, the National Coaching Foundation (NCF)/Sports Coach UK[8]. The code displays a wide variety of rules, principles, duties and general exhortations the type of which are likely to be familiar to the reader and, therefore, the one exemplar is chosen merely as representative of the kind of analyses that might be made of the remainder of the code and, indeed, any other code of its kind. Consider, then, principle 3.3 in the Code of Practice for Sports Coaches:

PRINCIPLE OF PRACTICE 3.3

Coaches should not condone or engage in sexual harassment [. . .] with performers or colleagues. It is considered that sexual relationships with performers are *generally* inappropriate to the professional conduct of coaches.

(emphasis added)

There is no reasonable person who would not want to say that sexual harassment is wrong. Surely part of what 'harassment' actually means is the negative evaluation; 'wrongful' (in the same way that someone could not condone murder which is *defined* as 'wrongful killing'; if it were not wrongful it would have to be an act that fell under some other description). Surely this principle is heading in the right direction at least; it sets out wrongful conduct and allows us to blame would-be wrongdoers and enable sanctions to be taken against them.

What, though, are we to think of this principle? First, let us be clear that it is an odd principle that admits of exceptions.[9] What is the function of the word 'generally' in its midst? Isn't a principle something that is absolute? Consider some classic deontological principles that are commonplace to those in a Judaeo-Christian tradition at least: 'thou shalt not kill' or 'thou shalt not steal'. Imagine now, then, 'thou shalt not lie, generally speaking'. This would appear an odd commandment were Moses to have brought it down from Mount Sinai. This might appear a trivial point but it is not. It kicks out at the very idea of establishing principles that are designed to function as universal rules not mere guidelines.[10] This is, again, a very general difficulty with the universalisation of moral rules. Perhaps it would be better to follow Hart's (1955) jurisprudential idea that we have rules that are defeasible. In special circumstances, things that we might normally disapprove of or even abhor may become permissible. This is the function of the word 'generally'; perhaps it could be stronger put. By contrast, the American Psychological Association's (APA) code is less equivocal. It forbids sexual intimacies with existing clients or patients for a minimum of two years after professional contact. Of course, the client or patient relationship is of a different kind than that of coach and athlete yet the potential for abuse is also there. What is significant about the APA's code regarding sexual harassment is the further, explicit rule that its members shall accord the complainant dignity and respect. The idea that the victim of sexual harassment should be taken seriously, morally seriously that is, is an interesting one. What it points to is the institutional recognition of norms of acceptable and unacceptable practice in areas that can be ignored or ridden roughshod over because of the sometimes macho ethoses of sporting practices. Stories are legion in sports of sexual harassment being ignored, not taken seriously or considered as part and parcel of the whole package of elite sport (Brackenridge, 2001). Again, there are salient differences between coaching and psychology not least of all in respect of the control exercised over its members by a governing legislature. So much of sports coaching is carried out on a voluntary basis and there is little hope of exercising such a degree of control as could be exercised by the APA or the British Medical Council or the Law Society in Great Britain. Perhaps codes of conduct in sport are best viewed as forms of institutional posturing; important but without real bite.[11] I shall return to this point later.

Second, let us also be clear, as Wittgenstein points out in the *Philosophical Investigations*, that a rule cannot determine its own application. The sophistication of this insight is one that will be underdeveloped here.[12] I will explicate a little of the import of this remark by way of discussion of the scope, application and interpretation of rules and also by noting the different aspects of rule-following as distinct from merely acting in accordance with a rule.

How should I conceive of the scope of any given rule that I am supposed to follow? Is it properly the place of a code of conduct to govern the conduct of its members outside the role of coach given the many related and unrelated roles that a coach has to play? These roles range from parent, friend and counsellor merely in the coaching relationship; there are a plethora of others. Would it really be unethical, or 'inappropriate professional conduct' for someone to have sexual relations with a colleague? This is one of the points at which there is a salient distinction between coaching and psychology; we refer to those who seek their service as clients yet the service they offer, though conceivably similar in certain contexts, *is* clearly different. So then, let us agree that sexual harassment is wrong, but how did the formulation of the 'rule' concerning sexual harassment lead us here?

Perhaps we should ask 'what is the concept of "rule"?' or 'what does "rule" actually mean?' in order to begin. Fortunately, that question has already been asked. Baker and Hacker make the Wittgensteinian point that the concept of a rule does not adequately allow for an essentialist analysis; there are no common features to all the things we call 'rules' in virtue of which we call them 'rules'. The recognition of such need not paralyse us though, for even if it opens up a certain generality, that generality is of a specific kind, as Baker and Hacker write:

> The generality of a rule lies in its *use*, not (or not necessarily) in its form. We *guide* our actions by reference to rules: we teach and explain rule-governed activities by citing the rules that govern it. When in doubt as to how to proceed we consult the rules. [. . .] *But the forms of guidance by a rule are most varied.*
>
> (Baker and Hacker, 1985: 45; emphasis added)

An important cautionary note is embodied in the final sentence regarding the variability of the forms of guidance that rules take. A cursory glance at the types of rules in any particular code of conduct would make this evident. That

the rules refer to so many different types of activities and interests from con-
fidentiality and safety to informed consent makes this inevitable. For present
purposes let us take the type of rule that is of direct concern to codes of conduct: moral rules. This theme has been taken up by Edmund Pincoffs, in his
tirade against reductivism in ethics that I observed in the previous chapters.
He warns us to be wary of asking of moral rules what they cannot deliver by
attending to their divergent powers:

> Rules may be like general standing commands or like general standing
> orders; analogously they may be like general standing specific and non-
> specific prescriptions. They may allow no leeway in compliance or they
> may allow a great deal of compliance.
>
> Some moral rules are more like general standing orders than like gen-
> eral standing commands: for example, "Love thy neighbor" or "Do not
> cause suffering." They say what is wanted but do not say what to do. If,
> however, we concentrate upon rules that are like commands, such as "Do
> not kill" or "Never break promises," we are likely to think of moral rules
> much like criminal laws, in that they will consist for us, largely of specific
> injunctions and directions. But if we recognize that they can also be like
> orders, we will be more aware of the discretion they sometimes allow.
> They do not tell us exactly what to do so much as they indicate what we
> should struggle toward in our own way.
>
> (Pincoffs, 1986: 25)

We can see now, perhaps, the unavoidable disparity of the *kinds* of rules that
are on offer in codes of conduct. For not only must attention be paid to their
differing roles, but also the comparative directness and ambiguity of their
application.

Third, following one of Wittgenstein's major theses against the 'private
language' argument, Baker and Hacker offer exegesis on the distinction
between rule-following and acting merely in accordance with the rule. (It will
repay attention for my present purpose even if I attend only to the consequences of this point, though its original target is significantly different, and
significantly more profound in philosophical terms, than that which I aim at.)
The distinction is apposite; it points to the discontinuity between the vogue
for codes of professional (and therefore ethical) conduct and much current
practice in elite sports that is characteristic of behavioural accordance rather
than rule-following proper. Baker and Hacker write:

> [I]t is not at all necessary that for an activity to be guided by a rule the rule
> should enter into the activity or even cross the minds of those engaged in
> it (chess players do not think about the rules of chess as they play; they
> know them too well) [. . .]. But neither is it enough that the behaviour of
> someone following a rule merely conforms with the rule (a chess
> computer follows no rules). Nor is it sufficient that he once learned the

rule – for that is past history [. . .] and the issue here is his present possession of an ability, not its genesis. Nor would it suffice that the rule might
be encoded in his brain (whatever that might mean); for being caused to
act by the encoding of a rule is precisely *not* to follow a rule [. . .]. That a
person's action is normative, that he is following a rule, that he is guided
by a rule (or better, guides himself by reference to a rule) is manifest in the
manner in which he uses rules, invokes rule-formulations, refers to rules
explaining what he did, *justifying* what he did in the face of criticism,
evaluating what he did and *correcting* what he did, *criticizing* his mistakes, and so forth.

(Baker and Hacker, 1985: 45)

As with the actions of our sports coaches, so with codes of conduct. Why do
we need a *rule* like that concerning sexual harassment? Well, let us be clear
that such actions are wrong and that we scarcely need a code to tell us this.
We can no more sexually harass our colleagues or athletes than we can any
other person in the street. So the rule, in this sense tells us nothing new. No,
to follow the rule with regard to sexual harassment is to understand the psychology of the situation: its thick, substantial richness. But rule-based theories do not work that way. What is the point then? Well, as an organisation,
the NCF/Sports Coach UK recognises clearly and properly that situations in
which coaches and athletes find themselves can introduce temptations into
human relationships. Such vicious behaviours as exploitation, domination,
extortion or bribery can and do occur. And with specific reference to sexual
harassment, oftentimes athletes are scantily clad and situations where the
coach is required to physically manipulate body positions are not rare.[13] The
rules are *intended* to preserve proper human relationships in the coaching situation. We use them for a variety of purposes as Baker and Hacker note; to
explain, justify, evaluate, correct and criticise. An example will better illuminate this point.

Consider the following scenario. I am the coach of some elite female ado-
lescent gymnasts. You are one of these gymnasts, aspiring to a full-time sporting career. Mine is a privileged position. The children are with me two or
three hours nearly every day of the week. They respond to me. I am a power
figure. I know my sport: its history; its techniques and skills; its hierarchy. I
hold a privileged position within that hierarchy. I am the gate through which
the successful gymnast must go first. I am esteemed in the community. I am
strong physically; I can catch you, literally, when you fall; I can lift you up
psychologically or I can destroy you and your career by various means; you
need me; above all perhaps, you trust me; your parents trust me. The sexual
harassment of you by me through the powers of my station violates that trust.
We do not need the rule book to guide our actions; we do not consult it to see
whether we do right or wrong, good or bad nor to explain, criticise or justify
those actions. (Though here again we must ask how, even when rules are clear
and unambiguous, such as that for sexual harassment, there are difficulties: 'it

wasn't harassment' says the coach 'of course that's wrong. But she gave me the come-on, she wanted it; that's not harassment' as the unfortunate script too often goes.) Instead we enquire as to what sort of person the coach is (we often ask for character witnesses); what his or her motivations might have been; whether he or she was disposed to other kinds of abuses; what his or her biography or institutional affiliations point towards and so on. The rules may allow us to blame, but they do not fully do the job of determining the context or evaluating the person; other considerations must come into play.

To consider the actual abuses that codes of professional conduct seek to highlight enables us to see the laudable work that the word 'generally' was trying to perform in our principle above. No rule book can anticipate all actions, nor can they describe, or predict, all possible actions that may be considered professional and unprofessional. Rule books just cannot do that sort of thing. And so what we have is an eclectic mix: some rules we make can perform specific tasks, others have more general application. We cannot expect them to be like a calculus table to be consulted prior to performance nor is this how they work in real life. And to capture coaches who are unprofessional in their conduct, we may very well wish to distinguish those who are genuinely following the rules (of course, not in the calculus-like parody) from those whose behaviour merely *appears* not to break the rule while appearing to act in accordance with it.

What becomes clear from this brief consideration of rules in codes of conduct, in addition to the diversity of rules and their action-guiding implications, is the need for something beyond mere rule-observance where this means the avoidance of rule-breaking actions. We can imagine, quite wrongly, that rule-responsibility is at the centre of ethical life. This is why Koehn's condition that a professional must have a highly developed sense of responsibility, though true, falls short of the mark. It is clear that it is not merely an important professional virtue, but that it is an essential social virtue; how could we get along if there were social anarchy or mere unpredictability and randomness of behaviour? What, of course, does not follow is the idea that ethics and ethical conduct can be simply *reduced* to the idea of rule-responsibility. To see why this is the case, we need to return to our earlier distinction of being and doing; of agency and acts. By turning to a non-reductivist vocabulary of the virtues we can prise open the reasons why such unprofessional conduct is reproachable; for the coach in our scenario is left in the care, or striking distance, of someone who is valuable in and of his or herself, and that trust has been violated by the coach. I shall develop this point in relation to the virtue of trust in the sections that follow.

One of the central reasons why we need either to replace or augment the notion of rules as exhaustively descriptive of ethical theory and conduct is, so to speak, their underdetermination. Put simply though they commonly tell us what not to do, often what to aim towards and, occasionally, what to do, they leave so much else in the void. Fried captures this point well: 'One cannot live one's life by the demands of the domain of the right. After having avoided wrong and doing one's duty, an infinity of choices is left to be made' (Fried, 1978: 13).

When, therefore, we consult the rules, to examine conduct that is under question, just as when we wish to commend conduct, the rule book will not do the work for us. The rule cannot determine its own application; we must do that from within the forms of life we inhabit. And in so doing we must try to work our way through the unavoidable pitfalls and fallibility of character evaluation in a spirit devoid of capriciousness or any of the forms of bias. But such actions as we will attempt to inspect and label 'professional' and 'unprofessional' will admit various, perhaps conflicting, interpretations. We are left to ask 'how we can possibly ground our interpretations, to know we have seen a situation aright?' and 'what underwrites our confidence?' to avoid the vertigo of subjectivity. These particular questions must be left for another day, but one thing is certain: if we are to discuss more fully such conduct as is to be characterised 'professional' and 'unprofessional', we must move to the language of virtues.

Virtue, virtues and virtue ethics

Let it be clear, however, that in making transparent some of the difficulties of rule-based ethics and in commending virtue-based ethics, at least with respect to my present concern with the theoretical and practical limitations codes of conduct, I must make similar caveats. First, the term 'virtue-based ethics' is itself a label for diverse modern and pre-modern theories of virtue and the good life. And I have only scratched the surface of these thus far while committing myself to a modified version of MacIntyre's conception of them. Second, I am not in any way committed to the thesis that rule-based considerations are always and everywhere either inferior, or reducible, to virtue considerations. It will be one of my conclusions that they may happily co-exist for the purposes of guiding professional conduct. I hold, instead, to the rather weaker claim that rules, principles and their like are not exhaustive of the basic facts of moral life, a picture of which is incomplete without reference to the virtues.

I shall argue that the pursuit of *eudaimonia* (human well-being or flourishing) is better served by certain sorts of characters rather than others. We prefer the just to the unjust, the courageous to the cowardly, the honest to the dishonest, and so forth. It is these virtue-based considerations that guide my conduct, not the moral rule book. In a sporting context there is a clear analogy. Are we not to prefer those who merely keep the rules for fear of being punished but those who keep them in order that the contest is a fair and equal test of relevant abilities and powers? And if sports are to flourish too, must we not have trustworthy coaches and wise administrators as well as honest performers all of whom keep the sporting faith; the spirit of the game?

The picture of the good life is one that is lived in accordance with virtue against a given background, for example, of the proper nature of human being (as in the pre-modern work of Aristotle) or the cultural and historical traditions I am heir to (as in the modern works of MacIntyre). *Aretē* (excellence) is that which enable persons to achieve their *telos* (proper end) of flourishing, yet *aretē* is also an ingredient of the attainment of that goal at the same time. As we have seen what constitutes the good life is socially and historically located, yet it will be achieved by persons who are possessed of a core of virtues that are acquired, displayed and produced in a variety of shared social practices that are themselves constitutive of broader cultural traditions.

When I am faced with a quandary, on a virtue-based account, it is not that I can simply consult a moral rule book that tells everyone, irrespective of context, not to do this and not to do that. I cannot write off the particularity of quandary. It is 'me', a grounded self, with particular goals, desires, needs, habits and roles. What will *I* do here in the light of what I conceive myself to be: just, cowardly, arrogant, sensitive, untrustworthy.

One of the key points in such a scheme is the notion of a virtue conceived not as an isolated act but as part of a narrative that is my life. This consideration points us toward the psycho-social aspects of my agency because the virtues or vices I display in this or that situation flow from relatively settled dispositions in qualitatively different ways. Virtues and vices are displayed in the *manner* in which I am disposed to act in regular and interrelated ways. This point is usually developed by remarking first that one cannot simply possess a virtue in isolation and second that the moral sphere is thereby extended to include a wider range of acts and appraisals that are found in rule-based accounts. MacDowell develops the point:

> Thus the particular virtues are not a batch of independent sensitivities. Rather, we use the concepts of the particular virtues to mark similarities and dissimilarities among the manifestations of a single sensitivity which is what virtue, in general, is: an ability to recognise requirements which situations impose on one's behaviour. It is a single complex sensitivity of this sort which we are aiming to instil when we aim to inculcate a moral outlook.
>
> (McDowell, 1981: 332–3)

But if there is no rule to guide us, how do we know which virtue, which sensitivity, ought properly to be triggered by this or that situation? One resort, analogous to the reduction to the 'master rule', is to pick out a 'master virtue' such as the disposition to be just. What can assure that my acts tend towards the appropriate amount of each virtue and fail not in excess or deficiency? Time and space do not allow further elaboration but a second example will show the more complete range of ethical considerations that virtue accounts would raise to the surface over and above mere rule-responsibility.

Trust and the virtuous coach

To enact and to evaluate trusting relationships necessarily requires a range of dispositions from courage to wickedness, spite, generosity, foolhardiness, benevolence and beyond. To dislocate trusting from the fuller gamut of dispositions and the contexts in which they are triggered is to focus on a partial aspect of the picture and thus to distort the grasp we have of it. There are, therefore, two reductive temptations that are to be avoided. We should neither consider isolated acts in our evaluation of the professional conduct of coaches nor should we focus too resolutely on single dispositions in evaluations thereof.

What is it then for the parent and performer to trust a coach? Social scientists have often talked about trust merely as reliance on another person or thing to perform some kind of act or function under conditions of limited knowledge.[14] But this understanding of trust is economistic; it lacks an explicit moral dimension. Sisela Bok was one of the first philosophers to recognise this dimension when she wrote: '*Whatever* matters to human beings, trust is the atmosphere in which it thrives' (Bok, 1978: 31). It is precisely because activities such as sport are inherently social that virtues such as trust are ineliminable. Developing this point Baier has offered a developed account of the moral concept of trust and its close conceptual relations.[15] Among other things, she highlights the importance of considering the notions of value and vulnerability in addition to reliance:

> [L]ook at the variety of sorts of goods or things one values or cares about, which can be left or put within the striking powers of others, and the variety of ways we can let or leave others "close" enough to what we value to be able to harm it. Then we can look at various reasons we might have for wanting or accepting such closeness of those with power to harm us, and for confidence that they will not use this power.
>
> (Baier, 1994: 100)

Now the coach is someone in whom discretion is invested. Parents value their children more than just about anything in the world. When they entrust the coach with their children they place within his or her sphere of influence a vulnerable person, one who can be damaged in a variety of ways. Yet they necessarily trust the coach as a professional. Expectations issue from the status of coach *as* professional as we have seen. Parents properly expect the coach not merely to be the bearer of expertise either with or without a fee. Loaded into the coaching situation are a set of normative expectations whereby the coach, implicitly at least, aims towards the good of the performer with appropriate knowledge and skills utilised in a framework of accumulated wisdom generated within the practice.

Consider, then, another scenario. My young gymnast, Johnny, shows great promise. He has the potential to be an Olympian. His parents are exceptionally keen. Perhaps their zealous guidance is motivated by their lowly socio-economic status (this would be a route to a good college scholarship, a lucrative career and so forth), perhaps it is vicarious success that makes them want their child to succeed. Whatever the motivation, I am told in no uncertain terms that I am to do whatever it takes to make Johnny the best gymnast that he can be. He is struggling with his flares on the pommel horse; he cannot perform sufficient repetitions and their quality is lacking owing to his own deficient amplitude in the adductors. And this afternoon he is tired after a heavy conditioning session this morning. Various options compete in my mind: shall I make him try that routine one more time?; is he too tired?; have I succeeded in achieving all I wanted to this session?; have I done enough for next week's championship? All these questions are invoked in everyday contexts that commonly fall well outside the rule-governed jurisdiction of the code of conduct (or perhaps better, beyond even the most comprehensive rule book), yet in each, as coach, I may have to ask myself 'what sort of person am I/would I be to act in this way or that?' And the spectrum of replies may range from considerate, sympathetic and supportive, to insensitive, myopic, arrogant, intolerant, vindictive and spiteful. How could any rule book cover such a range without tearing down all the rainforests in order to attempt to write rules for every possible occasion or eventuality? And yet the exaltation of the rule book mentality, 'moral minimalism' to invent a term of art for the occasion, is precisely that mentality whose character is raised by the exclamation 'we have done nothing wrong or immoral; we have broken no rules' as if the latter were synonymous with the former.

I decide that the only way Johnny will succeed is if I 'help' him gain the amplitude by further stretching exercises. I ask Johnny to go down into the splits and to get his chest as close to the floor as possible. He fails to get close. I continue to urge him with greater vociferousness. He complies, he utters no words of complaint. Then, while he is unaware I come behind him and with all my strength, force his chest down to the floor and hold him down. I prove to him his body's capabilities; I chastise him for his laziness and lack of willpower; I rebuke him for the ingratitude for his parent's sacrifices for his kit, travel expenses, coaching fees and so forth. And all the time I *may* have broken no rule. I may have complied with every consenting wish of his parents (perhaps even Jonny himself, after he has recovered his tearful fit) and I have reinforced the 'no pain, no gain' ethic in him. Yet on the way home I reflect: what sort of person am I that I should do such a thing; shall I convince myself that I have done nothing wrong since I have broken no rules and in any case it is all in the child's long-term financial and performative interests; his parents sanctioned it; without my intervention there is no way he would have . . . and so on. Such a view *may* be underwritten by our rule-based ethic. I am comforted. But perhaps I reflect upon considerations that perhaps should have weighed with me as the boy's coach, a figure esteemed in the community, a role model. I think to myself 'Johnny trusted me, and his parents trusted me with a son whose respect I have complied with only under the auspices of potential star performer.'

What are we to think of this not uncommon scenario? Let us accept that there is no clear application of a rule that will help us unequivocally here. The situation, if not a moral dilemma, is deeply ambiguous. Given that we impart to the trusted coach a valued child, within limits of discretionary power we run the risks of verbal, physical or psychological abuse. Anyone who has been engaged with elite sport knows how cruel it can be. Yet this is not something that can be avoided lest we attempt to live in a bubble or indeed to wrap our children in cotton wool; it comes part and parcel both of sports and of trust itself:

> To understand the moral risks of trust, it is important to see the special sort of vulnerability it introduces. Yet the discretionary element which introduces this special danger is essential to that which trust at its best makes possible. To elaborate Hume: "'Tis impossible to separate the chance of good from the risk of ill."
>
> (Baier, 1994: 104)

Trust, then, on Baier's analysis is characterised as letting persons take care of something that is cared for or valued, where such caring involves the use of discretionary powers about the reliance and competence of the trusted. Risk, as she reminds us, is of the very essence in trusting. But there are good and bad bets. In accepting this Baier builds in a normative dimension that inescapably requires good judgement. To leave your baby with the nearest passer by while you go into a store to buy some provisions while on a shopping trip to London or New York is not trusting but *ceteris paribus* foolishness. We should be wary of jumping to the conclusion that the proper attitude to adopt in such a situation is to distrust. The consequences of distrust are dire; it is, as Baier reminds us, a fragile plant that does not long survive the inspection of its roots. This point is reinforced that we must view trust, as any other disposition, in the context of the person as a whole and the community in which they reside.

We do not, of course, expect to read in any code of ethics a rule confirming the trustworthiness of the coach. Under the cloak of moral minimalism coaches may sell themselves the story that where no rules are broken there is no moral difficulty. Yet, as we have seen, the rules underdetermine the ethical sphere in everyday life as well as in professional interactions. There is no rule to trust; it is almost a matter of volitional necessity. We have no choice in the matter most of the time. Like our health, which is foregrounded as a concern only when we are ill, so we attend to trust only when it is broken. And what would be the cost of continual distrust? Is not paranoia the name for such a condition?

The latter considerations are brought before us *only* under the aspect of a proper consideration of the place and role of virtue in ethical situations, whether everyday or climactic. And these considerations are to be prioritised not simply by asking whether I have broken any rules, but by asking what a person in my situation might do in the light of the kind of life that they consider 'good'. And this cannot be done by the methodological trick of making dispositions generalisable under principled propositions, though this is, I think, precisely what codes of conduct illicitly do; code writers attempt to make rules do the work of virtue requirements by replacing the need for particularity. They attempt to relegate context-sensitive judgement to the rule of law.

One needn't throw the baby out with the bath water. What we might say by way of temporary conclusion is, first, that the scope of rule-based ethics is underdetermining; there is still oftentimes a wide range of options and corresponding dispositions to fill the void after the rules have been laid out. Second, the rules do not specify their own scope and interpretation; agents who are variously virtuous and vicious do. Likewise, third, even after the rule is specified it will only be *followed*, in the strong sense, by the virtuous agent. Mere robot-like rule-observance is an inappropriate point of departure for our description of ethical lives, professional and otherwise. And worse, it can lead to the further entrenchment of the ethos of rule-bending in its extreme as is characteristic of so much conduct in modern sports.

This is precisely the case of our gym coach whose actions are those of the technocrat. His reasoning is instrumental. He sets out his ends unreflectively in accordance with the relevant dominant ethoses and chants slogans around his workhouse: 'no guts, no glory'; 'just do it'; 'nobody remembers who came second'. What justifies the selection of means is technical efficiency and economy. Ethical discourse is suspended under various guises such as 'nice guys come last'. Bend the rules as much as you can but don't break them or if you do, whatever else, don't get caught. Here the professional as craftsman/woman finds no home; their dedication, care and commitment to the defining excellences of the practice, moral *and* technical, are relegated to the sole, justifying, end: winning performance whose services have been bought and paid for, whose contractual labour measured only against that reductivist end.

Conclusion

What kind of communities are developed in professional sports practices is a question insufficiently asked in the education of coaches whose typical agendas are narrowly conceived in instrumental and technicist terms. Two witticisms spring to mind. First, I think it was Samuel Becket who once said that, at 50, we get the face we deserve. Perhaps, at the beginning of the twenty-first century we are getting the sporting milieu we deserve too. Too readily, journalists, administrators, performers and coaches refer to sports and athletes as professionals merely by virtue of their grossly inflated remuneration or their expert knowledge, without recognising what by virtue of that normative description is entrusted to them; the demands that the term places upon them. Their mien is too often characteristic of Molière's remark about writing, a profession 'like prostitution: First you do it because you enjoy it; then you do

6 Racism, racist acts and courageous role models

Racism and responsibility

Having argued the case for the possibility of ethical development in and through sports, I now want to argue further what this development does and does not consist in. One obvious challenge to such a claim is the sheer ubiquity of vicious behaviours in sports. Social scientific research abounds that shows how sports can be a vehicle for child abuse, misogyny, sexism and of course racism. To my knowledge, however, despite the voluminous literature on racism and sport, there has been no attempt to give an aretaic account of it: that is to say, of racism as a vice. This chapter attempts to articulate a clearer picture of the repugnance of racism as it manifests itself in sport and to develop a virtue-ethical perspective by considering racism as a vice. In particular, I explore questions of responsibility and culpability for both committed and less-entrenched racism in sports.

I argue against the binary understanding of persons as either racist/not racist which brings with it an undifferentiated moral response. Thus understood, the almost universal acceptance that racism is wrong somewhat ironically brings its own problems. It is sometimes suggested by anti-racist scholars that there is an unwillingness to acknowledge certain practices, within and outside sport, as racist because that might require us to recognise, at least potentially, the racism within ourselves. More importantly, for my purposes at least, the homogeneity of moral opprobrium attached to racist attitudes, policies or utterances effectively carries disproportionate sanctions and thereby threatens to jeopardise more considered, and perhaps more productive, ethical responses to it. I explore here the desirability of imagining a scale of severity rather than the more common but analytically crude binary categories of racist/non racist. In an attempt to do justice to the complexities of the debate I offer what I hope is a more nuanced appreciation of racism, taking account of context, intentionality and the centrality of the trait to the identity of the person alleged to be racist. To do this I consider the case of a high-profile football commentator and former manager, Ron Atkinson, whose racist remarks lost him his job in 2004. In arguing for an ethically salient distinction between a racist act and a racist character I offer a clearer it for a few friends, then you do it for money.'[16] We must remind ourselves continuously that professionalism demands *much* more.

I am conscious that the burden of my argument has rested on the explication of theoretical weaknesses as applied to a single principle for professional conduct. Ironically enough my argument requires that it be taken on that trust which I have briefly argued is definitive of professionalism; that, indeed, extrapolation can further be made to other principles, rules and codes.[17] This is one of the areas that needs far greater explication in the same way as we need to explicate more fully the relationships that exist between rules and virtues themselves. There is, of course, no use in philosophers who favour rule-based ethics castigating their otherwise inclined colleagues as 'allergic to principles', or in virtue theorists characterising rule-reliant adversaries disparagingly as 'psychologically phobic'. The debate must instead focus on the complexity of their unavoidable relations. I have not eschewed rules altogether from codes of conduct but have instead focused on their variety, the difficulties necessarily entailed in their interpretation and application as well as their characteristic underdetermination. Codes of conduct are indeed indispensable to the safety-net task of catching those who will be unprofessional in their conduct and enabling their punishment and/or expulsion. What they cannot do, and what they should not be expected to do, is to have any great effect in ensuring ethical behaviour per se. In highlighting this shortfall, I have focused positively on the role that virtues play in professional life and ethical explanation and have argued the necessary incompleteness of ethical evaluation and motivation in their absence. I have hinted at difficulties entailed in conceiving professionals as technocrats, whether merely as hired hands or providers of expertise and how, following Koehn, we might more profitably look to the notion of trust as characteristic of the basis of professionalism rather than to mere rule-responsibility and the legally inspired 'moral minimalism' that so often accompanies it. In the particularity and richness of personal relationships such as that exists most commonly between coach and performer, the rules, I fancy, play very little motivating or explanatory roles.[18]

conceptual schema for evaluating beliefs and behaviour in this highly charged arena. I conclude the chapter with one of the finest examples of role modelling by sportspersons, the Zimbabwean cricketers Andrew Flower and Henry Olonga, who were prepared to forego their participation in the Cricket World Cup of 2003 in order to declare objectionable the racism of their own nation's political policies.

Understanding racism

Among social scientific scholars the concept of 'race' is a discredited biological concept. Hence in sociological writings 'race' commonly appears within inverted commas, and is taken to refer to the antipathy that people experience because of their appearance/inheritance, which arises from other people's designation of them as 'others'. But this discredit has a longer history than might be assumed. The invidious tendency to consider racial characteristics as scientifically endorsed rather than as the product of a merely convenient biological classification as Darwin had intended (Appiah, 1996) often goes unnoticed even in modern times. Yet Ralph Waldo Emerson had challenged and discredited the convenient race classification well over a century ago:

> An ingenious anatomist has written a book to prove that races are imperishable, but nations are pliant constructions, easily changed or destroyed. But this write did not found his assumed races on any necessary law, disclosing their idea or metaphysical necessity; nor did he on the other hand count with precision the existing races and settle the true bounds; a point of nicety, and the popular test of his theory. The individuals at the extremes of divergence in one race of men are as unalike as the wolf to the lapdog. Yet each variety shades down imperceptibly into the next, and you cannot draw the line where one race begins or ends. Hence every writer makes a different count. Blumenbach reckons five races; Humboldt three; and Mr Pickering, who lately in our Exploring Expedition thinks he saw all kinds of men that can be on the planet, makes eleven.
>
> (cited in Appiah, 1996: 68–9)

The emergence of genetic discoveries threw into the dustbin of scientific anachronism the idea of there existing separate races in nature. Nevertheless, despite its redundancy the continuing significance of racism as a social process and lived experienced still resonates today and shows no ready signs of giving way. Wieviorka (1995) draws on Guillaumin's (1972: 63) explanation that 'imaginary and real races play the same role in the social processes and are therefore identical as regards their social function'. As a falsehood or product of bad science Massara (2007: 498–9) argues that race is ontologically false. Although, in opposition to the ideas put forward here, he neatly captures their stance: 'race cannot tell us anything about who we really are as individuals – it does not function, that is as a causal explanation of behaviour – however strategically necessary in the short term the concept may prove for political resistance'. The use of the concept of 'racism' has been extended to a consideration of the treatment of ethnic groups and a range of signifiers that may or may not include skin colour (e.g. Miles, 1989). Whether or not it can legitimately be applied to the treatment of religious groups is a matter of some dispute in the literature (Hall, 1992; Modood, 1997; Solomos and Back, 1996).

In other writings the term 'racism' has been re-labelled to as the 'new racism' or 'cultural racism' (e.g. Back, 1996; Barker, 1981; Gilroy, 1987; Parekh, 1995). The terminology is designed to indicate a more defensive mode of racism that seeks (allegedly) more to preserve a given way of life against the incursions of those labelled 'outsiders' rather than a direct assault on those so labelled. This can raise uncomfortable issues around the difference between asserting one's identity as a statement of difference, and racism. Paradoxically, as Solomos and Back (1996: 27) put it, this line of argument 'can produce a racist effect while denying that this effect is the result of racism'.

Some writers, such as Connolly (2000), suggest it is not just direct actions, but all those beliefs, behaviours, practices and processes that contribute either directly or indirectly to the racialisation of certain groups that can be designated as racist. Connolly also notes that this is seen to arise because of the way in which the signification of certain groups comes to 'shape the development of future social relations, institutions and processes' (2000: 503). Similarly, in a passage where it is easy to draw parallels with sport, Macpherson (1999: 17) noted:

> Unwitting racism can arise because of lack of understanding, ignorance or mistaken beliefs. It can arise from well intentioned but patronising words or actions. It can arise from unfamiliarity with the behaviour or cultural traditions of people or families from minority ethnic communities. It can arise from racist stereotyping of black people as potential criminals or troublemakers. Often this arises out of uncritical self-understanding born out of an inflexible police ethos of the 'traditional' way of doing things. Furthermore such attitudes can thrive in a tightly knit community, so that there can be a collective failure to detect and to outlaw this breed of racism.

In keeping with these anti-racist positions, it is necessary to hold on to the ideas of 'race' and 'racism' despite their having no genuine ontology because they function wrongly to privilege or derogate social groups. Within the broad framework that this represents, the basis for prejudice and discrimination is multidimensional, embracing culture, ethnicity and nationality.

D'Souza (1995: 27) presents an account of racism as 'an ideology of intellectual or moral superiority based upon the biological characteristics of race'.

This hierarchical portrayal of superior and inferior races is obviously central to white supremacists, but offers an incomplete definition of racism. This can be seen particularly clearly in the sporting arena where the apparent and widespread celebration of black sporting prowess has failed to eradicate racism.

More subtle variations of racism play along the borders of ethnocentrism. It is not always clear where to draw the line when what is perceived as benign ethnocentrism may be perceived as more exclusionary and properly deserving of the label racism. In an effort to counteract protestations of innocence it has been suggested that an action should be deemed to be racist if it is perceived as such by the person subjected to that action (see, for example, the report of the inquiry into the police investigation into the murder of the British African-Caribbean schoolboy, Stephen Lawrence: Macpherson, 1999). This position effectively embodies a relativistic argument (typical of some social constructivists) that reflects an inadequate way of conceptualizing the phenomenon of racism. If it is desirable to argue that people may be being racist even when they protest their innocence (as I do), then it is necessary to argue that people may not be being racist when others believe they are. Racism, to corrupt a well-known phrase, cannot therefore merely be 'in the eye of the beholder'.

Other writers have sought to dismantle conceptions of what they see as falsely unified accounts of racism, drawing attention to its variegated nature, its different forms and levels. Carrington and McDonald (2001), for example, illustrate dimensions of racism in cricket that extend beyond the immediate form of crude racial abuse. They see two further levels evidenced through racial stereotyping of cultural essentialisms that discriminate against black and Asian people, and racial exclusion based on a conception of white Englishness that creates a form of institutional racism serving to limit access to socially valued opportunities. Others have stressed the importance of analysing racism within the triplex of concepts: 'race', 'class' and 'nation' (e.g. Balibar and Wallerstein, 1991).

Wellman attempts to demonstrate that racism is not simply reducible to the concepts of 'bigotry' or 'prejudice'. Instead he sees racism as 'culturally acceptable beliefs that defend social advantages that are based on race' (Wellman, 1993: 4). I have considerable sympathy with the proposition that we all have embedded racial constructions affecting the way we think and behave towards each other, and that most, if not all, of us in the West at least, operate within social structures that favour certain ethnic groups. Indeed, it is important that people recognise this before they become too free in their criticism of others.

Without gainsaying the possibility of institutional racism, or the defence of social advantage, there is an important distinction to be noted between sometimes behaving in a way that reflects thinking grounded in racially prejudicial thought and being 'a committed racist'. Note this distinction is not backsliding. Nor is it intended to exculpate those whose racism is simply not as strong as others'. The distinction is clearly put in Aristotle's *Nichomachean Ethics* between an act and a character (see Williams, 1980: 190). It is important to uphold in order to not treat as equals those who behave in a racist manner unknowingly and those who do so characteristically and reflectively as part of a chosen way of life.

To examine whether one might exhibit racist behaviour without properly being a racist, consider a paradigmatic case of racist language. In his discussion of the use of the word 'nigger' in the context of the legacy of white supremacy, Blum (2002: 19) notes that its use by certain young blacks as a term of affection and bonding is a context-bound use that has confused many whites, and is objected to by many, especially older, blacks. This leads to the point that our evaluations of racism, though not relativistic, are deeply context-sensitive (cf. Wellman, 1993). To treat them otherwise is not (socio)logical. True, there are actions that require little understanding of context to be appreciated, but some knowledge of context is always necessary to evaluate social action.

In order to appreciate the intentionality of racism we need to appreciate historically the shifting attitudes towards racism. Nonetheless, as Blum (2002: 18) argues:

> In general, people beyond a certain age should recognise what is racist; their moral responsibility for perpetrating racism when they do not recognise it is analogous to the fault of citizens who cause injury through negligence rather than direct intent. They could be reasonably expected to recognise or anticipate the moral damage. Except for people with extraordinarily sheltered lives and upbringings, ignorance of racism does not absolve one from responsibility, although, everything else being equal, intentionally demeaning a racial group is morally more blameworthy than unintentionally doing so.

To some the possibility of racist actions or attitudes being 'innocent' or 'ignorant' is politically indefensible. Nevertheless, it *is* logically possible. And if we find those to whom it might apply, however unlikely, our position is that we should not treat it in the same way as fully conscious or premeditated racism. In estimating the potential grounds for latitude the following questions might be useful:

1   Can racist beliefs be held, or racist acts be performed, by persons we *ought* not to label 'racists'?
2   Is it helpful to articulate an underlying scale of racism?
3   When does racist thought, feeling or action genuinely form a part of one's character *as* racist?

There are those who will reject (1) the logical possibility, and/or (2) the normative justification that such questions attempt to create a space for. I believe, however, that the preservation of these possibilities is both logically possible and morally desirable.

If sociological understandings of action are always to be context-sensitive, then our moral responses should be the same. Children raised in a racist family who merely mouth racist sentiments are, however, less culpable than their elders. If it is true that our moral responses to racism should be sensitive to these features, perhaps we can extend that list. Consider the level of entrenchment of racist beliefs. Some, who though prejudiced (and thus deserving of moral opprobrium), when challenged might concede that their views are based on ignorance or prejudice born of reprehensible socialisation. To what extent ought we to treat such a person *in the same way* as an otherwise intelligent white supremacist? In such a case might it not be better to think of them as 'ethically disabled' (Jacobs, 2001) and therefore not fully responsible for their agency? The level of awareness of one's racism appears to be an important contextual feature to be taken into account in the moral register of racism presented below.

The level of premeditation or reflective awareness should also be considered. Contrast the deliberate use of racist language to antagonise an opponent (e.g. 'sledging' in cricket or 'trash talking' in basketball) with an abusive racial remark blurted out in the heat of the moment. It might be appropriate to ask to what extent the racist remark is characteristic of the person's other conduct or 'merely a lapse'. This is not an apology for the equivalent of racist Freudian slips. Yet if we acknowledge that, for the sake of argument, anyone over 50 years old (in Britain or the USA at least) was brought up in a society that harboured deep and widespread racist prejudices, then it is reasonable to suspect that their early socialisation contained at least some pernicious social and moral views based improperly on racialised characteristics.

While modern moral theories in some sense mirror the rationalist idea of universal reason – and hence universal moral registers (impartiality, universality, prescriptivity) – virtue-theoretical evaluations of moral character and agency, as we have seen, pay significant attention to the forces of habituation in the learning of our im/moral responses as patterns of thought, feeling and action. Of course the questions remain open as to what we should do with our knowledge of such habituation in and outside sport; how it is that people come to hold racist views, feel racist emotions and act in racist ways. We need to consider this properly in our evaluation of persons, but not to use it as a ready excuse for racists proper, whose acts and attitudes are not merely 'disabled' but self-consciously vicious. Of the latter, the more vicious end of the racist register, there are others for whom such abuse is not out of character in time of stress, but reveals their 'true' character.

Such non-benign contextual features require moral responses to racism to be classified in a more subtle manner than the in/out, yes/no binary divide of racist/not-racist. We need a vocabulary that qualitatively discriminates appropriately and does so in an ethically self-conscious way. The philosophical task as I see it is to set out the moral scales of racism from innocence, ignorance and ambivalence on to outright bigotry, and show why this more conceptually and morally nuanced vocabulary is important. Only after this is done can we consider the extent to which racist actions or utterances genuinely form part of the character of the person labelled 'racist'.

Articulating the moral repugnance of racism

To help resolve these questions I draw heavily on the work of Lawrence Blum (2002). Blum draws upon the widely used distinctions of personal, social and institutional racism, and we concur with his suggestion that merely to consider racism individualistically (Allport, 1987) or socially (Ture and Hamilton, 1992) is to replace one partial definition with another. However, we focus here on the individual while being aware that, in its ontology, racism can never in reality be separated from other levels. Blum (2002: 9–10) writes:

> We do better to accept the plurality of items that can be racist (beliefs, institutions, systems, attitudes, acts and so on), without thinking that one of these needs to be the foundation of all the others. Personal, social and institutional racism are each morally problematic, in at least partially distinct ways.

His starting point is a categorisation of racial discrimination/differentiation derived from his assertion that all forms of racism relate to two general themes or paradigms: *inferiorisation* and *antipathy*. Blum's inferiorising racism is expressed in attitudes and actions that variously show disrespect, contempt, derision, derogation or are demeaning. While an inferiorising racist generally thinks that the racial other is inferior, sometimes people believe their own group to be inferior. In sport we have witnessed interesting reversals in this process. For example, the previous common presumption of the inferiority of black athletes has been inverted in many events. The populist position has become one that asserts that black athletes are 'naturally' better equipped to run the 100 metres and other power-based activities involved in, for example, American football. But even on its own terms this prejudice is limited since one cannot ignore how many more Olympic and World Championship medals are won over 800 and 1500 metres by Sudanese and Moroccan athletes, nor the complete dominance of Kenyan long-distance runners on the track. The implication is that black athletes have an unfair advantage so there is no point in 'our' valiant men and women trying to compete. In the 1990s there was even discussion of limiting athletes from African nations on the televised American running circuit.

In Blum's construction, inferiorising and antipathy racists are distinct because the former do not necessarily hate the target of their beliefs. It is quite possible for them to have a paternalistic concern for people they regard as their inferiors. So not every race-hater is supremacist, nor is every supremacist a race-hater. Moreover, antipathy might be based on feelings of inferiority as well as superiority. Blum argues that 'racial prejudice' is illustrative of the antipathy theme. Although the linguistic root suggests a prejudging of something precipitously, racial prejudice, he suggests, is a generalised antipathy towards another racial group, or members thereof, merely in virtue of that membership. He draws upon Allport's (1987) definition that prejudice is antipathy based on erroneous generalisation, but argues in addition that all antipathy to a racial group must be considered prejudicial since the variegated nature of the group would deny the validity of grounds for antipathy to the entire group based on race-founded suppositions. The notion of racial prejudice, as we have noted, can cut across the conscious/unconscious division. One may have prejudices towards others and be unaware of it. Much racism falls into the category of racist views without the people holding them necessarily identifying self-consciously with those views. A reasonable anti-racist expectation in those circumstances is that, when made aware of the damaging consequences of such prejudice, those who do not on reflection subscribe to racist values ought to seek to instigate change in themselves. Blum (2002: 13) modifies Allport's definition:

> [P]rejudice is a kind of antipathy, toward a race-defined group and would by my definition appear to count as a form of 'racism'. Indeed racial prejudice is often called 'racism'. But, 'prejudice' often implies dislike or antipathy, but not necessarily hatred or strong antipathy. . . . Because prejudice is, in general, a less malevolent attitude than hatred and intense hostility, it is less morally evil. It is not clear whether we should call weaker forms of racial prejudice 'racism'. These forms should, in any case, evoke opprobrium in their own right.

Thus, someone who might typically be considered as racist may yet have grounds for less than total moral condemnation. There are a few cases where a lack of moral agency (e.g. the very young, the severely intellectually challenged) may to a certain extent yield cases where there cannot be ascription of responsibility. There are also clear-cut cases of vicious racists whose attitudes may be the result of inferiorising or antipathy or both. While the former may be racial supremacists in less corrosive ways, still heavy moral opprobrium attaches to them while antipathy-based racists appear to be *ceteris paribus* the group to be most morally reviled. There is a rather grey area, then, involving those who hold racist views, beliefs or attitudes, or who commit racist acts on a non-regular basis, that we need to consider more fully. If vice is typically the opposite of virtue, what grounds are there for thinking that a certain person exhibits the vice of racism? Which beliefs mould it? What language evidences this? Which acts typify it?

Racism and a vice

While the dominant moral theories of utilitarianism and deontology are diametrically opposed to each other in the direction of their moral schemes, they are similar in form. Just as deontological concerns direct our moral salience to universal rights and duties that we 'know' to be true before we act (don't harm people, don't disrespect them, allow free speech and movement to all, etc.), utilitarianism pushes us to maximise good outcomes while at the same time treating all persons as equal in our calculations. As guides to the moral life deontology, or duty-based ethics, is thought of as an ethics of the 'right action', whereas utilitarianism is a teleological theory of the 'good living'.[1] It may at first be difficult to see how utilitarianism can make sense of the idea of racial wrongs. One of the foundational premises of utilitarianism is that everyone must be treated as equals so racism is ruled out *ab initio*. Beyond arguing that maximising the good entails the calculation of pleasures/utility of all relevant persons, utilitarianism offers little in the way of theoretical resources to understand the wrongness of racism, though its consistent application (the impartial treatment of all, considered equally, in order to maximize happiness in the world) might help significantly to remove racism.

Deontology fares better. Sharing the principle of impartial treatment of all persons, and the universalisation of rights and duties, it illuminates proper guides to conduct in its foundational ideas such as equal treatment, respect and autonomy among others. Nevertheless, deontology with its resolute focus on moral *reasons* is commonly held to be inadequate in terms of moral psychology. It holds, in the classic form of moral cognitivism from Kant and Plato, that merely by knowing the right thing to do one will act in accordance with the dictates of moral reason; moral reasoning and moral action are one. Such a theory holds no space for either weakness of will or for inconsistencies of thought and action. In Chapter 8 I attempt, in some small way, to defend Kant against this pernicious characterisation by considering some remarks within his theory of virtue as opposed to his overall moral philosophy of duties. Virtue ethics is more hospitable to social and psychological factors, attempting to take seriously the agency of embedded and embodied agents in the particularity of time and place.

To think of someone as a racist is a particular way of conceiving someone as possessed of a vicious character. A racist character is not typically revealed in a one-time activation, but through a complex and interrelated pattern of thoughts, feelings and acts relating to inferiorising and/or antipathy racism over time. The particular configuration of this patterning will be person-specific and derivative of the usual catalogue of social indexicals: age, embodiment, class, gender, intelligence, sexual orientation, wealth and so on. It may range, as we have seen, from unacceptable paternalism to wicked subjugation and violence. Equally, contrast the disaffected youth for whom overtly racist political parties become a source of self-esteem with the controlling mind of the organisation; or with the international sportsmen who were apologists for apartheid sport. All are racists, but surely of different depth and intensity. Racists are not a 'natural kind'; they do not form a homogeneous class. What can be said more generally though, is that to ascribe the condemnatory title 'racist' to a person, like any other aspect of their character, it should be one that typically informs their modes of being in the world in relatively consistent ways that they understand to be part of their identity:

> A racist *person* is not merely someone who commits one racist act or acts on a racist motive on a small number of occasions. Motives and attitudes such as bigotry, antipathy, and contempt must be embedded in the person's psychological makeup as traits of character. In this sense being a racist is like being hateful, dishonest, or cruel, in implying an ingrained pattern of thought and feeling as well as action.
>
> (Blum, 2002: 14–15)

Rather than a binary thing, perhaps it is better to think of racism in subtle gradations, and/or subtle inflections activated by particular contexts. This is why the question 'When is a racist a racist?' is unhelpful. There may be cases when one act is sufficiently malevolent, but more typically there will not be. Blum argues that holding one racist view, or making one racist remark, or telling one racist joke ought not necessarily induce the label racist:

> The beliefs themselves were genuinely racist, but belief in them had not been deeply enough rooted in her psychological makeup to make her 'a racist'. She must be *genuinely committed* to and invested in racist beliefs in order to be a racist.
>
> (Blum, 2002: 21; emphasis added)

Of course, everything hangs on what is meant by the elliptical phrase 'genuinely committed' here. The committed racist in his or her actions is ethically inexcusable. No one would seriously dispute that (except, presumably, a racist). However, defining a person as 'racist' may not require so strict a condition as 'genuine commitment'; reserving the term only for 'genuinely committed' racists may be to 'throw the baby out with the bathwater':

> Calling the belief in question, or the believing of it, racist, emotionally overloads a discussion of the validity or worthiness of the belief and leads us to think that because a view may have undesirable racial implications, it should be dismissed prior to discussion.
>
> (Blum, 2002: 22).

The point is well made, but fails to accord fully with some of the more subtle ways in which racist attitudes move from embryo to actuality. We need to attend to the processes of racialisation that are present in contextualised evaluations of those we consider more or less racists. These are captured well by Connolly (2000: 503) who, following Miles, notes:

> The signification of certain groups is not only grounded in the specific social relations that exist, but will also come to inform and shape the

Sources and degrees of race-related actions/feelings/thoughts		
Ethically excusable	← →	Ethically inexcusable
↕		↕
ethically disabled	ethically immature	committed racist
ignorance	misperception/misrecognition	evil
one-off racist remark (out of character)	occasional	typical (in character)
unintentional	negligent	pre-meditated
incapable of change	amenable to change/education	entrenched

Figure 6.1 A racist register

> development of future social relations, institutions and processes. As
> such . . . all those beliefs, behaviours practices and processes that con-
> tribute, either directly or indirectly, to the racialisation of certain groups
> can be designated as racist . . . [I]t is not just overt racist attitudes and dis-
> criminatory and exclusionary practices that constitute racism, but all of
> the more subtle ideas and processes, however indirect and unintentional,
> that tend to maintain and reproduce the racialisation.

There can be no sharp distinctions here that will be conceptually felicitous,
though those more politically inclined may say that the price of greater subtlety is simply not worth paying given the scope of the problem. A register of
race as a vice would need to pay attention at least to the factors outlined in
Figure 6.1.

What no typology can achieve is a complex grasp of the relationality of
agency, context and structure. Nor should it aim to. In articulating this register I am merely trying in a preliminary way to draw attention to the degrees
of viciousness that are often unhelpfully lumped together under the label
'racist'. Yet the moral economy of racism must be more differentiated than
this. By contrast, I am suggesting that there exist degrees of culpability that
allow us to differentiate the viciousness of different kinds of characters
labelled racist. Consider the following example:

Cricketers and baseball players commonly rail against the decisions of
umpires. In a recent study of cricketers in the north of England, Long *et al.*
(1997) report that one of the Asian batters in the study protested that he had
been the victim of a bad decision by an umpire, protesting: 'I was never "out".
He gave me out because I'm Asian . . . and he did that for three others.' The
perception of racist behaviour makes it a racial issue, but does not mean that

any racism has necessarily been committed. That is to say, a perception of racism by an apparently maltreated other is neither a necessary nor sufficient condition of its existence. In this case, the umpire may indeed have been racist, but he may also have been an incompetent umpire judging them incorrectly out (or struck out in baseball). Or he may not be racist in any way shape or form and the batter is merely using the racist slur to bring pressure to bear on the umpire for future decisions or to mask their own incompetence. There is also the possibility that the umpire is indeed a repugnant racist but feels bound in this situation by the ethos and laws of cricket to make impartial decisions.

Just as the belief that one is the subject of racist sentiments does not automatically mean that another is a racist, so another's denial that they are being racist is insufficient to deny the truth of the assertion. The remark or behaviour does not stand alone. Consider a circumstance in which a player or official has told a racist joke, used racial abuse or made a decision on the basis of some racial presumption. Interpretation of the significance of that might vary depending upon whether the perpetrator: says sorry (then or later) or shakes hands with a 'Well played mate' at the end of the game; insists it was 'just in the heat of the moment'; does so in a team founded on the principles of cultural pluralism; or elsewhere engages in actions to counter racism. Even then there are other contextual layers that those involved will use to arrive at their interpretation of meaning. It was clear that the black players in Long *et al.* (2000) viewed and responded to incidents in a differentiated manner depending upon the context. Quite properly, it seems to me, they attached varying degrees of moral opprobrium to those whom they perceived had acted in the 'heat of the moment incidents' to those whose behaviours displayed a clearer pattern of consistency.

If virtues and vices are enduring traits of character, it should mean that the idea of a one-off racist would be an oxymoron. To be a racist it must be part of one's character; one's relatively settled dispositions to think, feel and act in regular and interrelated ways. As I have said above, this makes judging whether a person is a racist, in the light of the register above, a more complex matter than some allow.

In their discussion of identity and agency, Rorty and Wong (1997: 20) attempt to explore the questions one might ask in order to judge whether a given trait is central to one's character. Their questions have salience for a more nuanced understanding of racism as a vice. They list seven ways in which a trait may be central in virtue of:

- the degree of its objective ramification, the extent to which other traits (that is dispositions to beliefs, desires, habits, attitudes and actions) are dependent on it;
- the degree of its contextual or regional ramification, that is, the extent to which a trait is exemplified across distinctive spheres (e.g. public and private domains, work and leisure) and across different types of

relationships (as they are differentiated by gender, status, class, age, etc.);

- the degree for which it is difficult for a person to change the trait (which is often a function of its temporal persistence);
- the degree of its social ramification, the extent to which the trait affects the way the person is categorized and treated by others;
- the extent to which it is dominant in situations that require coping with stress or conflict;
- the extent to which it is dominant when it conflicts with other traits (e.g. when generosity conflicts with vengefulness); and
- the degree to which it is appropriated as important in that the person regards herself as radically changed if the trait is lost or strongly modified. Such appropriations may, but need not be, explicitly articulated; they can be sporadic or contextualized; a person can appropriate a trait without succeeding in acting from it habitually. Sometimes what matters to a person's identity is that she centrally strives to strengthen and exercise a trait. Important traits are often also the focus of self-evaluation and self-esteem.

It is useful to illustrate the power of these questions in the context of a real example from sports. In 2004 the veteran English football manager, commentator and pundit, Ron Atkinson, resigned from his job immediately upon hearing that remarks he had made about the lacklustre performance of Chelsea's French defender Marcel Desailly in the European Champions League had in fact not been completely "off-air" but had been broadcast to several international audiences. Big Ron (as he was affectionately referred to) remarked: 'He's what is known in some schools as a fucking lazy thick nigger.' Naturally, and properly, the media frenzy that followed was immediate and severe. But where ought we to place Atkinson on the racist register above?

At first sight it appears to be a one-off racist remark that was not premeditated. But does this make him merely ethically disabled? His immediate resignation shows some level of remorse and recognition of the wrong committed. Much will hang on whether the remark was the product on an entrenched disposition or whether it was "out of character" so to speak. This is where things get philosophically interesting. To go further down this road we need to ask some conceptual questions about the centrality of the disposition to this attitude/remark and some empirical ones about his biography. Rorty and Wong's questions become particularly helpful here and I want to situate them in the Atkinson case along with the remarks of other media commentators from within and outside of sport.

Atkinson's remarks seem to be without objective ramification. That is to say, the racist trait does not appear to form a central part of his identity. After his resignation and the widespread condemnation of his comments, Atkinson made several protestations about his career being one that had been supportive of players of colour. During the 1970s, as a manager Atkinson had helped to develop several British African-Caribbean players not only to top division football but also the point where they represented their national team: England. This is one reason why so many people were shocked. Atkinson remarked himself: 'What I said is racist, I understand that, but I'm not a racist.' Moreover, he insisted in an interview with the editor of *New Nation* (a leading newspaper of the black community): 'I've offended nobody more than me at the moment. Christ almighty it's cost me roughly a million quid. I've done my penance.' Beyond the blasphemy that some might take offence at, one must ask whether Atkinson has the conceptual wherewithal to distinguish between penance and sanction. It's clear he has lost out financially and that, to his credit, he did not wait to be sacked. What is there to be said of the contextual ramification of the trait? Is Big Ron a racist in private but not in public (or at least not normally in public)? Critics have suggested that this is not the first such slip he has made. I shall discuss them further below. The point seems ambiguous but resonates with the idea of the social ramification of the trait. Clearly Atkinson's capital has fallen through the floor with nearly all sports fans and the wider public. He has not been associated with racist remarks and they hitherto formed no part of his social standing – unlike those whose standing, say, in a white supremacist movement is predicated on their racist credentials, Atkinson's certainly is not. Moreover, in his interview, Atkinson inadvertently displayed all of his non-politically correct credentials in his casual acceptance of the historical use of derisory language (queer, nigger etc.). One thing in Atkinson's defence is the clear idea that his remark is at odds with his promotion of black players within the football teams he has managed. Whether this is equity or expediency (it might be argued, though I think unfairly, that the black players were simply the only ones of any quality he could afford or attract) is open to question though certain black players who played for him appear to give support to his testimony. He has succeeded in his career without the trait; he does not depend on it for his success or self-esteem. It seems clear that the trait of racism is not central to his identity. Though the opprobrium that flew his way was well deserved, and though his utterance was utterly repugnant, it seems fair to conclude that despite his racist act(s) he himself is not possessed of a committed racist character.

Ron's racism, sports reporting and other courageous role models

Some media colleagues offered levels of support for Atkinson's person though not his remarks. A fellow football TV pundit, the septuagenarian[2] Jimmy Hill, offered the quasi defence that the remarks were no more than 'fun' between footballers. Hill, a former anchor man of the most popular British football programme of the last 30 or so years is reported to have said the following on the web site for Football Against Racism in Europe (2004):

> In that context, you wouldn't think that words like 'n****r' were particularly insulting: it would be funny. Without meaning to insult any black

men, it's us having fun. What about people who make jokes about my long chin? I mean, n****r is black – so we have jokes where we call them n****rs because they're black. Why should that be any more of an offence than someone calling me chinny?

Now Hill is well known in the UK to have a pronounced chin but to equate his facial characteristic with the use of a word so historically loaded with disrespect and the fundamental denial of human rights, coupled with abusive derogation of Desailly's character, seems not so much bizarre but the product of a limited intellect. Despite Hill's being in his seventies, and Atkinson in his sixties, it seems clear that both person's character have been forged in racist times and neither has been able to break free of those limiting shackles.

On the basis that racial groups have been historically subjected to destructive forms of prejudice, stigma, exclusion and discrimination, Blum (2002: 96) notes that 'a somewhat greater wrongfulness attaches to racial differentiations than to others. Race *is* an especially invidious category, both uniquely inferiorising and uniquely divisive'. In a similar vein, Muhammad Ali taunted Joe Frazier before their first fight for the Heavyweight Championship of the World. This was in response to Frazier's refuse to call Ali by his adopted Islamic name and, instead, by his former name Cassius Clay Ali had called Frazier an 'Uncle Tom' meaning to demean Frazier whom he mocked as a gorilla; an unthinking beast, a person of colour insufficiently intelligent or articulate enough to challenge the hegemonic racial order, one happy (and with complicity) to preserve the racially based social hierarchies. Moreover, in the one-sided and bitter fight that followed, Ali berated Frazier 'what's my name? . . . what's my name?' repeatedly whilst brutally beating him. In 2001 Ali offered an apology in the *New York Times* but Frazier, though appearing to accept it, later remarked that the apology had been made to the paper rather than him. In Atkinson's case, the instant apology might incline us to move Atkinson to the centre of the register in Figure 6.1, but if subsequent events confirm that this is representative of an underlying trait we would return him to the right of the register.

If Hill's remarks are those of denial, how much better are the inflammatory remarks of the columnist Darcus Howe?:

> Football managers tend to be dictatorial brutes. They treat their charges with a paternal brutality that would have any father hauled up in court for child abuse. These men, almost all of them white, behave in a way that would not be tolerated in any other area of modern society. They infect the players with the brutishness they dispense. As a consequence, women and blacks – perceived as the weaker sections of society – are deemed the lowest of the low. Gang sex and racial barracking are the stock-in-trade of players. The game has become a sewer containing all sorts of filth not permitted elsewhere.

Atkinson is up to his neck in it. He pleaded a lapse in an otherwise unblemished career, which included signing several black players when he was manager of West Bromwich Albion. Yet Atkinson once alluded to a Cameroonian player's mother who, he claimed, lived up a tree in Africa. He boasted about how he had made Cyrille Regis, one of the blacks he signed while at West Brom, travel to away games at the back of the bus, as blacks were once forced to travel in the American South. Ian Wright, the Arsenal and England player, once asked a players' representative to warn Atkinson about his racial jibes.

(Howe, 2004)

It appears then that, given the truth of the claims above, Atkinson was no one-off racist. The trait had surfaced elsewhere in public but was clearly at odds with others in his character. But having made his point, Howe then descends into a diatribe of disrespect that robs him of the moral high ground. He continued:

So steeped is football in racist muck that nobody thought Atkinson's behaviour exceptional. Even black people accepted it. He demanded from them, and got, gratitude for letting darkies into the game. Hence several black players were at the front of the queue saying that, though his remarks on Desailly were wrong, he is no racist.

Then what is he? A leader in the vanguard of anti-racism? All I have to say to Atkinson is: "Get thee hence." In case he doesn't know what that means, I'll translate into dressing-room jargon: "Fuck off."

(Howe, 2004)

But if we are to understand racism in sport in the round, it is appropriate to ask what kind of response is ethically called for to such situations; what is the virtuous response to racist sports journalism or reporting? At first sight it appears that Howe's diatribe has some provenance from no lesser figure than Aristotle, who argued that anger was the virtuous response to injustice. As we read on though, we find that it is not simply the angry response that is just:

[A]nyone can be angry – that is easy – or give or spend money; but to do this to the right person, to the right extent, at the right time, with the right motive, and in the right way, *that* is not for everyone, nor is it easy; wherefore goodness is both rare and laudable and noble.

(NE II Bk. 9; 1109a25–30)

And later, in a slightly different context, Aristotle notes: 'It is not easy to determine both how and with whom and on what provocation and how long one should be angry . . .' (*NE* II Bk. 9; 1109b14–16).

Of course there is some irony in quoting Aristotle here. For like other great philosophers he too was a hostage to the times. He had a conception of aristocratic nobility that appeared to influence heavily his conception of the good life for 'man'. Slaves and women were distinctly second class.

The idea of racism in sports has a long history. Though shorter, there is also a history of defiance against racial barriers, which perhaps achieved its epitome when in front of the Aryan supremacist Adolf Hitler, Jesse Owens won his Olympic sprint title in 1936 in Berlin. More recently, and against the racially segregated and vengeful backlash against white imperial rule in Zimbabwe, one black and one white cricketer stood together in defiance of the widespread racially motivated violent repatriation of land, and unlawful acquisition of property under the acquiescence (and some would say active support of) President Mugabe. On the eve of the Cricket World Cup, to be hosted by Zimbabwe for the first time, Andrew Flower and Henry Olonga, two of their leading players, wore black arm bands during a World Cup match to protest at their nation's racist policies. Not since the 'black power' protest of Tommy Smith and his fellow American athlete John Carlos in the Mexico Olympics had sportsmen or women put their head above the parapet to enter the political arena. Flower and Olonga jointly made the following pronouncement to the media:

> It is a great honour for us to take the field today to play for Zimbabwe in the World Cup.
>
> We feel privileged and proud to have been able to represent our country.
>
> We are, however, deeply distressed about what is taking place in Zimbabwe in the midst of the World Cup and do not feel that we can take the field without indicating our feelings in a dignified manner and in keeping with the spirit of cricket.
>
> We cannot in good conscience take to the field and ignore the fact that millions of our compatriots are starving, unemployed and oppressed.
>
> We are aware that hundreds of thousands of Zimbabweans may even die in the coming months through a combination of starvation, poverty and Aids.
>
> We are aware that many people have been unjustly imprisoned and tortured simply for expressing their opinions about what is happening in the country.
>
> We have heard a torrent of racist hate speech directed at minority groups.
>
> We are aware that thousands of Zimbabweans are routinely denied their right to freedom of expression.
>
> We are aware that people have been murdered, raped, beaten and had their homes destroyed because of their beliefs and that many of those responsible have not been prosecuted.
>
> We are also aware that many patriotic Zimbabweans oppose us even playing in the World Cup because of what is happening.

It is impossible to ignore what is happening in Zimbabwe. Although we are just professional cricketers, we do have a conscience and feelings.

We believe that if we remain silent that will be taken as a sign that either we do not care or we condone what is happening in Zimbabwe.

We believe that it is important to stand up for what is right.

We have struggled to think of an action that would be appropriate and that would not demean the game we love so much.

We have decided that we should act alone without other members of the team being involved because our decision is deeply personal and we did not want to use our senior status to unfairly influence more junior members of the squad.

We would like to stress that we greatly respect the ICC (International Cricket Council) and are grateful for all the hard work it has done in bringing the World Cup to Zimbabwe.

In all the circumstances we have decided that we will each wear a black armband for the duration of the World Cup.

In doing so we are mourning the death of democracy in our beloved Zimbabwe.

In doing so we are making a silent plea to those responsible to stop the abuse of human rights in Zimbabwe.

In doing so we pray that our small action may help to restore sanity and dignity to our nation.

Andrew Flower, Henry Olonga
(http: //news.bbc.co.uk/sport3/cwc2003/hi/newsid_2740000/newsid_
2744700/2744795.stm; accessed 10.4.06)

It seems to me this is as moving and powerful an example of a virtuous response to racism in society through the equally powerful medium of commercialised sports. Their act was courageous. They knew in publicly articulating the racism of the ruling regime they not merely ended their international sporting careers but would in all likelihood face retribution from the governmental security forces, not known for their polite treatment of political dissenters. And it did. The proclamation led to a warrant for the arrest of Olonga on the grounds of treason and the pair were forced into hiding and then to move from the country. Finally, their statement expresses the anger and indignation that is apt in response to injustice even if others will merely see it as a small corrective of the vicious historical white domination of that continent. It also shows how sport, far from standing outside of the ordinary business of living, can seek to act as a powerful agent for social change.

On a final note, I am conscious that the examples mentioned here are both males and I certainly do not wish to give the impression, perhaps suggested by Rorty (1980) that courage as bravery needs detoxifying. Rather these examples of courage show its fortitudinal aspect and not merely its risk-engendering aspects. Some examples to counter this tendency would include Julie Krone who, in 2004, won the Wilma Rudolph Courage Award recognising her

18-year career as a top-flight female jockey fighting both injury and prejudice alike. Equally, Hassiba Boulmerka had to overcome considerable sexist prejudice and threats against her performing in immodest Western athletics clothing in order to represent her country and eventually win the 1991 1500m gold medal at the World Championships (see Morgan, 1998). It is a sad fact indeed, then, that the less noble role models who so often attract the media's attention, such as Mike Tyson and Michael Vick, regrettably endure as racially stereotyped role models. Whether this is indicative of some unacknowledged racism in sports journalism is itself a moot point.

Conclusion

Research on racism in sport has tended to adopt an on/off conceptualisation of racism: either that person is a racist or they are not; that it was a racist incident or it was not. Such certitude is enviable, but does scant justice to a complex phenomenon. I recognise the problem with facilitating the nuanced appreciation of racism set out here, with its degrees of severity. Nonetheless, an appreciation of the register suggests the need for more subtly differentiated anti-racism campaigns and targeted actions in the playing, administering and reporting of sport. Of course, there is the danger that it may give succour to those not inclined to act to counter racism if they can justify inaction on the basis that there are others who are worse than they are. It might, however, be counter-productive to alienate potential allies in campaigns against racism in sport by berating them for what they consider to be minor indiscretions. In presenting this register of racism I have tried to open up a space for an appreciation of the significance of context, the possibility of a dynamic process of alignment on racial issues and the moral opprobrium that ought differentially to attach according to these factors.

7   Hubris, humility and humiliation

Vice and virtue in sporting communities

Introduction

In this chapter I extend the virtue-ethical discussion into a much talked of vice. In modern parlance it is typically, though with a certain loss of meaning, called arrogance. In the popular psychology of sports, some even go as far as to say it is a necessary condition of athletic success. In the Ancient Greek catalogue of virtues and vices it was known as hubris. In its moral gravitational field is its opposite, humility, and the emotion of humiliation, which is often spoken of in sports journalism. I argue that humiliation felt as a response to sporting defeat may indeed be rational. In distinguishing weak from strong humiliation I show that while the latter is reserved to those cases where one's moral status as a person has been assaulted, the former may be experienced by sportspersons who fail to observe certain standards of character and conduct. To make this case I argue that it is necessary to locate the felt humiliation against the hierarchical nature of sports identities and practice communities where the notion of honour still resonates. This context makes the idea of a highly committed sportsperson's humiliation more plausible than the idea that a heavy or unsuspected defeat necessarily occasions a mere blow to their self-esteem. I develop an account of humiliation in close relation to its conceptual cousins: shame, embarrassment, dignity and humility. I show how, paradigmatically, those who display the vice of hubris are predisposed to weak humiliation and illustrate such in a case study of the boxing contest between two of the greatest ever welterweight boxers, (Sugar) Ray Leonard and Roberto Duran.

Sports as practices: hierarchy and honour

I discussed in Chapter 3 the relevance of MacIntyre's thesis that modernity has loosened the bonds between fact and value, role and identity to the contexts of sports. Who we are and what we ought and ought not to do and be are commonly supposed to occupy separate realms. Unlike many other cultural practices, however, sports retain a strong vestige of the view that our roles still issue in clear directives for personal action and life-commitments.

Sports, with their structural exultation of the heroic, still offer a partial vision of what is honourable. While it may be the case that we are less clear of our role-related expectations in our everyday (post)modern lives, sports by contrast offer themselves as a bastion of social conservatism. How is this so? First, at an individual level, there is a strong explicitness surrounding the specified roles we occupy in the sports arenas. As goalkeeper, or umpire, or coach, the expectations attached to our positions are relatively circumscribed. Second, sports' ethoses too can be tightly bracketed in an explicit system of social structure that is notably hierarchical. It is in these structures, and the expectations that flow from the roles we occupy within them, that sports share many similarities with honour-based heroic societies.

I have noted how it has become commonplace in the literature to eschew previously dominant analytical accounts of sports and instead consider them under some social aspect as a 'practice'. One aspect commonly ignored in the application of a MacIntyrean account of social practices is the notion of ritual. I have argued in Chapter 1, following Sansone's (1988) anthropological thesis of sports as the sacrifice of energy, that the conceptualisation of sport as *inherently* social urges upon us a picture of elite sports at least as forms of public ceremonies and all forms of sports as partly both play and display. So I simply assert here that sports are the object of practice communities and that they are essentially forms of ritual and ceremony in and through, and for, those communities. The shared background presupposed in the very idea of sporting communities is essential. In more abstract political debates it can be difficult to make much sense of communitarian ideas such as 'shared ideals', 'shared goals' and 'shared purposes'. In the less diverse and less complex worlds of sports one scarcely has to work hard to conceptualise their contents and contexts. And it is in this idea, coupled with the Western heritage of sports as play and display, where spectators are thought to be part and parcel of the activity and not mere adornments, that the crucial structural context to the moral psychology of sports is given. Here individualised evaluations of winning and losing, of bragging and moaning about lost opportunities or refereeing incompetence are seen in the life of an evolving tradition of each and every sport, told and re-told by deed of print or word of mouth, of hard-earned success and undeserved 'tragedies', of hollow victories and glorious defeats.

It is often difficult to dislocate talk of ungracious or hollow victories, humbling defeats, or of moral winners and losers from our self-evaluations regarding winning and defeat.[1] The idea that Western sports have emerged from a civilization that made pre-eminent the honour ethic is one that I will not sufficiently analyse here.[2] Nevertheless, conceptions of honourable conduct are always in the background, with attendant virtues and vices displayed by the winner and loser. What I wish to do is draw on Miller's quasi anthropological theses about shame and humiliation. This, at least, will help to gain some conceptual clarity concerning humiliation and hubris in sports. So, just as the Greek myths and legends give birth to an agonal context that allowed sports to flourish, so the agonal warrior ethic can be found in Norse sagas such as Beowulf too. And these can help to illuminate a modern sense of emotions such as shame and humiliation in sport. It will repay attention if we bear in mind the structural similarities of honour societies and elite competitive sports, especially those that involve direct competition involving physical contact (such as football, boxing, rugby, hockey). So we might say that the concept of 'honour' is deeply intertwined with hierarchical societies. Thus Miller writes:

> Honor was more than just a set of rules for governing behavior. Honor permeated every aspect of consciousness: how you thought about yourself and others, how you held your body, the expectations you could reasonably have and the demands you could make on others [. . .]. It was your very being. For in an honor based culture there was no self-respect independent of the respect of others, no private sense of 'hey, I'm quite something' unless it was confirmed publicly. Honor was then not just a matter of the individual; it necessarily involved a group, and the group included all those people worthy of competing with you for honor. For the most part, people acted as if the mechanics of honor had the structure of a zero-sum game or less-than-zero-sum game. The shortest road to honor was thus to take someone else's [. . .].
>
> (1993: 116–17)

Nowhere is this better exemplified in late modernity than in the zero-sum structure of sports. And it is almost deified in sports such as boxing, where the language of the 'champion' and 'contender' is most obvious, where the claims to be 'the greatest' are the strongest. Honour though is not merely to be thought of as representing oneself appropriately in a social structure. It is noteworthy that, like other dispositions, honour predisposes us to feel and act in regular and interrelated ways. Those who value honour necessarily value reputation and above all the appearance of that reputation. A 'loss of face' is the modern vernacular for loss of honour. It follows then that how others see us is critical to our standing in the scheme of things. This is why in premodern societies (among other reasons of course) the social concept of shame is the powerful regulator of our thoughts and deeds. Lest it appear that I have some nostalgic view of honour, it is worth acknowledging the dangers to the powerful social structures that weave our identities and actions so tightly. Characteristically such structures function to preclude critical self and other reflection and comment. Moreover, in sports as in academic lives, shame is commonly the fruit of envy. Academics covet the positions and status held by colleagues who get tenure first, or publish most prolifically, or who attract prestigious national funds. Individual sportspersons are characteristically thought to covet the number one slot in leagues or drafts. Responses to that shame in tight social structures can be equally problematic to (post)modern minds. Falling on one's sword (perhaps the ultimate act of masculine honour in shame-cultures) is widely thought unacceptable now, though retiring gracefully after a drunken fall at a party is not. Emotional economies scarcely stand still. How we match social failings and their analogue feelings and subjective judgements are themselves subject to cultural change.

The ancient warrior ethic, if you like, operates tightly since the background beliefs, the framework or supporting structure, is itself tight; there are no gaps or interstices. Nowhere is the tightness of roles and their expectations developed so effectively than in the conflicts of Greek tragedy such as in King Creone who, to execute his role-duties, must execute his daughter for her defiance of the law. Creone knows what he must do because he knows who he is. As MacIntyre puts it:

> Every individual has a given role and status within a well-defined and highly determinate system of roles and statuses. [. . .] In such a society a man knows who he is by knowing his role in these structures; and in knowing this he knows also what he owes and what is owed him by the occupant of every other role and status. [. . .]
>
> But it is not just that there is for each status a prescribed set of duties and privileges. There is a clear understanding of actions that are required to perform these and what actions fall short of what is required. For what are required are actions. A man in heroic society is what he does.
>
> (MacIntyre, 1985: 122)

What is so interesting about these role-related commitments is how an appreciation of them can illuminate our understanding of the moral psychology of winning and losing in sports. Both Dixon (1992) and Hardman *et al.* (1996) highlight the ranking function in sportspersons' self-evaluations in terms of comparative measurements of athletic ability. But there is more to it than this. I have proposed that attention be paid not merely to the fact that certain sports (though surely not all – compare the ethoses of heavyweight boxing and ice-skating) still retain a vestige of honour codes. But more importantly I think the relation between differentia – how players are ranked in that structure (favourites, no-hopers, new-stars, fading stars and so on) – need to be apprehended. What merit is accorded to sportspersons and their sporting status rests partly on how they themselves evaluate their worth within the scheme. The expectations of how they comport themselves alter according to the places they register in the social scales of sports. Tolerance may be given to the new kids on the block who shout their mouths off a little too quickly; it is less easily afforded to those who are old enough, or experienced enough, to know better. What will be termed 'structural pretension' within a system of rankings will be crucial to understand felt-humiliation in sports I will argue. The idea that one judges oneself worthy of esteem beyond that which one merits makes one easy prey to the emotion. In sporting practices, as I have said, we come to know who we are, not merely as athletic performers, in our understandings of what we stand for and where we stand in the catalogue of those who come before us and are the canons of excellence in that activity. And proof of that standing comes not in verbal forms but as action. If we are first or twenty-first we come to know our place, which is verified in the public forum of sporting competition. Virtuosity and incompetence are there for all to see, and esteem and derision follow hard on their heels. Sports are not intellectually complex. They are scarcely comparable to the high arts in terms of their (im)penetrability by the masses. And this brings me to speak of recognition and esteem; for both notions lie close to an understanding of honour and expectations of conduct in the execution of role-related behaviour.

I want to re-affirm why, as I argued in Chapter 3, what MacIntyre sets out generically as external goods (e.g. wealth, status and social esteem) are not simply to be thought of as the necessarily corrupting components of modern commercialised sports. I argued there that external goods *justly conferred* are proper signifiers that our (sporting) lives are going well. A better way to talk of this relation is not to slip into the old intrinsic/extrinsic dichotomy but to think of the sportsperson who relationally values the sport for the esteem it brings him or her. To be sure, esteem can be wrought from a range of activities beyond sports, but it is a clear (and for some people, perhaps, the only) means to that particular end. Talk of esteem as an external good of sports, one that is merely extrinsically valuable, is too crude. Moreover, given that elite sports have historically been associated with certain of what are called external goods, there comes a point when one wants to ask the role that the word 'external' is playing here. In ancient schemes death or glory was the chant of virtuous soldiers and clearly was intrinsic to their motivational set. I see no reason why this need not still be part of the ethical-emotional stance of many elite athletes, and particularly in those sports in which there is considerable physical contact where putting bodies on the line is not so much metaphor as reality.

Of course there are ways of pursuing these ends, such as esteem, that are more and less morally acceptable. Tony Skillen's discussion of Rousseau and the fall of 'social man' captures important points about competitive status ranking and the proper means of their pursuit:

> This is the sort of thing we find in Thrasymachus, Glaucon and Adeimantus' defence of injustice in Plato's *Republic*. They argue that the reputation of virtue is desirable because it brings material rewards. [. . .] But this is not what Rousseau is on about. He is not primarily concerned with people's pursuing social reputation as a means to materialistic, asocial ends, but rather with their quest for esteem as a confirmation of their social identities. [. . .] And without shared 'recognition' of superiority, such distinction is worth-less.
>
> (Skillen, 1985: 114)

What I think we have in sports then is the demonstration of who we are *in the way* that we play sports and the myriad of ways in which we make comparisons of athletic excellence. And when our sports are played and officiated properly, when we develop our talents and capacities, when we pit them against others, we visit an inner sporting oracle; we come to know the limits of our sporting world, and the sporting world comes to know our limits too. That is the central function of ranking systems such as leagues and titles, demotions, promotions and so on. But *how* we win and lose speaks crucially of who we are. Keeping a close eye on the relations between ends and means is critical; perceptions of their natures are an inherent part of the context. But we also have to reflect upon the self-conceptions of performers (how, for example, they saw themselves win or lose) if we are to understand properly the weak humiliation visited on or felt by them. Below I argue that, in cases of strong humiliation, the context is relatively unimportant. I will argue that strong humiliation entails an awareness of the violation of basic respect of a person, not the deflation of their self-esteem. I will then show how weak humiliation may be the proper emotional corollary of defeat.

'Strong' and 'weak' humiliation and structural pretension

It has been argued by Dixon (1992, 1998) that humiliation is not a proper emotional response to a sporting defeat, since it conflates humiliation with a mere loss of self-esteem, which is the appropriate emotional response. Since the defeat itself does not *morally reduce* the opposition as persons, it cannot therefore be considered as an example of strong humiliation:

> In general, a loss of self-esteem is a regrettable but morally acceptable consequence of many legitimate actions in the pursuit of legitimate goals. In contrast, inflicting strong humiliation, which brings moral shame and disgrace on a person, is a more serious harm that requires a more substantial justification.
>
> (Dixon, 1998: 67)

This is not quite right. Dixon persuasively distinguishes between a loss of self-esteem and strong humiliation. But he pays little attention to what might be called 'weak humiliation', whose conceptual territory is different from the individualistic evaluation entailed in 'self-esteem'. Furthermore, he fails to clarify sufficiently what 'strong humiliation' actually is and presupposes that justification thereof is possible. By way of extending this discussion I will begin with the distinction between loss of self-esteem and strong humiliation. Dixon argues that not all lowerings of self-esteem are strongly humiliating. Yet the difference between a lowering of self-esteem and weak humiliation should not be thought of merely as a matter of degree. Dixon fails throughout to distinguish strong humiliation from shame and disgrace and merely says that strong humiliation is a 'different beast' (1998: 67) from weak humiliation. It essentially involves a lowering of moral standing that is not a necessary condition of weak humiliation:

> An athlete who competes fairly and with dignity, who prepares assiduously and performs to the best of her ability, and who has a decent minimal level of competence at the game, is absolutely not shamed or disgraced (i.e. strongly humiliated) by a lop-sided defeat.
>
> (Dixon, 1998: 67)

Dixon is absolutely right that the lop-sidedness of the defeat is independent of the humiliation felt, justifiably or unjustifiably, by the humiliated. Nevertheless, the criteria relate only to the loser and not the quality of defeat nor the broader social context that is necessarily to be understood if the actions themselves are properly to be characterised. In all acts of strong humiliation, the context is relatively unimportant for the actions to be understood as humiliating. In Margalit's (1996) discussion of the decent society, 'humiliation' is tied to the most basic respect for persons. It is indeed the kind of thing a torturer seeks to inflict on a victim. We need to know little of the context to appreciate the humiliation of the torturer/tortured variety. In such strong humiliation the humiliated are passive at the hands of the tormentor, whereas in weaker cases the power balance is not as dramatic. So clear is the denial of the status of personhood to the subject of strong humiliation that the imposition of powerless degradation requires little or no awareness of a moral and conceptual vocabulary to modern minds.[3] In contrast, sports require at least a minimal conceptual background to be understood before winning and losing, and the deflation of recognised status, can be perceived. Moreover, in terms of the violence done to one's status as a person in strong humiliation, we may say that sports never reach this depth. But are there instances of 'weak humiliation' to the serious sportsperson (amateur or professional) rather than merely a loss of self-esteem?

To explore this question requires further attention to the nature of humiliation and related concepts. One's self-awareness of shame, honour and humiliation presupposes the transgression of moral boundaries. They relate to actions that are evaluated in light of shared, public norms. As a precursor to his discussion of humiliation, Miller laments the passing of shame proper.[4] He notes how it has contracted from the large role it played in honour societies concerned with saving face or reputation (notwithstanding huge problems in itself, e.g. gendered ideas such as protecting one's honour by having dresses down to the ankles) into a mere association with not feeling good about oneself or having low self-esteem.[5] Here, everyday locutions, 'shame on you', 'you ought to be ashamed', point to a stronger status-related concept rather than a mere subjective feeling.

Miller argues that shame and humiliation are to be distinguished along the lines of status pretension. Humiliation, he argues, is tied to a mode or quality of self-presentation. He writes:

> They seek deference from others, they mean to cut figures before others, and in doing so they presume on others; those others will get even. It is the presumption that enables the humiliation and justifies it. Vanity begs for humiliation.
>
> One of the most salient distinctions between shame and humiliation is that, at root, humiliation depends on the deflation of pretension.
>
> (Miller, 1993: 139)

Before we develop the argument further, we should enquire where this distinction fits with the humiliating blowout literature. In concentrating predominantly on the score itself and quantitatively the margin between victor and vanquished, neither Dixon nor Hardman *et al.* developed their theses in relation to the modes of self-presentation of the contestants. In order to give a virtue-ethical account of these episodes it seems to me that this is critical. To be fair, Dixon makes the point that one may be humiliated where one shows character flaws but fails to expand the point. Pugilistic examples can be particularly relevant here, since the boxing world is saturated with machismo. The mode of self-presentation is critical to boxers, since part of their identity as much as their chances of winning rests in the (self-)deception they can generate both to gird themselves and psychologically to terrorise the opposition; 'respect' here is no Kantian notion, but a cultural shorthand for embodied power.

Notwithstanding this, blowout scenarios, however various they may be, are not tied to shame necessarily. For, as we have noted above, shame is linked with a failure in reaching a designated *moral* as opposed to technical standard. In addition, there is nothing in losing by a large margin that would indicate the appropriateness of such a weighty emotion. One might say that embarrassment was the proper response to a failure against inferior opposition because of poor preparation. Shame will characteristically be thought too serious an emotional response. Yet if shame occupies itself with the transgression of issues of cultural, moral or religious rules, humiliation in its attenuated form is only tied to the conventional or the decorous. Many authors have noted that it holds a perversely incongruous grip on the psyche of some. One might think of those for whom humility had descended to the pathological. Instead of weighing their talents and achievements in a proper way, their self-evaluations never reach beyond mere self-loathing. Likewise, there are others over-sensitive to 'proper' conduct who feel that any and all transgressions of etiquette are self-imposed attacks on their integrity. A form of alienation is the end point of this view. We can see its development in accounts of those who argue that they feel they do not belong within certain milieux. Their experiences are to be found in early accounts of racism encountered at golf clubs, or sexism within football cultures, where blacks and women respectively report to being acutely sensitive about observing intricate social codes or conventions. Perhaps the pathological grip is strongest though on those who act not in ignorance or gaucherie but rather in pretence. Later I will argue that those who display an arrogant form of pretension are particularly ripe for weak humiliation.

In order to develop the account of humiliation and hubris I need to appropriate some important distinctions from Miller that open the door to thinking about weak humiliation in sports. He talks of pretensions of accident where a person merely finds oneself superior in some respect to another, which is to be distinguished from an active putting on of 'airs'. It is the latter that is interesting for our purposes. It is not difficult for sports fans to remember any number of pre-fight hypes where challengers for titles describe in rich and colourful terms how bad the champion is; how he has only been matched against cherry-picked opponents; how he's past his best and should have retired before this fight to save him from the impending woe the challenger will visit on him. The litany of abuse is depressingly familiar. Why is such a person, lacking in both humility and due-respect, ripe for a humiliating defeat? Miller writes:

> Structural pretension is not merely a matter of fowl among fish. It depends on the fowl occupying, by the usual social conventions of status demarcation, the higher position. The setting must be one in which the fowl has no moral or social right to assert the higher status, but also is likely to be seen as making such a claim because the context calls for special attention to status differential.
>
> (Miller, 1993: 142)

Now one can innocently occupy the high ground, but our boxers do not fit this scenario. The boxing world has an honour code; it represents an honour community, where virtues and vices are displayed under fire and the public's gaze. So the disrespectful boxer's quest for esteem and status is cheaply sought at the price of disrespect for the champion who has earned his right to that status and can now play the role of champion (what in Ancient Greek thought would be honorifically described as *megalospuchia* – the great souled man) with the dignity appropriate to a champion. In Aristotle, we find an idea that jars on moderns: the idea that a certain level of pride is appropriate to those who are recognised for their greatness. Nevertheless, the idea that a certain status attaches to a role still remains in the strongly structured world of boxing as in other martial sports. Working out whether in particular circumstances embarrassment or humiliation attach will not be a mechanical application of criteria. Nevertheless, something general needs to be said to demarcate cases. Again, Miller writes: 'If shame is the consequence of not living up to what we ought to, then humiliation is the consequence of trying to live up to what we have no right to' (1993: 145).

As the mealy-mouthed pretender to the throne is beaten in the first few rounds, few shed tears. Where are all his hollow threats now? Where is his vaunted jab, stout defence or granite chin? He is indeed humiliated before the boxing community and perhaps the entire audience to the extent that they appreciate the standards of the practice and the significance of status ranking therein. In sports, unlike so many other practices, we are positioned publicly. He can lay no such right to that ground again without fear of ridicule.[6] So in these cases, the public deflation of a status beyond our merit occasions weak humiliation. While the negative emotion felt is a form of 'emotional punishment' for the flouting of recognised, socially conferred status it does not amount to an assault on the basic condition of the sportsperson *as* person and therefore cannot be considered a case of strong humiliation. What must be shown below is that it can amount to more than a mere loss of self-esteem.

Hubris, humility and the modes of self-presentation

What I want to do now is to show how hubris, thought of as an exaggerated pride in oneself, specifically in one's powers and status, is crucially related to the possibility of suffering weak humiliation in sports. Hubris takes its original meaning from the Greek description of those who thought themselves superior to the gods. It entails the moral failing of not knowing one's place in a hierarchical scheme and vaingloriously sticking to it. Boxing, perhaps the closest sporting cousin to war, provides the case study.

In the first title fight between (Sugar) Ray Leonard and Roberto Duran in Montreal, much bad blood was spilt in the pre-match promotion. Duran had wanted to unsettle his opponent and reduce him to an angry fighter. He did this by a number of taunts and provocations that challenged, among other things, Leonard's sexuality and heart for a battle. In the fight, Leonard eschewed his usual highly technical skills in favour of a brawl. Naturally, he lost to Duran who had seduced him into contesting the match in a manner that conduced to Duran's abrasive style. In the rematch, however, Leonard set out to prove that he had learnt his lesson. The contest was set up as a grudge match wherein two classic styles of boxing were in the starkest of contrasts. In addition to this dichotomy of 'artist' and 'slugger', much was made of personal contrasts between the two. Here there was the pitting of an articulate, college-educated, stylish, beautiful black man against a hungry and hardened opponent, notorious for never taking a backward step, who had never been knocked out, and whose overweening pride now manifested itself in an arrogance that went well beyond an all-consuming self-esteem.

In the early rounds Leonard's technical virtuosity was clearly on display. He was quicker of mind as well as fist and foot. He hit Duran so many times and with the full array of combinations. It was simply remarkable. Duran just could not get near enough to hit him with any effect. And often when he tried, and he tried often, Leonard's fluid defensive manoeuvres meant that he slipped punches by inches in with aesthetic élan, making Duran appear an amateur.

When Duran did land a punch, Leonard's elastic movements assuaged the full force, and with beautiful balance he simply countered to greater effect.

By the middle rounds, Duran was tired and frustrated at his inabilities, and this was compounded by Leonard's public demonstration of his own pugilistic excellence and Duran's limitations. Without verbal assault, Leonard's entire performances exuded élan, an aesthetic dimension of which Duran's own mien was the antithesis. In his biography of Leonard, Toperoff writes:

> In the eighth round, a round that has already become an indelible part of boxing history, one that will forever tarnish the Duran legend, Ray Leonard sensed the level of Roberto Duran's frustration at not being able to have his own way. Now it was Sugar's turn to taunt and mock the man with hands of stone. A payback for all the insults and humiliations in Montreal. Ray dropped his hands in mid-ring and exposed his chin, a look of teasing stupidity playing on his face. By merely twisting this way and that, he made Duran miss the too-tempting target. Frustration mounted. A few seconds later, again in the center of the ring, Ray wound his right arm like a pantomiming softball pitcher. The so called bolo motion is not one of boxing's classic punches, but as Duran watched the right hand warming up, Ray popped him with a quick left jab right on the schnoz [nose]. It was the sort of move my old man would have pulled on me during our first few weeks of sparring. Duran heard the crowd's derisive laughter.
>
> With only sixteen seconds left in the round, and with Ray working *him* along the ropes, Roberto Duran turned away and said to Octavio Meyeran, the referee, *"no mas no mas"* [no more, no more].
>
> Meyran said "Por que?"
>
> Duran's non-answer "No mas"
>
> Roberto Duran's quitting, unhurt in mid-fight, was so big a story that Ray Leonard's strategic and technical brilliance was overlooked. [. . .] There were strong rumors of mysterious drugs that had sapped his will. More logical was the explanation that the macho man could handle anything except being made a fool of in public – it had never happened during his life on the planet: now it was happening for the world to see. So he chose dishonor over humiliation.
>
> (Toperoff, 1989: 140–1)

Now this was no blowout victory. To be sure, Leonard was well ahead on points but, notoriously in boxing, one punch can finish the contest. As long as an opponent is standing, one had better beware. It was rather Duran's hubristic machismo, his strutting airs of masculine invincibility, which made him ripe for the humiliation. Of course, had Leonard fought him toe to toe (man to man as some may say), he would surely have lost again. For Duran was a fighter of frightening will and physical power. Leonard simply out-thought and out-boxed him and did it so publicly that he demonstrated Duran's limitations for the world to see. I think that this case is probably the limit case of weak humiliation. For the professional sportspersons, their chosen profession constitutes an identity-constituting commitment. Leonard's assault on Duran's identity as boxer was considerably harder to bear than the physical blows he received. Because of the significance of those commitments and the public deflation of his honour as boxer, the loss to Duran exceeds characterisation as a loss of self-esteem. It's not simply that he thinks a little less of himself now. Rather, in full view of the adoring public and the boxing community, his legend lost much of its lustre in the nature of his defeat. Though he may recover some of his self-esteem in the future, he can do nothing to erase the record of that humiliation.[7]

Just so it is not thought that I am putting the victor on a pedestal or engaging in some variant of ethical hegemony against a culturally specific machismo, some critical remarks are in order.[8] Having established that weak humiliation is not necessarily tied to the quantitative measure of defeat but rather its quality, and in particular the character of the humiliated, a word or two is in order of the potential viciousness of the victor. Of course, Leonard was now ripe himself for being brought down a peg or two. But not in the manner that had behoved Duran. To be sure he had mocked Duran but not in the vicious manner in which Duran had questioned his integrity. He had not 'shot his mouth off' to use the vernacular. He had not abused Duran – though this may have been as much out of prudence as virtue. To have bad-mouthed Duran may have been to motivate him further. There is an old Aesopian tale about crowing one's eminence only to be brought low by a creature greater than oneself. Even the greatest of sportsmen and women do well to mind its moral. Such is the nature of sports: they are temporal affairs; they offer time-related goods. The one sure fact a champion must come to know and to obey is that he or she will not be champion forever. Time will have its way and usually sooner rather than later.

It is worthy of note that, after Mackinnon (1999), virtue theorists have tended to focus on a range of positive dispositions and rather neglected the negative ones. So it is in the sport philosophical literature that there is little discussion of the vices that are commonplace and the qualities they take on in sporting contexts. So in our potential evaluation of humiliators we must take into account whether we will characterise their acts as vicious, and if so, enquire as to the nature of that viciousness. To what extent do they pursue the humiliation of their opponents in ignorance or full knowledge of their actions and consequences? Are their failings mere weaknesses of will or outright wickedness?

I have little doubt that the full lists of vices display themselves in and across all ranges of sports. What is less clear, but more interesting is the extent to which vicious acts are the products of 'weak' and 'strong evaluation', which was discussed in Chapter 2. Recall, that the weak evaluator is no more than a means–ends reasoner. The ends of his or her actions or desires are never problematised nor alternative visions explored. Here we have a paradigm of sports talk; winning is taken unproblematically to be the exclusive goal of professional sports. How wins are secured is only considered in terms of models of technical reason, where criteria such as efficiency and effectiveness dominate. There are exceptions of course. And the exceptions betoken a particular problem for those who wish to generalise in the ethics of sports. For the heterogeneity of sports and sports cultures makes generalisations problematic. Honda (2005) in his defence of the sportisation of the ancient art of Kendo notes how shifts from its underlying warrior ethic (*budo*) to a sporting one, have angered traditionalists. They have argued that the deployment of strategy and tactics is deceitful, ignoble and unworthy of the Kendo master. The loss of this ethic, however problematic it may be in its own right and in modern times, also represents a certain shift in ethical language from strong to weak evaluation.

Nevertheless, in the West it is clear that such technical criteria dominate and not merely at elite levels. It may well be the case that Dixon's athletes bent on achieving the widest margins fall most easily into this category of weak-evaluating sportspersons. We might think the vice of hubris and the viciousness of strong humiliation-infliction are the products of the weak evaluator, one who is simply morally negligent. Where the margin of victory and defeat are not relevant, there appears little justification for the all-out pursuit of the widest margins. Though the viciousness of such athletes or coaches cannot inflict strong humiliation, we can still ask what good it achieves for the victor, the vanquished, or even the sport itself. But that is to stray beyond my stated purpose. What is the point of the comparison of the abilities? This is the question of the strong evaluator, someone who is capable of critically reflecting the quality of the relations between means and ends and indeed of the ends themselves. How we pursue our goals necessitates discussion of virtue and vice. Here, any deontological or utilitarian vocabulary insufficiently grasps the adverbial nature of ethical discourses. Having said that an aretaic vocabulary is required to capture the phenomenology of victory and defeat, a further caveat is required. How we describe and evaluate action in sport must not be reduced to an individualistic framework. The ethos of various sports sub-cultures sometimes fosters viciousness as part of the everyday business-as-usual background of the activity. In particular, coaches who subject young athletes to regimes of physical and verbal abuse in order to improve performances are apt to be described by such a vocabulary. Humiliation may here be the product of a mere weak evaluator but we should reserve our deepest approbation for those who knowingly humiliate their athletes merely for economic gain, or sporting glory, or in the worst-case scenario, who use humiliatory strategies to bolster their domination as in the coach–coached relation.[9] To capture the wrongness in terms of respect may be apposite, but to dig beneath that disrespect requires a vocabulary more psychologically robust.

Of course, it is the case that virtues and vices display many formal similarities. As virtues are innervated through particular perceptions, so are vices. As virtues are habituated, so too are vices as patterns of feeling, judging and acting. As virtues are chosen and ramified by supporting traits, so too are vices.

And similarly, the catalogues of virtue and vice are heterogeneous. As I noted in Chapter 4, Kohlberg (1981) was not without prescience when he noted that the trouble with virtue approaches is that everyone has their own bag with its preferred contents. This is precisely why he urged developmental psychologists to move to a system of rational universal principles to evaluate moral development. Only with a consistent scale could one compare developmental stages of persons in different time and place. To the extent that this is true, it would of course follow that vices varied too in scope and significance. It would be difficult to conceive of anything we might call a society these days in which certain fundamental virtues such as justice and honesty were necessary. Yet each culture, or horizon of significance as Taylor puts it, lauds and laments particular persons and personalities. Humility played no part in Ancient Greek schemes of thought, nor later in Hume's writings when he derided it pejoratively as a 'monkish virtue'. Yet chief among the theological vices of medieval Christendom was pride. Indeed Gregory the Great labelled it the root of all evil. Similar to hubris, the proud man failed to understand his limitations in the place of the pantheon of gods and men and thereby alienated himself from both. It seems too that an understanding of status within or without a theological horizon is crucial to understanding the nature of hubris or arrogance, which is probably our closest approximation to it, as a vice.[10] I do not take the two to be synonymous. In the absence of detailed analysis, I suggest that arrogance entails hubris, though hubris does not necessitate the haughtiness or dismissiveness that arrogance demands.

In modern professional sport no less than in the great sagas, self-knowledge and self-understanding are part and parcel of the good life. Hubris, if we can situate it in modernity, is a presumption of power in excess of one's capabilities. But I want to hold to an idea that can distinguish it from mere ignorance. The arrogant know their power, but they fail to situate it properly in the contexts that give rise to their overweening pride. A crucial component then of both humiliation and hubris is the idea I set out above of thinking rather too much of oneself. It is the direct opposite of humility, which requires an understated though reasonable estimation of one's powers and status. It need not entail the failure to give others their due in an active sense. It is too self-centred, too egoistic. One may be dismissive of others without claiming greatness for oneself. So, though a dismissive attitude often accompanies hubris, it is not logically tied to it.

What fuels hubris in sports, and what makes those who display the vice so ripe for humiliation, is the bloated importance of big-time commercialised sports and sportspersons. Too many veils of economic interest cloud the athlete's own critical self-interrogation. Irresponsible agents and journalists promote players in the most outrageous of styles. Florid language conduces to the formation of would-be heroic reputations based on the shifting sands of falsely conceived superhuman abilities. Athletes too often live a cocooned world where critical coaches and commentators can either be ignored or dismissed in favour of others who will sing more sycophantic songs. To such athletes then, we may view weak humiliation as a corrective to their conceited self-conceptions. But even where we judge this to be a good, this does not license in any way a triumphalism on the part of those who render the corrective. Humility in victory and graciousness in defeat may be the stock-in-trade platitudes of the physical educator, but have a genuinely deeper import. The virtues are indeed our best travelling companions in good sporting careers no less than in good lives.

Although there is a limited place for weak humiliation, there can be no such place for its stronger counterpart. Perhaps some linguistic stipulation is necessary here. To be humbled may be no bad thing in the great scheme of things; but no one (except a masochist) is grateful for humiliation in the strong sense. So the humiliator who seeks pleasure in the degradation of another is simply wicked. The sooner a professional ethics of coaching emerges to outlaw the verbal torture that many athletes old and (especially) young endure, the better for us all.

How, as philosophers of sport or reflective coaches or physical education teachers, we are to cultivate greater powers of reflection in our sports cultures is no easy matter. One philosophical challenge is to create better taxonomies of the emotionally laden virtues and vices of our sportsmen and women. Sharper distinctions can indeed help all involved in sport to mark out the ethically acceptable from the unacceptable territories. Crucially, that will entail the analysis of concepts but in a way that is historically sensitive and socially situated. In articulating the shared roots of hubris and humiliation, we can help deliver the resources critically to initiate practitioners.

Hubris, honour, and power on loan from the gods

The honour societies of Greece and Scandinavia, where one was how one acted, and certain modern-day sports are still rich in ethical instruction – even if we must learn the modern lessons of non-discrimination to detoxify ancient honour. How one comports oneself is ethically significant. The broad-chested swagger of hubris still is as vicious now as it was in the days of Agamemnon. Yet we might also ask whether our desire for modest millionaires is merely egoistic. We want sports superstars to retain touch with the herd, with a common humanity. How then are we to think of keeping such hubris in check? Is it even possible? The worst excesses of sports talk and posturing can and must be kept in check by sports institutions that are paradoxically in the position both of exploiters and guardians of sports practices and communities. What are called the external goods of sport, such as recognition, wealth, esteem and status, are perfectly proper in sports when justly conferred. And the muscles of the institutions can indeed be flexed when badmouthing and egregious arrogance offends the best traditions of those sports. To understand the nature and sometimes positive functions of weak humiliation is in part to know the price of hubris and what makes sport the power for good it can be.

Of course, as inheritors of the Greek scheme, we are left with some of its pieces in a puzzle that just does not hang together. Phillipa Foot, long before MacIntyre and others, warned us of this. But in sports, and especially sports such as boxing, the heritage is closer to that brutal time. Even if the gods or 'fate' as sources of equilibrium between hubris and humility are no longer available, we can take a lead from Weil's recognition of the need to appropriate and rein in the power of 'force' in such warrior-sports:

> Thus it happens that those who have force on loan from fate count on it too much and are destroyed.
>
> But at the time their own destruction seems impossible to them. For they do not see that the force in their possession is only a limited quantity; nor do they see their relations with other human beings as a kind of balance between unequal amounts of force. Since other people do not impose on their movements that hold, that interval of hesitation, wherein lies all our consideration for our brothers in humanity, they conclude that destiny has given complete license to them, and none at all to their inferiors. And at this point they exceed the actual measure of force that is at their disposal. Inevitably, they exceed it, since they are not aware that it is limited. And now we see them committed irretrievably to chance; suddenly things cease to obey them. Sometimes chance is kind to them, sometimes cruel. But in any case there they are, exposed, open to misfortune, gone is the armor of power that formerly protected their naked souls; nothing; no shield, stands between them and tears.
>
> This retribution, which has a geometrical rigor, which operates automatically to penalize the abuse of power, was the mainstay of Greek thought. It is the soul of the epic. [. . .] conceptions of limit, measure, equilibrium, which ought to determine the conduct of life are, in the West, restricted to the service function in the vocabulary of technics. We are only geometricians of matter; the Greeks were, first of all geometricians in their apprenticeship to virtue.
>
> (Weil, 1983: 231)

Conclusion

I have argued that sporting contests cannot occasion 'strong humiliation', where this is taken to mean the denial of the basis of respect as a person. I have argued, however, that something more than a mere loss of self-esteem may be effected by a sporting loss and, moreover, that this is independent of the mere margin of the loss. I have argued that structural pretension is logically tied to what has been called 'weak humiliation'. In illustrating the vice of hubris, I have shown how such weak humiliation may occur and also highlighted the corrective role that humiliation may play for those who opt for hubris over humiliation. In sports, more than most cultural pursuits, greatness is indeed on loan temporarily from the gods.

8 *Schadenfreude* in sports
Envy, justice and self-esteem

Introduction

Sports administrators, media commentators and policy makers have tended to focus on the big ethical issues such as child abuse, doping and violence in their pronouncements upon the moral health and ailments of sports. Yet it is often the smaller acts of kindness and unkindness that are better indications of the moral health of sporting practices. Following directly on from the previous chapter, we are left with the worry that in celebrating (Sugar) Ray Leonard's humiliation of Roberto Duran we are endorsing the humiliation of another human who is clearly suffering. The aim of this chapter is to scrutinise that feeling crystallised in the concept of *schadenfreude* – the pleasure felt at another's misfortune – and argue that one's feeling it is both a culpable and, at the very least, undesirable aspect of the ethico-emotional ecologies of sport.

   In order to attempt to show that *schadenfreude* is a morally objectionable emotion in sport as elsewhere, and one that can be curbed, I first offer some conceptual remarks about emotions generally and their differential treatment in philosophical discussions. Second, I argue that the rationality of the emotions is crucial to our self-understanding as persons in general and sportspersons in particular, attempting to live good lives and play good sport. I situate this point within an understanding drawn from both Aristotle and Kant. Third, I argue for its undesirability in the character of the one who feels the emotion (the *schadenfroh*) and their relations to those who suffer. I offer a critique of the argument for the ethical excusability of *schadenfreude* in Portmann (2000) and argue that he fails to defend his position coherently. Specifically, I show how his defence of the emotion's genesis in low self-esteem and a commitment to justice is not compelling and suggest that one's feeling *schadenfreude* is itself evidence of poor sporting character and sporting culture.

Ir/rationality and the emotions: Kant and Aristotle

When an actor at an audition says to his or her fellow actor 'break a leg', it is ordinarily understood that the saying is one of encouragement. When some sporting competitors utter the same remark, I fear, it is often tinged with a less metaphorical desire. When we see the delight on the face of a contestant whose competitor falls at the last hurdle, fails their final jump, or injures themselves in the warm-up, some of us at least are troubled by this. Ought we to be? *Schadenfreude*, the joy or pleasure felt at another's harm, is something sportspersons and coaches undeniably feel. Is it felt for reasons good or ill, one may ask? Whichever is the case, we ought first to ask, more generally, what it means to say that one feels an emotion and to consider why it is worthwhile paying philosophical attention to the emotions. I want first to observe what Bernard Williams wrote more than a quarter of a century ago, and which has applied to much recent sports ethics talk:

> Recent moral philosophy in Britain has not had much to say about the emotions. Its descriptions of the moral agent, its analyses of moral choice and moral judgement, have made free use of such notions as attitude, principle and policy, but have found no essential place for the agent's emotions, except perhaps for recognising them in one of their traditional roles as possible motives for backsliding, and thus potentially destructive of moral rationality and consistency.
>
> (Williams, 1973: 207)

The thought that emotions are themselves irrational has a long and varied history spanning folk psychology and a number of academic disciplines. Emotions appear to have a dual nature; on the one hand they refer to bodily sensations and on the other to expressions of judgement. In philosophy, no less than in certain scientific writings, a peculiarly pejorative and simplified picture of emotions emerged only to be dismissed. And this disposition is no new one. Plato talks in the *Republic* (1974: 440a) of 'reason and its civil war with desire'. He also writes in the *Phaedrus* (1962: 246a8) of the Soul being a composite power, a pair of winged horses and a charioteer. Reason, our ruling part, is the charioteer of course, and while one of the horses is of good and honourable stock, the other is not and 'makes our chariot wayward and difficult to drive' (1962: 246a8).

This picture of rationality both controlling and prosecuting the emotions remained dominant in philosophy and religion into modernity, where Kant gave it particular prominence. As I noted in Chapters 2 and 4, this picture demands correction if we are to understand engagement with sports in a manner that is more than one of mortal machines. I noted there how as part of an evaluation of the moral emotions Wollheim referred to Kant's position as being a 'singularly bleached moral psychology' (1993). Kant is traditionally attributed with denying the rationality of the emotions and therefore derogating their value, both of which are said to be conceived of as obstacles to rational moral action (Williams, 1973). More recently, however, scholars have been at pains both to look for similarities in the ethical writings of Aristotle and Kant (Engstrom and Whiting, 1998) and to give a more generous evaluation of Kant, particularly in relation to his writings in the

Metaphysical Principles of Virtue and *Anthropology from a Pragmatic Point of View* (Baron, 1995; Sherman, 1997).[1]

The widespread, though less favourable, Kantian interpretation is summarised by Montada (1993: 295) thus: (1) that emotions are transitory and capricious; (2) that conduct issuing from emotions is therefore unreliable and unprincipled, even irrational; (3) that the moral perception of right and wrong entails abstraction from our emotions; (4) that emotions are passively experienced and we are not responsible for them; and (5) being attached to particular persons and not universal principles, they are partial and therefore not belonging to the moral realm.

I will comment below partly in defence of Kant's position. I draw out some counterpoints to Montada's characterisation in respect of the relations between passivity and responsibility in our emotional experiences they often held to be part of the Kantian position. Depicting the difficulties that attend to the passivity of, and responsibility for, emotional experiences may help us to understand better the ethical import of emotions generally, but specifically here in relation to human suffering or misfortune, and the experience of *schadenfreude*.

Baldly put, Montada asserts that under a Kantian description we experience emotions passively and that, therefore, we are not responsible for them. This position, though not wholly wrong, lacks precision. Specifically, it is based on an inaccurate reading of Kant since it fails to recognise that, as a response to Hume and others, Kant distinguished between affects or emotions on the one hand, and passions, on the other in his *Metaphysical Principles of Virtue*. A point about nomenclature is necessary here. Kant refers both to '*Affekt*' and '*Leidenschaften*'. In the Mary Gregor translation '*Affekt*' is affect whereas in the Ellington translation it is referred to as 'emotion'.[2] Thus if we use the term emotion – in some recognisably modern sense – we may both (1) obscure the distinction; or worse (2) take his more negative stance to *passions* and apply it inappropriately to what we call emotions. In the Gregor translation Kant says:

> *Affects* and *passions* are essentially different from each other. Affects belong to *feeling* insofar as, preceding reflection, it makes this impossible or more difficult. Hence an affect is called *precipitate* or *rash* (*animus praeceps*), and reason says, through the concept of virtue, that one should *get hold of* oneself. [. . .] Accordingly a propensity to an affect (e.g., *anger*) does not enter into kinship with vice so readily as does a passion. A *passion* is a sensible desire that has become a lasting inclination (e.g., *hatred*, as opposed to anger). The calm with which one gives oneself up to it permits reflection and allows the mind to form principles upon it and so, if inclination lights upon something contrary to the law, to brood upon it, to get it rooted deeply, and so to take up what is evil (as something premeditated) into its maxim. And the evil is then *properly* evil, that is, a true *vice*.
>
> (Kant, 1991: 208)

To give a fairer reading to Kant, especially in respect of our emotional responses to human suffering or misfortune we must bear this distinction in mind. One important aspect of this distinction for Kant's understanding the emotions (in this case elicited by the suffering of others) is that in passions a 'lasting inclination' is formed and that this entails choice and judgement, which in turn carry the agent's experience into the realm of responsibility. I shall comment further on this point in the section on the culpability of *schadenfreude* below. A second point pertains to the passivity of the experience and is brought out nicely by Baron when commenting on a section from *Anthropology from a Pragmatic Point of View*:

> Kant's distinction between sensitivity and sentimentality is further evidence that in his view we play a significant role as agents in determining how we respond affectively. 'Sensitivity is a *power* and *strength* by which we grant or refuse permission for the state of pleasure or displeasure to enter our mind, so that it implies a choice.' By contrast 'sentimentality is a weakness by which we can be affected, even against our will, by sympathy for another's plight' (Kant, 1974: 236). Clearly, then, we are not always passive with respect to our emotions and feelings: sensitivity does not involve such passivity.
>
> (Baron, 1995: 196)

Sherman too offers a useful summary of Kant's point here: that his intention is to 'repudiate sentimentalism, not sentiment' (1997: 153). So, let us first allow that Montada's position is Kantian, rather than Kant's. Second, and more substantively, despite Baron's protest at the lack of agency ascribed to Kantian emotion, our passivity in the experience of sentimentality entails a lack of responsibility. But, with Kant's distinction above in mind, we should say that the point refers to emotions as affects (i.e. sentimentality) – rather than passions (i.e. sensitivity). And this is important in his consideration of the cultivation of sympathy as a moral duty. One point that Baron takes from all this, and one that I am in *sympathy* with (if you will excuse the pun) is that we should not use feelings and emotions as objects to excuse our moral responsibility. And this, I contend, is often what happens when people say that the experience of an emotion such as *schadenfreude* is felt by someone in relation to a suffering other. But the experience of emotions such as *schadenfreude* need not be considered like what might be termed 'immediate natural responses' such as a knee-jerk or anxiety at the onset of a sharp toothache.

Consider a sports physician who refuses pain relief to the athlete on the grounds that they do not believe the level of pain reported is either accurate or authentic. On reflection the physician wonders whether their mistrust and hostility to the patient is, for the purposes of example, driven by their guilt-ridden recollection of giving a questionably high dose of pain killer to an ageing athlete who played on in ignorance of the damage being done to him, and was forced subsequently to retire. In such cases colleagues might claim that the physician's judgement was 'clouded by emotion.' Thinking carefully through such scenarios requires a consideration of the relations between cognition and the relevant emotions at play.

All cognitive theorists of emotion have argued that simply characterising emotions as subjective feelings – as biological theorists do – ignores two important aspects: first, that emotions entail judgements and second that they are to a considerable degree influenced by space and time. One important part of this strategy is to argue that feelings and modes that are not in some way suffused with some cognition are not emotions proper (G. Taylor, 1985), and the very fact of our making linguistic choices signifies this. Early analyses of emotions, inspired by Wittgenstein's anti-essentialism in conceptual analysis, conceived of emotions-talk as illustrating the family resemblances idea: there is neither an essence nor unifying set of properties to them. Some are voluntary, some involuntary, some passive yet others are active. Likewise, their intensity, though typically greater than felt moods, can vary too; compare a punch in anger in the playground, to the studied resentment of a colleague's unmerited promotion where one may stew for days, weeks, even years in one's own acidic feelings, memories and thoughts. Those familiar with British soccer may recall the Manchester United player Roy Keane in his recent autobiography revealing that he harboured resentment for an opposing Norwegian player (Alfe Haaland) for a full year before exacting revenge in a violent, career-threatening tackle. Even allowing for their biological bases, we must agree with Rorty (1988: 1) that 'the emotions do not form a natural kind'. Sometimes the emotions are felt in anticipation of action; at other times they succeed it. Sometimes they are directly motivational, at other times they are not. Moreover, certain emotions such as panic are experienced as self-referring while other emotions such as humiliation or shame have a very significant interpersonal role in preserving boundaries of conduct by reinforcing norms of the acceptable and unacceptable. Emotions such as guilt, remorse, regret and shame all have a negative power that we typically seek to avoid or to work off.

The emotions can be allowed a much more positive role in our identification of what matters to us in both fleeting and more considered ways. While it is easy to recall instances when emotions have got in the way of good judgement, or indeed been obstacles to right action, we can also think of examples where our emotionally driven responses of, say, compassion or mercy are salient. To conceive of the emotions more generously opens a conceptual space in which we can consider more broadly the roles they play in our lives beyond exculpation and the denial of responsibility. To elicit the ethical import of the emotion of *schadenfreude* (or any of its close cousins in the emotional field – envy, spite, resentment, to name a few[3]) we must accept that the feeling is imbued with a judgement or an interpretation of their situation as I argued in Chapter 2.

Aristotle's writings are typically taken to afford a more generous interpretation of the emotions in the good life than Kant's, though as I hoped to illustrate above, perhaps too much has been made of the contrast. Aristotelian commentators note how the emotions record and convey our values in a manner that is constitutive of ethically defensible and desirable living (Sherman, 1989). Of course they can only perform these functions when attuned habitually to (wise) judgement. His account of emotions is not, however, encumbered, by the top-down Kantian approach where the absolute value of the moral law and the autonomous will 'shape and regulate the emotions' (Sherman, 1997: 157). Precisely what form the judgement takes is highly disputed in the literature on the philosophy of emotions. Few cognitive theorists would deny that the desires, motivations and feelings we experience involve a sense of our situation. The strongest account of the cognitive element is found in what Griffiths (1997) labels the 'propositional attitude school'.[4] Griffiths argues that in its strongest form, in Solomon's early writings, the emotion simply is a judgement about ourselves and the world. Other accounts (e.g. Roberts (1988) and Armon-Jones (1991)) have shied away from the propositional reductionism that can be attributed to Solomon and others. What is at issue among them is the extent to which language captures the construal. Charles Taylor's writings, which I employed in Chapter 2, might be criticised for having emphasised the linguistic dimension of emotional experience whereas Roberts' (1988) and Armon-Jones' (1991) accounts lean towards less propositional elements of emotion and view them under the aspect of some kind of 'construal' of events. Nevertheless, it is sufficient for my purposes here to note that in both cases language and the construal are internally related to the experienced emotion.[5]

What I shall do now is to interrogate the specific emotion of *schadenfreude* and to consider the extent to which the occurrence of the emotion in a sportsperson might make it a reason for us to think of them as lacking virtue or exhibiting vice.

Emotions, good sportspersons and good sporting lives

So, far from being blind passions, as Hume would have it, or wayward steeds as Plato preferred, I have tried to show how our emotions can shape our moral responses. We feel guilt properly at transgressions, remorse at serious violations, and shame at our inability to match well-founded social expectations. These negative emotions can act as powerful sensitisers to the worth of respective courses of action just as they can give evidence of our sensitivities, or lack of them in consequence. Whether sportspersons do experience these emotions is of course not guaranteed, however strong the social expectations for them might be. Thus, for example, many people could not understand the Argentine footballer Diego Maradona's *post facto* rationalisations of his cheating in the 1986 football World Cup quarter-final when he deceived the officials into thinking that he had headed the ball past the English goalkeeper, though in fact he had illegally punched it. His now infamous remark – that it was the 'Hand of God' – was later retracted and explained by him with reference to the more obvious motive that he was seeking a competitive advantage by a strategy that he had used successfully before. What is central to his reaction is the lack of regret (let alone remorse) expressed for his actions. (At least Ron Atkinson had publicly expressed his deep chagrin in the wake of his racist remarks.) So it is not merely, then, that we hold sportspersons responsible for their emotions and emotional outbursts, but a fortiori that we properly hold them culpable at times for their failure to experience and signal them too.

It is in this vein that Nancy Sherman writes of seeing through the emotions:

> We can think of them [emotions] as modes of attention enabling us to notice what is morally salient, important, or urgent in ourselves and our surroundings. They help us to track the morally relevant "news". . . . In addition to their role as modes of attention, emotion plays a role in communicating information to others. They are modes of responding. Putting the two together, emotions become modes both for receiving information and signalling it. Through the emotions we both track and convey what we care about.
>
> (Sherman, 1989: 40)

As I argued in Chapter 2, after Taylor, in making a strong evaluation, we are articulating the import to which the feeling aspect of emotion relates. And in doing so, we display our own moral sensitivities and insensitivities. Our emotions typically carry information to our reflections. Frequently, after a sporting encounter, and occasionally in the midst of one, we may ask ourselves, 'Why did I do and feel this and not that?', 'To what extent am I a worse or better person for feeling this and not that?' In this vein, consider the example of a recent international cricket match between Sri Lanka and England that descended into a bitter farce when members from both teams deceived and harassed each other and the umpires to such an extent that the debacle sparked a near crisis in a game renowned for its civility. After all, in how many sports does the opposing team welcome the opposing batter(s) to the crease by clapping them? In this scenario, what were thought of as hitherto unreflective professional sportsmen began asking themselves how their actions may be seen to tarnish the game irreparably. Without recourse to convenient exculpations such as the pressure of the event, the heat of the moment and so on, players came to think of themselves as having diminished a noble tradition. The players from both sides began to speak of (and therein to reconceptualise) themselves as 'custodians' of the game whose conduct and character had failed to appropriately reflect that role. The inner dialogue that prompts such questioning frequently follows our pre-reflective responses to situations that are typical of our emotional life. It was a direct consequence of the regret and even the shame many of them felt and acknowledged publicly in respect of their actions. The game emerged stronger in response to their public self-purging. Envy, like resentment and spite, can simmer. I do not want, therefore, to make too much mileage out of the episodic nature of many emotions. In a fuller discussion of the emotions in sport, and their ethical significance, there would need to be room for the full array of associated concepts such as the ranges of cognitive components and their significance. The sources of retaliatory acts of violence, for example, have a quite different aetiology than the premeditated ones that are cultivated in the locker room and practised with more or less conscientiousness on the playing field. What is important to note, however, is that our habituation into certain modes of emotionally laden attributions and responses is central to our self-development as characters of a given kind.

Thus far I have argued against the naive irrational feeling model of emotion. I have also suggested how the cognitive element of emotion renders intelligible our evaluations of good lives. It is worth developing this idea a little while connecting it more closely to the idea of virtuous and vicious character. What is required now is to interrogate the specific emotion of *schadenfreude* and to consider the extent to which the emotion is good or bad and whether the person who experiences it is necessarily to that extent a person of good or bad character.

What is *schadenfreude*?

The idea of taking pleasure in another's misfortune is one that probably translates across the world without remainder. Precisely why it is that, in modern times, only the Germans have a word for it (or as is quite often the case in German, two words joined together) is something imponderable.[6] Quite literally the word means 'harmjoy'. Before analysing the concept of *schadenfreude* and evaluating its normative status, it is worth illuminating some comical observations beyond the paradigmatic Germanic sense. Terry Lane has defined *schadenfreude* as the sensation experienced when you see two Mercedes Benz collide, but that may reflect a preference for Australian-made cars more than his misplaced egalitarianism. Philip Howard, parodying Oscar Wilde's famous remark about homosexuality, describes it as the sentiment that dares not speak its name (in English). In a similar vein, Clive James admits to feeling *schadenfreude* when he sees his rival's books in the remainders bin. Is there something distinct about the source of the feeling, which effectively designates two emotions, not one? There is something more than the comic at play in James', albeit witty, construal. One of my fellow competitors is suffering in contrast to me. What this emotion resonates with is me and my self-esteem. What seems to lie behind the first example might at least be the murky construal that the Mercedes drivers in some way deserved their comeuppance by virtue of their wealth.

Is there a morally righteous and morally repugnant conception of *schadenfreude*? Imagine a basketball player who has consistently fouled his way through a game, and done it so slyly that his actions have gone unnoticed and unpunished by the officials. In the last second of a tied match, he drives for the

basket, misjudges his approach, trips over your foot, and tears his ankle liga-
ments without making the shot. You smile wryly to yourself. Are you really
any the worse for your reaction? Are you thereby a sportsperson of deficient
character? Part of a reasoned evaluation of this type of scenario must always
be particularised; it must always take account of the relations between the
sufferer and the judger. Another part of our response or evaluation should
concern the normative codes that structure their relations. Is the *schadenfroh*
deserving of the harm? Of course, again, for these questions to make sense,
we must reject the anti-cognitivist picture of the emotions. For to appreciate
their sense and value is already to be committed to the cognitive dimension of
emotions and thereby their rationality.

We need to be able to distinguish when what seems to be *schadenfreude* is
an emotional corollary of justice – if indeed this is the case – and when it is
really envy or resentment in disguise. It is clearly not born of a sense of justice
when the emotion becomes active and turns into a malicious glee. In some
cases of course, the experience of the emotion is not spontaneous or episodic.
On the contrary, we cultivate it; sometimes cherish it; it curdles over time, and
if not attended to, depletes our moral resources. This is why I have sketched
the non-episodic account of *schadenfreude* in the example above. We can
only attend to this task of recognition and (re)appropriation if, as Neu (2002)
notes, we are able to discriminate among the sources of our emotions and
thereby to understand and evaluate ourselves more judiciously. The experience of *schadenfreude* is clearly not born of a sense of justice when the emotion becomes active and turns into a malicious glee. This is the point made
specifically by Kant about the experience passion being turned into a lasting
inclination. Indeed he writes specifically of *schadenfreude* (translated as
'malice' in both the Ellington and Gregor editions) in this regard:

> Malice, which is directly contrary to sympathy, is also not foreign to
> human nature; when it goes as far promoting evil or wickedness itself,
> then as a special kind of malice it reveals a hatred of mankind, and
> appears in all its horrors.
>
> (Kant cited in Ellington, 1994: 124–5)

This malicious glee is not, according to Portmann, *schadenfreude* proper
despite the widespread understanding of it under such a description. What
the matter hangs on, so to speak, is the idea of whether the harm is deserved
or undeserved, and whether indeed one can take an attitude of detached
impartiality towards the suffering wrongdoer.

If we wish to appraise the character of the one who feels *schadenfreude*, we
need to determine the extent to which, when judging the pleasure felt at
another's misfortune, they are active or passive in the generation of the emotion. Now, to intend that another be harmed is part of an active strategy –
Portmann argues that the pleasure, which is consequent upon this, is not
schadenfreude proper but rather a malicious glee. Portmann argues that

schadenfreude proper requires the re-drawing of the emotion away from that particular misconception. As part of his recognition of the passivity of *schadenfreude*, he goes on to suggest an analogy between sympathy and *schadenfreude* – both come uninvited or not at all. Just as manufactured sympathy is not sympathy proper, so in experiencing *schadenfreude*, we experience a pleasure *that* they are harmed without a prior desire for them to be harmed. When set against our earlier account of emotions being necessarily partly constituted by a cognitive element (a construal), this looks odd. What sort of construal is going on then? *Schadenfreude* surely does not visit us uninvited as a guest might. Portmann (17: 27–8), in his defence, says:

> In speaking of the passivity of *Schadenfreude* I do not mean to imply that we are victims of our emotions in the sense that emotions seem to toss us about like ships in a storm. I do not claim that either malicious glee is beyond our control; indeed because we are not purely passive in the fact of feelings and emotions, our efforts to manage our emotions sometimes succeed. Alternatively, we can rationalise our enjoyment of the suffering of another; we can tell ourselves that we take pleasure in the fact that another suffers (as opposed to pleasure in the actual suffering) and that this pleasure results from the love of justice. Such mental dodges attest to the rationality of *Schadenfreude*, as well as to our responsibility for it.

The passivity of all emotions was, perhaps too swiftly, attributed to the Kantian picture of emotion and their non-existence in morally autonomous persons. And Portmann is surely right not to give in to that particular temptation in his defence of *schadenfreude*. But the key to his position is his use of the word 'rationalisation'. For that is exactly what, I will argue below, his position is. That an ethically defensible (praiseworthy?) sense of *schadenfreude* exists, where one can love a sinner while hating the sin and take pleasure in justice being served is precisely that: a rationalisation. Can we hate the foul but love the fouler? Love the cheat but hate the cheating? I will argue that this, in the context of stratified and hierarchically structured activities such as sports, is no more than a rationalisation and that its genesis is typically envy and not a love of justice or low self-esteem, as Portmann argues. But that is to move ahead of the game. Let us next consider the genesis of *schadenfreude*.

The genesis of *schadenfreude*

Articulating the genesis of *schadenfreude*, precisely why the *schadenfroh* feels pleasure at another's misfortune, should open the door to an evaluation of the ethical status of the emotion and the character of the *schadenfroh*. I take the categories from Portmann. He argues that *schadenfreude* may be born of: (1) low self-esteem; (2) loyalty and commitments to justice; (3) the comical; and (4) malice. I shall be concerned here only with the first and second categories. While Portmann maintains that the first three are still liable to be appraised in the guilt and blame we apportion to the *schadenfroh*, the latter is always to be condemned. My position, which I merely assert at this point, is that the third and fourth categories are not philosophically interesting, since the third is not a paradigmatic sense of the concept,[7] because it relates properly to instances of embarrassment rather than harm, while the fourth is obviously despicable and therefore uncontentious.

Let us consider, then, the idea that low self-esteem might give birth to feelings of *schadenfreude* that are ethically excusable. Early on in Christine Mackinnon's consideration of the cultivation of the self in virtue theory, she remarks that 'everybody is faced with the task of constructing a self, but not every-body starts with the same equipment' (1999: 37). Is it the case for those who feel *schadenfreude* that they necessarily think so little of themselves?

Francis Bacon captured something like the point nicely when he said that a recognition of others' sufferings can redeem our own.[8] This seems to be the case with our basketball player. He was on the wrong end of his opponent's cheating, made to look bad because of it, and feels relieved that the game has not been lost by virtue of his inability to master his cheating opponent. Of course, the precise identity of the other sufferer and their relation to us is a crucial variable. This is what generates remarks such as Clive James's above: it is *his* competitor's book in the remainder bin. Portmann argues that self-esteem enhances our sense that we are leading good lives. More specifically, he asserts: 'Self-esteem does not blind us to interpersonal differences; rather, it prevents us from concluding that the superiority of one person signifies the worthlessness or inherent defect in another' (2000: 33).

It seems clear to me here that he is talking about self-respect, which is not exclusive – the possession of self-respect by one does not entail its exclusion in another. Where, however, our sense of our own worth in relation to others is set in a competitive structure (going for the head coach position, achieving a promotion from one division to the next, breaking the record), it seems that self-esteem is characteristically exclusive.[9] My having won entails your loss, and vice versa. The objects of envy are typically positional goods. This is precisely the theme of a remark attributed to Gore Vidal that 'whenever a friend succeeds a little something in me dies'. Now the distinction is crucial for Portmann, since the *schadenfreude* born of low self-esteem is of a deficient sense of self; it is a weakness of character. He takes this to entail its ethical excusability. He takes his cue here from Rawls' (1972: 534–40) remarks on envy and, in quoting Rawls approvingly, conflates self-esteem with self-respect:[10] 'When envy is a reaction to the loss of self-respect in circumstances where it would be unreasonable to expect someone to feel differently, I shall say it is excusable' (Portmann, 2000: 34).

Now where resentment is felt as an affront to one's dignity – and here we can say he has shifted to self-respect again – the feeling of anger may be justified. He says it reflects a healthy self-esteem, but here he is trading again on self-respect. While self-respect has a categorical status (one either has it or not), self-esteem derives and is measured from our evaluations of ourselves in social structures according to a good or range of goods or abilities.[11] He concludes: 'To the extent that a feeling of inferiority seems to invite celebration of other's woes, condemning a *Schadenfroh* person is a bit like blaming him or her for dissatisfaction with an unjust social framework' (Portmann, 2000: 35).

Now it is clear that if we feel pleasure when someone has, for example, strongly humiliated another (where the limit case is torture), then Rawls' exculpation might be reasonable. Other cases of celebration of loss by others in sport are worthy of consideration. Consider someone who is a not a regular player in the starting line-up, but is a solid and reliable substitute 'quarterback' (in American Football) or 'stand-off' (the equivalent in Rugby Union), whose fitness levels and tactical and technical abilities are not developed to the elite level of his starting team-mate. When the starting player is stretchered from the field of play, the substitute rejoices inwardly at his chance to shine and to show his talents. Where this feeling is not directly driven by the player's negative attitude towards the starting 'quarterback' or 'stand-off', I think we ought to be careful not to excuse the pleasure he experiences. On the one hand, what should rankle with us is not merely the lack of empathy and sympathy with a team-mate but the egoistic quality of his celebration, which is dependent upon a teammate's suffering. Nevertheless, the relationship between his joy and the harm of the star player is not one of cause and effect but rather mere correlation. So the concept of *schadenfreude* does not apply properly here even if we think of the substitute's inward celebration as disrespectful or callous. It is not clear to me that sports are unique in this matter. I see no reason why one would not find considerable evidence for this emotion in a whole range of competitively structured practices from work to politics. We might, however, think that paradigm cases of *schadenfreude* were those in which persons were pitted against each other in some antagonistic way. What may be slightly unusual in this example is the fact that the type of emotion can perhaps as easily be felt in relation to those with whom I share goals and aspirations. I do not want to make too much of this, however, since it is perfectly possible that competition and the exclusivity of goods on offer (especially the positional ones, such as status, ranking, hierarchy and power) might as easily obtain in other practices of an inherently competitive kind. I shall return to this issue below with a slightly more difficult example from a recent Ryder Cup contest.

Part of why I think *schadenfreude* is problematic is because of the envy that often accompanies the emotion. Both Solomon (2000) and Herzog (2000) get much closer to the relationship between envy and *schadenfreude* than Portmann. Everyone seems to agree that envy is a 'loser's emotion' resulting from a failure accurately to assess one's self-worth. We might conclude that *schadenfreude* harms no one but the *schadenfrohe* themselves. Let them stew in their bitter juices, we might think. Harm them nonetheless it does by generating false pictures of their relations with those who facilitate what it is they are committed to – sporting excellence. In developing our attitudes to these

emotions dependent on self-evaluation, we might also consider the patholog-
ically 'humble' who ritually deprecate themselves and seek to defer to and
emulate others. Of course, we might then see envy as emulation gone bad. For
emulation is, on the face of it, a good thing, and in virtue theory in particular,
it is the wise person (in Aristotle, the *phronimos*) whom we seek to model our
choices and character upon. In envy, however, our admiration goes awry; the
negativity overtakes what benefits could be had from emulation. If we are to
believe the Catholic tradition, then envy first leads to sadness, then to gossip,
then to *schadenfreude*, then to hatred (Solomon, 2000). If indeed this is so,
then although the lack of self-esteem that can give birth to *schadenfreude* may
not be as vicious as resentment, or spite or malicious glee, it is nevertheless
something we should be on our toes to avoid and/or acknowledge on our path
to making ourselves better (sports) persons.

In respect of the slide between emotions of lesser and more corrosive
power, Herzog picks out the comic dimension sometimes associated with
schadenfreude that is morally unobjectionable. I have asserted above that this
emotion is better conceptualised in terms of the concept of embarrassment
because of the relative seriousness or significance that attaches to each.
Herzog shows how our comical responses to embarrassment can slide into
the deeper, nastier emotion, which can find root in envy at the same time as
being productive of it:

> The heart that's heavy seeing other men more worthy in anything is the
> motive for a certain kind of *Schadenfreude*. Not the snicker that greets
> the pompous speaker who rises to the lectern with resolute gravity, obliv-
> ious to the lobster bisque splattered across his tie; so much doesn't
> require any antecedent envy. But suppose you had previously noted your
> dismay that he cut a more imposing figure in public than you, that the
> thought rankled, and that now you rejoice in seeing the fates bring him
> low precisely because his humiliation makes him less of a threat to your
> self-esteem.
>
> (Herzog, 2000: 148)

So it is often the case, and is by no means ethically excusable, that the
schadenfreude born of low esteem masks a more or less bitter envy, not
because one has been robbed of one's self-respect, but rather because one has
suffered a blow to one's self-esteem that one simply cannot handle.

In this vein, Dr Johnson remarks that envy, not selfishness, is the mother
of all malevolence:

> Most of the misery which the defamation of blameless actions, or the
> obstruction of honest endeavours brings upon the world, is inflicted by
> men that propose no advantage to themselves but the satisfaction of poi-
> soning the banquet which they cannot taste, and blasting the harvest
> which they have no right to reap.
>
> (Cited in Herzog, 2000: 149)

Moreover, when we think of envy, it is important to consider who is envied and what are its characteristic objects (from material goods, to appearances and talents). Like *schadenfreude*, envy is felt paradigmatically, but not exclusively, in relation to those in whom we have antagonistic relations. Consider the jealousy that drives so many of the characters of *The Iliad* against both friend and foe alike as they seek to claim that most competitive of goods, honour, from the gods. What often drives envy is not so much the desire to be the greatest; that is too limited a preserve to be psychologically credible. Rather, what motivates a sportsperson's emotional set more frequently is the desire to be seen to be (even a little bit) better than one's nearest rival. Two qualities of this desire for status strike me as important in an attempt to better understand what is going on when *schadenfreude* is felt, either in terms of opponents or indeed of team-mates occupying the starting line-up. First, it is the narcissism of minor differences, in Freud's term, that seems to drive the emotion. Second, the joy felt at our antagonist's harm is therefore driven by our familiarity with them. Or, as Hume puts it, 'tis not the great disproportion betwixt ourself and one another, which produces it, but on the contrary, our proximity' (cited in Herzog, 2000: 155).

There is a further, related point that is worthy of notice. Ought we to think of the celebration of a loss by one team, or indeed a vital mistake by our opponent, as being born necessarily of *schadenfreude*? The much discussed response of the American Ryder Cup team of 1999 who ran across the eighteenth green before the hole had been finished is paradigmatic of this category. Were they celebrating their European opponent's failed putt or their own win? It seems to me, although the matter is open to subsequent empirical refutation, that in the heat of the moment, the relief and joy expressed in their actions was symptomatic of mere catharsis and not inherently the rejoicing at their opponent's suffering. If my reading of this is correct, then it would be improper to think of their actions under the description of *schadenfreude*. It was of course still highly undesirable; the best that one can say is that it evidenced a lack of respect – and against the grain of what is undeniably among the nobler sports. This is not to say that in all such cases, the celebration of such an incident could not be classified as *schadenfreude*. If they were genuinely rejoicing the miserable failing of their opposition, and the celebration of their victory was secondary in importance, then it is clear that the description of *schadenfreude* would be properly applied – and our responses to it should alter accordingly.

I see no reason to suppose that any particular sports culture is more given to *schadenfreude* than another. What strikes me as noteworthy, if you will pardon the pun, is that in the sport where direct harm is intentionally and legally inflicted, boxing, *schadenfreude* is almost conspicuous by its absence among the boxers themselves. It might be argued more generally that spectators or followers of clubs, teams, and individual sports stars revel in opponents' harms rather more so than the players themselves. Where the clubs have intense geographical and cultural rivalries, it seems that this is perfectly plausible, though no less regrettable. For my own part, this might well be explained by a deficient sense of self, where spectators appear to believe that their self-worth is vicariously tendered by their identification with a successful other (be it team, club or player). Further exploration of this issue is, however, beyond the scope of the present discussion.

That we can reflect on the antecedents to our emotions is one clue as to how we may think about working upon our emotions and perceptions of others and selves, in order to go about educating ourselves in that respect.[12] They do not *all* visit us as uninvited guests might. Moreover, correct perceptions of others and selves are surely part of what we call a good life. And I want to emphasise that it is only a virtue-theoretical position that attempts to take this feature of our experience seriously. For to act well is not merely to do so for the right reasons, to the right extent, at the right time, and so on, but also to feel these reasons and responses while so construing and responding. And this, I fear, is simply ignored, not merely in much of the flourishing sports ethics literature but also in the sociology of sport.[13] Having rejected Portmann's first defence of *schadenfreude*, I will consider his second, rather stronger account for excusability: a loyalty to justice. If he is right that the feeling of *schadenfreude* may be justified as a function of justice then it might be seen as a virtuous rather than a vicious emotional response.

The sense that most of us may feel both familiar and warranted is in the *schadenfreude* felt by those who believe that another has violated an expectation or obligation and suffers in relation to their transgression. (How many times have you heard in post-match conferences: 'They got their just desserts!'; or 'I am glad they got their comeuppance', or, in both anticipation and desire, 'What goes around comes around'? Portmann writes:

> There is an important difference between enjoying *that* someone suffers and enjoying actual suffering. The former case must be held apart from *Schadenfreude*, for the attendant pleasure is not properly in seeing someone suffer but in the hope that someone will learn a valuable lesson in having suffered. Thus we take pleasure not in the suffering of another, but in the hope that he or she will correct a mistake.
>
> (Portmann, 2000: 48)

The pleasure felt at seeing justice done, he argues, must not be confused with a pleasure that a given person is actually suffering themselves. But it seems to me that 'pleasure' is not the right concept here. To take pleasure in suffering is too active, too destructive of human sympathy to be evidence of a love of justice. Now lest it be suggested that I am promoting a picture of sport devoid of intense commitment, let me make it clear that I do not approve of a sporting ethics of indifference. To the contrary, anger is an entirely appropriate emotional response to injustice as was noted in Chapter 6.

How it is registered, how accounted for and how exacted – these are further questions. I am merely arguing that pleasure felt at another's suffering is itself not desirable, even when the suffering is experienced by a wrongdoer. I think the more appropriate model may be a legal one. What one seeks through the courts is often described as 'satisfaction'. I want my transgressor to be adjudged wrong in public and admonished. A more appropriate emotional response, then, will be a less hedonistic or egoistic one; not cold, impartial, empathy-lacking justice, and certainly not an active, hand-rubbing glee. It strikes me that the proper emotional response to justice being served, and subsequent harm befalling the wrongdoer is captured by the concept of 'satisfaction'. Such is the feeling that ought to characterise our basketball player's emotional response. This concept denotes emotional neutrality and a certain passivity that is entirely absent in the positive and corrosive *schadenfreude*.

Of course this distinction regarding our rejoicing in the seeing of justice done begs wider questions about the role of human suffering in our lives. The position here is in debt to St Augustine in *Summa Theologiae*: Love the sinner, hate the sin is the exhortation. But Portmann's gloss seems unreal. 'We take pleasure in hoping they will correct the mistake' (2000: 156), he says. Well this *may* be the emotion felt by the zealous reformer, but the attitude of the *schadenfroh* seems not of this kind. 'You're bad but look how good in contrast I am', seems closer to the mark. What is missing here is any reference to sympathy – note, *not* empathy – with the sufferer. Of course, the resenting sportsperson may well, like Keane above, have empathy with his opponent, as he writhes on the floor in agony; it is precisely that empathy that fuels his enjoyment.

Schadenfreude and sporting sympathy

I have tried to show that Portmann's defences for *schadenfreude* are unacceptable. In the first instance, his conflation of self-respect and self-esteem undercuts his defence of the emotion. Second, the idea that low self-esteem and a commitment to justice might drive an excusable pleasure at another's suffering is at odds with any basic notion of human sympathy that will be at the core of all moralities I (perhaps too boldly) assert.

In summary, it seems more felicitous to link *schadenfreude* with a lack of spirit – an othering[14] of my opponent or competitor, or a failure to connect with their humanity as opposed to a deficiency in one's self-esteem. It is clear that our attitudes towards *schadenfreude* will alter accordingly with the severity of the suffering and the greatness of their deficiencies in conduct and character. What seems clear, however, is that the 'trick' of loving the sinner but hating the sin is a perception that will not find a home in the capriciousness of human character (however much we might want to cheer with the angels). Better that we recognise the nature of the occurrence and reflect on our own motivations in relation to the sufferer before we revel too much in the baseness of others and, by contrast, our own righteousness. In sports practice communities, no less than in social science research, we do well to observe Owen Flanagan's principle of minimal psychological realism. 'Make sure when constructing a moral theory or proposing a moral ideal that the character, decision-processing, and behavior are possible, or are perceived to be possible, for creatures like us' (Flanagan, 1991: 32).

This dictum could be seen to work both for and against the position I have set out above. It is natural that our responses to competitors' sufferings will not be driven by feelings so impartial that their losses strike us as heavily as our own. To an extent this is obviously true. Of course, one cannot hope to develop in sportspersons so detached a consideration of human interests, a point made more frequently these days against modern moralities of both utilitarian and deontological persuasion. But the active pleasure at another's misfortune goes beyond the asymmetry of self and other. *Schadenfreude* passes beyond the excusable and into both the realms of culpable and responsible emotion. Worse, where it is cultivated or merely utilised to enhance and celebrate our own esteem and achievements, *pace* Gore Vidal, a little something in us dies too.

Part III

Sports ethics, medicine and technology

9   Suffering in and for sport

In the previous two chapters I have explored the emotional ecology of winning and losing and tied it closely the virtues and vices frequently found in sport. The arrogant are lowered; those who relish their suffering are to be thought of as undesirable characters. I want to extend this ethical discussion further into the limit cases of suffering, which is manifest in many ways in sports. Compare the tears of Mary Decker Slaney, the hot favourite for the women's 5,000m final of the 1984 Olympics at Los Angeles with the uncontrolled weeping of British rower Matthew Pinsent on the podium in Athens in 2004, as he won his fourth consecutive Olympic gold medal in rowing. These extreme examples of intense emotions in sport should warn us against simple classifications of the emotions. In this chapter I want to make sense of how we can better understand and appreciate the emotionally saturated concept of suffering by first distinguishing more carefully between pain and suffering than is typically done in sports medicine or sports anthropology, where they are often conflated and treated as synonymous with private or subjective feelings. I go on to present critically some philosophical accounts of the concept of suffering and in doing so begin to draw together threads of shared interest between sports ethics and medical ethics. I articulate and exemplify a range of issues that arises from thinking of suffering in sport as an extended emotional experience, which is inherently linked to the projects that we care about, are committed to, and that partly constitute our identities as sportspersons.

On suffering and pain: some conceptual geography

There is not a developed philosophical literature on pain and suffering in sport.[1] Jeff Fry (2002) recently published a very insightful overview of the theodicy of pain and suffering as it applies (and where it does not apply) to sports. In sports anthropology, David Howe (2004) has catalogued the habitus of injury-acceptance as part and parcel of the practices that are elite sport. Neither Fry nor Howe, however, directs attention significantly to the relations between the two concepts. What I shall do in this section is to set out some analytical remarks concerning the two concepts – and only hint at the theological similarities and dissimilarities in an attempt to enquire as to whether a consideration of suffering might have something interesting to say about the nature and purposes of sport, and the sportspersons' emotional components seen as part of the living of a good life.

There is often conceptual confusion in sports talk surrounding these thorny concepts. Typically suffering and pain are conflated. One is thought to be suffering when in pain, and concomitantly when pained, to be suffering. One of the ways of dealing with the complexity of the conceptual connections of pain and suffering is crudely to dualise them in the aspect of the person. Under such a dualism, pain is physical, suffering is mental. Thus Howe writes: 'Pain is a highly subjective phenomenon, and this has led to its exclusion from much discussion of injury, which may be seen as more objective' (2004: 74).

Despite disavowals to the contrary throughout the book, it is difficult to read passages in Howe's book in any way other than dualistically.[2] After Descartes, and dominating Western philosophy until Gilbert Ryle's brilliant debunking in *The Concept of Mind* (1949), people were thought to be comprised of separate substances – minds and bodies – whose natures were distinct. Howe's writing, like that of many other social scientists (especially with the rise of the sociology of the body, with authors who are not naturally inclined to a phenomenological mien) and even sports psychologists (who really should know better), has difficulty in escaping the language that separates mind and body as distinct substances. So in Howe's critical ethnographies of living with pain and injury, it is perhaps not surprising that 'mental' concepts such as 'anguish' or 'suffering' do not appear in the index. It seems clear that physical pain is the paradigmatic object of discussion. And there is of course nothing necessarily wrong with this. What is problematic, and what is found in many places elsewhere, is a particular set of relations between pain and suffering. On the one hand there is an apparently non-dualistic position where writers casually refer to 'bodily suffering' as a sensation 'usually' in the body. On the other hand there is the dualistic one: suffering is supposed to be the felt marker: pain indicates suffering.[3]

A further and less frequently observed aspect of suffering and pain is brought out by Ivan Illich[4] (1987):

> The Old Testament is very rich in words that express a deep, deep sense of suffering: anguish, fear, bitterness, the experience of being lost, forlorn, beaten up, exposed to the wrath of the Lord. It was only very much later, during the Christian epoch, that rabbis felt the need to assign a specific word for that which we moderns now call pain. When these same rabbis had to talk about physical pain they used the word that designated punishments which I inflict. The English word pain comes from the Latin poena, from being punished. The concept of a physical pain, one specifically physical, comes from the experience of being chastised by another. In our language pain does not come from the inside; it is imposed on us from outside.

In what follows I will assume that the concepts of suffering and pain are closely related and will develop some ideas more concerned with suffering that is not driven by pain. To do this I shall draw upon analyses of suffering from the medical ethics literature.

Concepts of 'suffering' in medical ethics

In a well-known medical ethics text, Cassell (1991: 33) offers the following definition of suffering:

> [S]uffering occurs when an impending destruction of the person is perceived; it continues until the threat of disintegration has occurred or until the integrity of the person can be restored in some other manner. [...] suffering extends beyond the physical.

And later says that 'suffering can be defined as the state of severe distress associated with events that threaten the intactness of person' (Cassell, 1991: 33).

The two features of this definition might be called the (1) feeling and (2) integrity criteria.[5] It is worth observing how these criteria relate to aspects of privacy and subjectivity. There can be times when there seems to be a simple causal relationship between pain and suffering – though it must be noted Cassell avoids the simple dualism of caused in the body, suffered in the mind. In such cases one suffers because one is in pain. Cassell refers (1991: 25–6) to situations 'when the pain is so severe it is virtually overwhelming', 'when the patient believes the pain cannot be controlled' and also to 'pain that is not overwhelming but continues for a very long time'. It is not difficult to find sporting examples for these instances of suffering because of pain. They represent, perhaps, a kind of paradigm for sporting suffering in that they are at least the most obvious of cases of sporting suffering.

Cassell, however, makes a couple of further conceptual remarks that are interesting for our purposes. Like Howe, he too writes dualistically in the vein of an essentially private character of suffering: 'Suffering is ultimately a personal matter – something whose presence can only be known by the sufferer' (Cassell, 1991: 35).

This privatisation of suffering runs counter to the view I shall adopt and adapt later. In that account, suffering can indeed be attributed by another. Indeed, our predication of empathy as sports spectators rests on this point. As I watch the gymnast fall on the last movement of their routine my heart goes out to them. I can appreciate at least sufficient of their misery to see how and why they suffer. In later remarks, however, Cassell captures at least some of what I take to be the inherent sociality of suffering:

> Suffering must be distinguished from its uses. In some theologies, especially the Christian, suffering has been seen as presenting the opportunity of bringing the sufferer closer to God. This 'function' of suffering is at

once its glorification and relief. If, through great pain or deprivation, someone is brought closer to a cherished goal, that person may have no sense of having suffered but, instead, may feel enormous triumph. To an observer, the only thing apparent may be the deprivation. This cautionary note is especially important because people are often said to have suffered greatly, in a religious context, when we know only that they were injured, tortured or in pain, not whether they suffered.

(Cassell, 1991: 35)

He summarises: 'Although pain and suffering are closely identified in the minds of most people and in the medical literature, they are phenomenologically distinct' (1991: 35).

Given that the concepts are so frequently run together, we should ask: precisely what does it mean to say that pain and suffering are conceptually distinct? One could think of minor ailments, when one is in pain but not suffering. One could think of fleeting twinges – for example, the type which, in my early middle age, I encounter in my knee, back and ankles when I run where it would be a piece of gross conceptual inflation to say that I was suffering. Finally, one could imagine cases of minor injuries, knocks, bumps, soreness, that are inherent in contact sport. When we experience minor injury or dysfunction it is no more than the consequence of the graft and grind of any sporting life. These simple remarks serve to establish the point that pain and suffering are not synonymous. We may often be in pain but it does not follow that we should think of ourselves as suffering.

One further idea that might cut through the simplistic body–mind/ pain–suffering complex is the idea of significance. It can be argued that what the integrity criterion attempts to secure is a quality of 'depth' in our experience. Suffering under such a description necessarily draws on both significance (extent or duration) and psychological distress. It would be odd to speak of one who suffered momentarily or in the blinking of an eye. In what follows below I consider Edwards' critique of the 'feeling' and 'integrity' criteria of Cassell's account and his own analysis of the concept.

Edwards bases his criticisms of the concepts of suffering proposed by Cassell, among others, upon a more cautious appropriation of the concept. His leading point is a rejection of the essentialism entailed in the necessary and sufficient conditions they propose; that is to say he rejects their method on Wittgensteinian grounds. Edwards says that we should attend to the uses of the concept 'suffering' in order to establish its meaning. And following our appreciation of that heterogeneity we shall find no crystallised essence but rather a family of meanings that criss-cross and overlap without containing any indisputable linguistic essence. Suffering is the kind of experience that must be felt. To suffer is to be in a state that is necessarily felt by the agent. In this respect, it is like pain. He says: 'Would it make sense to say of a person "You're in pain" if this came as a complete surprise to them?' (2003: 65). Of course, stories are legion of sportspersons who are injured without consciousness of it as they perform heroic deeds – only later to collapse in agony. One image that springs to mind is that of the bandaged American gymnast Kelly Strug as she prepared to risk even more serious injury lining up for the vault, which won the American team the gold medal at the 1996 Olympic Games. While, however, one may be injured without being in pain, one cannot be said to suffer without the cognitive aspect of the emotion registered at some conscious level. This condition seems indisputable for human suffering. Put formally we might say that it – the awareness of some seriously negative happening – is a necessary condition of suffering but not a sufficient one. Well, for the moment we may say that. I think there are some grounds for denying even that much, as we shall see.

Second, Edwards argues that suffering must be extended in time. Something as fleeting as a pinprick, or stepping on a sharp stone, cannot count. Moreover, though this seems a separate point, he argues that pain is not a necessary condition of suffering, for we may grieve deeply while experiencing no pain – where this is taken to be the unpleasant sensation produced by physical causes. Third, he argues that one cannot be happy and suffer. To suffer is to have a shadow cast – for that time – over one's enjoyment of life. He does note that in theological accounts of suffering – martyrdom is the extreme – that suffering is a central part of one's conception of the good life but he argues here one merely has a stronger preference for the suffering.[6] Edwards summarises his threefold account thus:

> The first is a 'self' component; the sufferer must realise that it is he or she that is suffering, that the experiences are his or her own. Second, the phenomenological component, the distinct way or ways it feels to suffer. And third, a temporal component; this will signal the duration of the experience of suffering. Schematically we might express such experiences thus: [S, p, t]. Where the components are the self component S, the phenomenological component p, and the temporal component t, respectively.
>
> (Edwards, 2003: 65)

We can conclude that there is at least a generic meaning here; a conceptual core but nothing as strong as an essence conceived of as a set of necessary and sufficient conditions. That general sense of 'suffering' means little more than experiencing something significantly deleterious to our well-being. In relation to human suffering we typically qualify the nature of that suffering in an adverbial way by drawing out the qualities of mind and character that attend the suffering. In addition, I want to draw attention to a specific dimension – the emotionally saturated idea of suffering. It seems to me that much suffering in sport is merely the experience of distressing pain – and this is surely worthy of explanation. But I shall not address it below, preferring instead to highlight a few remarks about the emotionality of suffering in sport. By way of summary let us agree for the moment that suffering in sport is an extended emotional response to events that are significantly deleterious to our well-being. Where will that take us?

Emotionally laden suffering

Let us say that we can articulate human suffering as a felt emotion. This point arises from Edwards' first two conditions, though he does not employ the description of suffering as an emotion as such. The idea that suffering is an emotion is denied by some. Consider Meyerfeld (1999: 50) who argues that one may suffer without cognisance. He asserts that one may be stunned, inarticulate or confused. Yet it seems that here he is presupposing that for which he must argue. For while it is true of certain moods ('distress' being one candidate) that they are to a certain extent diffused or inchoate, I cannot see what conceptual advantage there is in thinking that the epistemological condition is not necessary.

In my discussion of emotion above, I included the cognitive element of emotion, which is typically in the form of a judgement. Imagine being told by someone who looked desolate that they are suffering but they had no idea why. We might think, quite reasonably, that they had taken leave of their senses. Of course they might be experiencing a sense of foreboding, anticipating some bad event, or simply be feeling melancholic. If this were the case though, we would have moved away from emotion-talk and back into the territory of moods, which have a lower cognitive threshold and no specific intentional object where the idea of emotional construal finds more obvious application. Moreover, that someone is inarticulate or stunned or confused is a psychological condition – one that need not impinge upon our conceptualisation of suffering as an emotion. So let me assume here that to suffer is to experience an emotion with an intentional object: we suffer because of our perceptions of something significantly bad about our condition. Nevertheless, this alone is insufficient to make sense of suffering. In the light of the foregoing we should say that to suffer is to undergo some unpleasant emotion for some significant duration. Now what is to count as 'significant duration' cannot be pre-specified in some abstract way. The particularity of the phenomenology of suffering means that what counts as extended in one context may be brief in another. But that does not open the door to subjectivity of meaning. Consider the intensity of effort of the 400m runner as he or she comes down the final straight, paradoxically trying to produce and remove lactates from her or his legs. I want to maintain that to use the word 'suffering' here, as commentators do, is inappropriate. Contrast the use of the word 'suffering' to describe the efforts of marathon runners in the last mile, or Tour de France cyclists going for the last climb of a mountain stage. Here the use of the word has a more natural home. Edwards does not develop this point and so I shall say a little by way of justification for the position.

For us to speak of emotionally saturated suffering, we must at least have time to dwell (should we so desire) on our misfortune in order for us to suffer.

In this sense we could contrast suffering with more episodic emotions – such as the joy of scoring a goal – which is brief, however much we recall, re-describe and relish it on later occasions. Now if we were to evaluate the benefit or disbenefit of an emotion we might well be required to consider its duration as well as its extent. Ought we to opt for a few years of adulation, status and wealth at the expense of a lifetime's suffering, as many elite sportspersons do? Typically, the experience of the emotion in sport does not last in time in the same way as the caring love of a parent or child. Equally, though pain can range from mild to excruciating, it seems to make little sense to say that suffering could be mild. This is not to say that suffering is all or nothing. We do not need to be absolutist about this. But it makes sense to say that there is a certain threshold before we meaningfully apply the concept.

By coalescing pain and suffering, by failing to keep them analytically distinct, Meyerfeld denies this attribution. He draws on the *locus classicus* of the pain register (Melzack and Torgerson, 1971), which describes pain as ranging from mild to discomforting, and then to distressing, horrible and, finally, excruciating. Meyerfeld goes further by saying: 'These words recognisably refer to the intensity of suffering not just pain' (1999: 39).

I fail to see the coherence of this application, and Meyerfeld offers no argument for it. In order that one may be said to suffer, one must experience a certain intensity or one cannot say one suffered. To suffer mildly makes little sense, *pace* Meyerfeld, though to describe a pain as mild does. Cassell is much clearer here. He says that we suffer – in relation to pain – 'when the pain is so severe it is virtually overwhelming' (1991: 36) and later 'when the patient believes the pain cannot be controlled' or 'in relation to pain that is not overwhelming but continues for a very long time' (1991: 36). It is not an accident that in the biomedical literature, where pain and suffering co-mingle, we find that chronic pain is the paradigmatic example. Extension in time, and a certain intensity, are all present in Cassell's examples. They are part of the condition of suffering. But an articulation of that condition is not complete without the articulation of a sense of meaning that attaches inherently to it.

In addition, it seems reasonable to say that we cannot suffer in relation to things to which we are indifferent. Whereof one does not care, thereof one cannot suffer. That for which we suffer we must, in some fairly strong sense, be committed to, or care for, or identify with. There must be some sense of both attachment and value. This is the direction in which Cassell's 'intactness' condition aims, but it sets too high a threshold. Equally, Edwards holds that suffering 'must have a fairly central place in the mental life of the subject'. And while I think that this is right, it does not have normative direction; it fails to specify the inherent negativity of the concept. In contrast to this point, Cassell merely asserts that the religious martyr suffers yet experiences the suffering positively. This seems to be too open-ended. I maintain that the negative normativity is, logically speaking, internal to the concept of human suffering. Where one embraces a painful death in what sense can one be said to suffer? It strikes me that that would be contradictory. It is a mistake founded on the generalisability of experience – yes, you and I might suffer in such circumstances but our *Weltanshauungen* are radically different.

What is at stake in suffering, as I have said, is something that is not a matter of indifference to us – it is something that is part of our 'horizon of significance' to use Charles Taylor's apt phrase. As Cassell observes, we can only *see* the Christian sufferer in pain. Perhaps we can put it more strongly by saying that martyrs do not suffer the pains of fire, rather they rejoice in it. Now a chief question will be whether sportspersons find, like religious martyrs, the depths of meaning in sport that their forebears did in Christianity.

Having merely hinted at the features that I consider critical to capture our emotional sense of human suffering, I will merely point to aspects of sports suffering that would bear further analysis and note certain social and theological parameters that might serve to deepen our understanding of suffering – especially for those such as physicians or physiotherapists or sports coaches who necessarily deal with the equally necessary sense of the inevitably tragic in sport.

Suffering in and for sport: three possibilities

As I have said, the paradigmatic cases of suffering in sport relate closely to those cases wherein pain drives the suffering over time in relation to something of significance to the sufferer. It strikes me that there are three categories where this conceptualisation could usefully be explored in sports-related literatures. They help to point to what I think of as the inherently tragic in sport. I do not mean by this the myth of continual progress so dear to global capitalism and crystallised in sports marketing. The point is simply that sport careers (however humble or exalted) are not best represented in a linear fashion. Rather they are cruelly, inescapably, elliptical. They rise, they peak and then, necessarily, they fall. The simple fact can be seen in three categories of sportspersons to whom we might look naturally for suffering: (1) the elite athlete; (2) the ageing athlete; (3) the retired athlete. In each of these cases the meaning of the suffering will be coloured in distinct ways; the manner in which the sport informs the life of the elite athlete – which may be almost suffocating in its exclusivity and intensity – will be quite distinct from the more chronic experiences of the ageing athlete and the desolation of the retired athlete who may wallow in a post-sport world devoid of emotional peaks and troughs (along with other lacunae).

If we were to agree that suffering in sport (as elsewhere) is best thought of as an emotional experience, then we should be able to point to the intentional objects involved. What might 'cause' such suffering? Some potential precursors might be (1) the anticipation of loss or the infliction of a defeat; (2) the recognition of consequences of injury; (3) distress of possible termination of career, perhaps most strongly for elite athletes; and (4) sports 'death' as it were: the loss of economic and social identity. Of course the list is not exhaustive and merely attempts to suggest where one might toil for more interesting phenomenological investigations. In these cases one could ask whether sportspersons, contra Huizinga, take their sports too seriously. Here the status of the sportsperson is all important. For professional players, sports may well be 'everything' – the phrase 'it's only a game' is a banal utterance in this context. The rest of us, however, need to find a place for the sports activities we care for, love and value, in ways that are not so totalising. It also opens up at least one significant normative question: ought we really to suffer for sport?

Having merely hinted at the meaning-driven facets of sports suffering it might be worth thinking how the duration element might draw us to look for central cases in sport. Where might we find suffering in the performance of sport – as opposed to the preparation for sport? The obvious point to look is at those endurance sports where performance is not merely extended over time – a round of golf after all takes three–four hours – but also those where there is a limited array of performance factors. Typically, sports where the production of power is not dominated by technical or aesthetic concerns seem rich candidates for sites of suffering. We find not merely temporal extension in marathon or ultra-distance running, biathlon, triathlon, and in cycle races such as the Tour de France, but a quality of extension where one has time and space for a welter of factors to impinge upon one's consciousness in the experience of the activity.

A recent incident may go some way to pointing up this interesting aspect in a literal way. At the 2004 Olympics the British runner Paula Radcliffe was the favourite for the marathon. She had posted the year's fastest times for 10,000m on the track and had recently smashed the world record for the marathon. Having struggled to control the pace, in heat that made even some African athletes retire earlier in the race, Radcliffe withdrew with only three miles to go to the finish, apparently in the knowledge that she would not win a medal. Clearly she suffered over the difficult, hilly, terrain in exhausting heat. Mile after mile her face grew more contorted, more anguished. What were her thoughts over those miles, those hours and minutes as she considered personal failure, in the certain knowledge that she had 'blown' probably her best chance to gain an Olympic gold? What kind of scathing introspection went on with her every stride? And just as one can experience emotion after the fact, what emotions fuelled her anticipation of the savage British sports press in the aftermath of what would be written as a national tragedy. Or as it was later written up, even in some of the most thoughtful quarters of the British media, not so much a national disgrace as a moment of personal egoism and cowardice. Robert Philip's (2004) article, entitled 'Radcliffe was a sore loser', was as critical of the national press that supported Radcliffe as a heroine as he was of the athlete herself:

> The Tears of a Hero proclaimed one headline alongside a picture of Paula Radcliffe. Well, if it's heroes you want, then I'll give you heroes: Japan's Mizuki Noguchi, who won the Olympic marathon, was a hero. So, too,

was Briton Liz Yelling, who produced a late sprint to overtake Maria Abel, of Spain, in a photo-finish for 25th place.

Nor should we forget her team-mate Tracey Morris, who ran in the same heat and up the same hills as Radcliffe to finish 29th only to be totally ignored by Fleet Street. And was there anyone more heroic than Mongolian Lursan Ikhundeg Otgonbayar, the 66th and last competitor across the line in the Panathanaiko Stadium, a full 30 minutes behind the woman in front and almost 1½ hours adrift of Noguchi?

But no, it is poor, distraught, anguished, heroic (I could go on but you get the drift) Radcliffe sitting in a gutter by the side of the road on whom we are expected to bestow the laurel leaf for Olympic gallantry.

Call me a cynic, but the way I see it is that unless the medics in Athens can come up with a physical reason why she quit just over three miles from the finish, Radcliffe stopped running and started blubbing for the simple reason that she had just seen gold, silver and bronze medals disappear into the distance [. . .].

What most observers appear to have overlooked is that, yes, while there are only three medals on offer, every runner who completes any marathon course is a winner. Radcliffe – as brave, heroic, and dedicated as she might have proved herself to be in the past – was a loser on Sunday night and, judging by her reaction when she opted out of the race having conceded third place, a pretty sore loser at that.

What is striking in this appraisal is the adverbial quality that Philip imports to the appraisal of the athlete's character. Without knowing it, Philip has charged Radcliffe and held her to account for her suffering. He has judged her character through an emotional evaluation. Yet he has only captured a small part of the aetiology of her suffering – the anticipated failure. It might be argued that he has failed himself (on a monumental scale) to empathise with the athlete in her suffering before moving to his strong critique. The significance of the goal, the preparation of a lifetime, the realisation of a lost dream, the estimation of one's fall from esteem (and then grace) all seem to meet our criteria for suffering to the point that make her devastation comprehensible. For Philip, all that is perceived is a wallowing, egoistic, pity. Now it might be held by others, properly, that Radcliffe's response lacked courage, that it was weak in some meaningful sense – but then that is not the position before us. It is clear that she experiences herself as suffering as she ran and eventually gave up. Ought she to have experienced this emotion? Is she entitled to the empathetic responses that are proper to the perception of a suffering one? These are the questions Philip fails to ask. Instead, he arrives too quickly at his conclusion: she is a shallow loser. For my own part, and based upon the analysis of suffering above, I think it makes every sense to see Radcliffe as suffering and worthy of an aptly felt empathy. I do not say that this makes her a model of good character; one to be admired or envied, simply one for whom we may feel, with justification, some considerable sadness.

To explore such suffering further – and our ethically responsible responses to it – we would need to evaluate the adverbial character of the emotion in a more compassionate manner. Precisely how does one suffer here? Is it wallowing in the failure to achieve one's expected goal? Is it more intense as one battles to dislocate one's sensory experiences, to dull the pain of chronic injuries or heat-driven distress? Again these are only suggestions as to where we might meaningfully further explore suffering in sport.

A set of interesting questions remains that is located beyond the individualised phenomenological conception that we are naturally drawn to in the West. I take my cue here from the socio-theological writings of the Catholic intellectual and polymath Ivan Illich. Illich (1987) writes of 'communities of suffering'. It is an idea rich in possibilities for understanding the places of suffering in sport. Of course this could refer to the suffering that is closely related to intense pain: the gym, weights room, the track, the pool. Commentators frequently remark about the camaraderie wrought by the masochistic mutuality of boxing, or the tacit acknowledgement of chronic neck and back pain suffered by front row players in rugby, or American footballers on the line of scrimmage, at the tight end, protecting the quarterback at the risk of life and limb.

If we eschew a model of emotion that is pejoratively characterised as mere moods, or as uncognitive – as feelings that visit rather like a thief in the night – it makes sense to ask questions regarding the history of suffering in sport. From whom do we learn to suffer? In what ways are we initiated to it? Do we embrace it as a friend or as an enemy? What coping strategies are authentic? Are such strategies for anti-suffering (such as withdrawal) somehow inauthentic? In what sense can coaches or team-mates or indeed opponents share in the suffering of others?

Suffering, sports medicine and the ethics of sport

Finally, there is a further set of Aristotelian-inspired ethical questions that we can ask in respect to the non-theological ethical significance of suffering under the physical and emotional aspects of the concept. Might there be virtuous responses to suffering? Could we think of the boxer, humiliated by his opponent, as acting courageously while he suffers? Or ought we to think of it as courage gone awry, as rash or reckless suffering? Is the boxer's suffering (especially where self-inflicted) in some sense wrenched from virtuous ends – and means? For virtue, if Aristotle is right, is always in the service of good ends. Not any amount of courage is to be thought of as bravery – a point that Philip might have borne in mind during his verbal lasceration of Radcliffe. Should we think differently of Stoic suffering in the face of unbearable pain forced on us by another – a model of passive suffering? Lance Armstrong talks of precisely such a disposition in his account of cycling in the Tour de France, of making his competitors endure the suffering he purposefully inflicted on them. To what point do we admire their forbearance? At what point does it become pathological? Is the quality of suffering conceptually relevant when that person is ourselves, pushing through the 'pain barrier', when we are active in the construction of our own suffering?

It seems best to think of suffering in sport in a teleological way. In medicine we suffer in rehabilitation. In Christian thought we suffer for redemption. What ends are served by suffering in and for sport? There will be no global answers here, only particular ones. But we are minded as philosophers to ask of coaches, players and physicians, especially in elite sports, a question put by Plato long ago (1974: 407a): what limits should we observe in our efforts to improve our bodily performance and remove causes of suffering?

In asking such a question, though not answering it, we would begin to challenge many myths in modern sport and sports medicine. There is a pressing need to understand the moral topography of sports medicine. Key to that challenge is the need to understand sports as well as sports medicine as social practices and, in particular, to uncover that which is often latent – the idea that medicine is merely a technical, unproblematic, means to unquestioned (and unquestionably valuable) ends.[7] So when we talk of medical professionals and professionalisation of sports, we need to ask: whose ethics? Surely there is no necessarily shared ethic between the doctors' cure, the physiotherapists' care, in relation to the players' career. How this is both gendered and loaded – or not – with emotional content will be worthy of exploration and explanation.

Rather than asking whether the pain is positive or negative we might ask: 'What qualities attend the suffering?' In what ways specifically do we suffer in sports? This requires us necessarily to arrange and argue about the adverbial qualities of our selves and our sufferings. These questions force us to deny the hegemony of physicalised, biomedically explainable pain as the paradigm of negative experiences in sport. They force us to take the social and emotional aspects of the emotion of suffering more seriously than hitherto has been the case. As Illich (1987) concluded:

> I am taking the liberty of speaking of suffering as the culturally shaped way of dealing with the shadow side of life rather than with its lighted, sunny side. I shall use the term suffering to indicate a particular socially and culturally acquired art of dealing with that shadow side, of bearing burdens which come with living. I'm speaking about the art of suffering. Pain is only one narrow, but very special, kind of condition in which one would properly need the art of suffering.

I hope, in the spirit of Illich's moving testimony, that I have at least offered a framework in which to consider suffering as an emotion loaded with ethical significance, and one that should be taken more seriously by philosophers and social scientists of sports and sports medicine. I shall now turn to a topic that has had no difficulty whatever in arresting the attention of these communities of scholars, the illicit enhancement of performance otherwise known as 'doping'.

10 Doping

Slippery slopes, *pleonexia* and shame

In Book II of *The Republic* Plato reports the well-known story of Gyges' ring. Gyges, a lowly shepherd, takes his flock into a cave and there finds a corpse wearing a beautiful ring that he subsequently steals. While talking with other shepherds, he fidgets with his fingers and turning the stone of the ring became invisible. Aware of his new-found possibilities, he uses the ring's powers to seduce the king's wife and take over the kingdom. In the Platonic dialogue that follows, Socrates' interlocutor, Glaucon, argues that any sane person would do the same as Gyges. The story throws into sharp relief the value of a life lived justly where one is at peace with oneself – but with little reward – as opposed to one that is lived ignobly while accruing wealth and power and (what seems at least to be) happiness. Is there a necessary relation between the flourishing life and an ethically praiseworthy one? In a number of respects, it will be argued, the myth of Gyges' ring is directly analogous to the problem of doping in elite sports.

In this chapter I will rehearse the central arguments against doping practices and substances and their rebuttal in the literature. I will then introduce the idea of slippery slopes, which has not been deployed in the sports ethics literature, and argue that it is a powerful logical argument against doping liberalisers. Finally, returning to an aretaic vocabulary and drawing upon the moral of the story of Gyges' ring, I will articulate the viciousness of those who unjustly acquire the goods and status their own athletic abilities do not merit as an example of what the ancient Greeks called *pleonexia*. Only in apparent paradox, I argue that the cultivation of shamefulness in elite sports might well assist in the necessary task of self-regulation by athletes and coaches in their strivings for dope-free sporting excellence.

What's wrong with doping? Some standard arguments

As one might imagine the problem of doping is not a new one (Dimeo, 2007; Hoberman, 2005; Houlihan, 1999). In the literature of sports ethics a familiar range of arguments are deployed and typically defused. As it is not my purpose here to review them critically in any detail I shall merely note examples of authors who have written more or less persuasively under the following headings: (1) that doping is all about performance enhancement; (2) that doping allows more training; (3) that doping is unnatural; (4) that doping is coercive; (5) that doping is harmful; (6) that doping confers an unfair advantage.

Doping is wrong because it enhances performance

The weakest of all anti-doping arguments is oddly enough one that is commonly proposed in sports bars and cafés. It is that doping is wrong because it enhances performance. The position is straightforward enough but clearly open to two types of initial rebuttal. In the first instance one might ask whether it is indeed true that the banned substances we see on lists of prohibitions are indeed performance enhancing. Among others, Nicholson (1987) claims that the evidence is far from clear. Much of their performance enhancing effect, he suggests, is down to a placebo effect. It would be fair to say that the body of sports scientists would argue that he is wrong as a matter of fact. It may well be true, however, that we are not, or at least not always, in a position to identify clear cut explanations for enhanced performance that are caused by the doping substance or process. To the contrary, it seems to me, sporting excellence – doped or otherwise – will always be a complex product of human heart and mind, as much as extreme bodily efforts. A second, less easily dismissed, aspect of this argument refers to the very possibility of gathering such information. If one suspected x, y or z substances were performance enhancing but also likely to cause harm, how would one proceed to gain ethical approval for the research that tried to demonstrate that? So, it is said, the very idea of gaining a large and reliable inventory of doping products would be scuppered at the first stage by the inability to gain research ethics approval by the relevant regulating authority. It seemed one could not in principle claim then to *know* that the alleged substances actually enhanced performance in a reliable and valid way.

Since the time these arguments were first raised, largely in the late 1980s, empirical work on performance enhancing products and substances has indeed emerged despite the scepticism concerning research ethics approval, on the grounds of potential harm to participants (McNamee *et al.*, 2007), ever being granted to gain sufficiently large and reliable data. Recent UK studies of body-building cultures both medical (e.g. Baker *et al.*, 2006) and sociological (e.g. Monaghan, 2001) offer clear evidence of risks outside healthcare and medically related doping abuse.

Doping allows athletes to train hard, too hard

In any event, it has been said by the sceptic, elite sports is all about enhancement, why worry specifically about pharmacological modes of enhancement. All elite competitors, and a good many below their elevated status, push themselves to the very limits of their own sporting capacities, looking for that extra degree of concentration, effort, speed, strength, or whichever capacity is prized in the various sports under discussion. One response to this problem is the idea that doping is wrong because, it is said, it allows some athletes to train harder.

In many spheres we admire those who, with exceptional focus, achieve goals of almost superhuman magnitude. Ought we to find ethically problematic athletes who dope in order to work harder? I might be on a caffeine high as I write; no one worries. A great many comedians and musicians are well known to suffer from a host of psychological deficiencies and can only face the audience when bolstered by alcohol or other drugs; no public outcry. Why should chemical or pharmaceutical means in sport to enhance performance provoke our ire? Moreover, access to new facilities, higher levels of specialised coaching, increased nutritional sophistication and equipment technology (such as isokinetic resistance machines or hyperbaric chambers) all improve training effects without so much as an eyebrow being raised? We encourage other training enhancement methods, it is said, why not pharmacological enhancement?

Doping is unnatural

One direct attack on pharmacological enhancement is the claim that doping is wrong because it is unnatural. Precisely what is natural is itself problematic. Nevertheless, even on the grounds of consistency it can be asked why approved substances and procedures such as sleeping in oxygen-deprived tents or chambers is thought to be any more 'natural' (see Fricker, 2005; Loland and Murray, 2007; Spriggs, 2005; Tamburrini, 2005; Tannsjo, 2005).

Another feature of this move that is open to attack, is the idea that sport itself is not natural but an artifice: a social construction and institutionalisation of the impulse to play. So why then should we be worried about doping as unnatural? What ethical leverage is the argument supposed to apply? If it is some unstated assumption that that which is natural is good and that which is unnatural is bad then one has only to wave that logical sword, the naturalistic fallacy, at such proponents. The naturalistic fallacy, in brief, holds that one may not move directly from statements of fact (what is the case) directly to moral conclusions (what ought to be). This is the move that is illicitly made between the jump that our natural bodies are good because they are natural, but unnatural ones are bad because they are unnatural (or analogously that natural performances are good and non-natural/artificial ones bad). And of course the conclusion *might* make for some indefensible positions on those with artificial limbs or replacement joints who (apparently) fall below the limit of what is a natural body. It is reasonable to suppose that those who naively put forward the naturalistic argument have failed to consider the implications for such people who engage in sports in both able bodied and disability sports. The idea that an athlete with prostheses is somehow morally inferior to natural athletes (which is the consequence of the view) is deeply offensive to our modern egalitarian ideals.

Yet there is something in the view that our human nature deserves respect that is not fully articulated in this view of the unnaturalness of doping whether pharmacological or genetic. As Miah (2004) correctly points out, part of it is objection to an irrational fear of some kind of mythical Frankenstein. Nevertheless, his particular rejection of the natural argument is not sound. He notes that the argument that sports ought only to measure natural performances which somehow can be divorced from artificial input, raises the following issues:

> This type of argument does not constitute a reason for prohibiting the use of genetic modification in sport because its definition of the natural is contested. Indeed, I suggest that the natural is, at best, a meaningless concept though, at worst, potentially divisive, since it would seem to lead to the conclusion that some kinds of human are more valuable than others.
>
> (Miah, 2004: 151)

It must be noted, however, that a distinction need not be absolutely clear for it to be useful. We cannot tell the precise point at which night becomes day yet we are able to apply the concepts without difficulty. One cannot point to an exact point at which orange becomes red but this does not prevent the traffic cop booking the driver for failing to stop at the traffic lights. And the very idea that *because* a concept is contested it follows that it must therefore be meaningless does not hold water. Consider what are referred to as essentially contested concepts (Gallie, 1956) such as education whose nature and purposes are contested by every political ideology. The very fact of their contestedness does not render them meaningless. To be sure Miah is right to be wary of the careless or the manipulative deployment of what is a fishy concept, but there is no reason to think that the normative utilisation of naturalness in arguments against doping leads us necessarily to condemn or disvalue disabled populations who rely on artificial or technological products in their daily living. Notwithstanding all this, the idea of a non-natural body enhanced from our ideas of normal human functioning is one that troubles many philosophers and scientists alike.[1] I will return to this idea specifically in the Chapter 11 when I consider the future sports and sports ethics in the light of biomedical technologies in society more generally.

Dopers coerce non-dopers to dope

It is sometimes said by athletes themselves that doping-related bans are justified to prevent their coercion into taking drugs. Or, as Ben Johnson's coach, Charlie Francis, famously put it: 'if you don't take it you won't make it'. Allowing athletes to dope, coerces other athletes into doing the same against their will it is said. There is a close relationship between the apparent coercion argument and the train harder argument. When a colleague eschews the model of a family life and, like a hermit, works 12 hours a day, 5 days a week, and 50 weeks a year, we may just as easily admire their industry as we may mock their lack of balance. Would we have grounds for saying, at the next promotion board, that the promotion ought not go to the super-industrious on the grounds that their work habits have a coercive effect on all those who wish to achieve the said promotion in the future?[2] Not any old social pressure may count as a coercive one. But if coercion means something like the wrongful restriction of an agent's freedom then one might be hard pressed to locate our fellow, dope-driven, athletes in the ascription 'coercers'. In what sense are they coercing their opponents? Can the clean not simply choose a dope-free option to training and performance? Is it not, rather, that a free choice not to participate, or to participate in legal and legitimate ways, is still possible? We do not say to our gut-busting, Stakhanovite, colleague that they ought to be prevented from accessing their workstation, or the library, or their personal computers after so many hours. We respect their autonomy even if we deride the narrowness of their industriousness. And on a point of consistency, if our arguments were truly about the concern that others inflicted upon us, that should apply to all practices such as athletes who run for more miles or in higher climates, swimmers who do more lengths, cross-country skiers who sleep in so-called oxygen tents to boost their production of red blood cells and improve oxygen transportation around the body. What about cyclists who wear aerodynamic hats, swimmers who wear fast-skin suits, or female gymnasts who are forced to discipline their bodies by calorific control to achieve outrageous morphological norms that are inappropriate for certain ages and body types and often deeply corrosive to their psychological well-being. What about jockeys who are 'coerced' to waste (to lose weight by the excessive use of fasting, saunas and often smoking) to achieve the weight that horse trainer believes is optimum for his or her thoroughbred?

Doping is harmful

The coercion argument is itself related to a more general justification of doping bans (and *mutatis mutandis* other allegedly unethical practices that are made impermissible by the rules), that of preventing harm to athletes. Doping substances, it is claimed, are harmful to the athletes concerned. Now, as I noted above, while there is a fair degree of consensus that some doping substances and processes are harmful, not all banned substances are harmful or at least not necessarily harmful. Might blood doping under medical conditions provide such a model (though certainly a more respectful version of the East German doping scandals of the 1970s and 1980s)?[3]

Even if it were true that doping products and substances were harmful we would again have to field questions as to why we should feel bad faith and not countenance the ranges of harms associated with doping, as opposed to our benign acceptance of other sports where harm is intrinsic to the activity or where it is statistically associated with it to a significant degree? Contrast the magnitude of harm that has been caused by elite athletes who dope with the panoply of boxers who engage in their sport in legitimate ways but endure in their careers, and long afterwards, seriously debilitating injuries. What about the deaths from equestrian sports, of horse and rider alike? What about the number of paraplegics whose disability has been caused from forceful contact with the ground and with other players in rugby and American football? Less dramatically, what about the legion of football players around the world with arthritic ankles, hips and knees? How do we honestly discount the magnitude of harm here?

As with the range of other practices that might be thought impermissible in the discussion on coercion, we find ourselves confronted with the question: 'what are the limits on "paternalistic interference" in sport?' Finding a satisfactory answer to this question ought properly to precede banning doping it might reasonably be objected.

Doping confers an unfair advantage

Perhaps the most commonly discussed criterion in support of banning doping has been the argument that it represents an unfair advantage to those who undergo it. Let us assume that the bans are based on the efficacy of the substances and processes so included. In this way we can set aside the fact that advantage does accrue to the doped athlete. The standard position against the unfairness argument is the sceptical one of inconsistency: unfair advantages abound in sport, why worry about pharmacological ones. Examples spring readily to mind. What should we say of athletes born in high altitude who develop greater oxygen carrying capacities? What about those born in wealthier nations who can rely on sophisticated technological systems support? What about teams that are sponsored by multinational companies or billionaire sugar-daddies compared to relatively impoverished opponents?

Perhaps the most problematical of all of the unfairness arguments concern our ready acceptance of those whose excellence is a direct product of genetic lottery? It is through no extra merit, nor is it fair, that I or you benefit from a wonderful genetic pool. To take this to its limit consider the case of Eero Mäntyranta and Miguel Indurain[4] both of whom were born with physical abnormalities that contributed directly to their athletic excellence. Eero Mäntyranta, the Finnish Olympic skier in the 1960, 1964 and 1968 Olympic Games won three golds, two silver and two bronze medals and won a very similar tally in the World Championships during that time. He clearly was a phenomenal skier.[5] Undoubtedly, part of his quite exceptional ability is based upon a biomedical abnormality. Mäntyranta was born with unnaturally high levels of haemoglobin because of a mutation in the ethrypoetin (EPO) receptor gene which allowed for more sustained maximal performance, discovered during familial genetic screening (de la Chapelle, *et al.*, 1993). Second, there is the case of Miguel Indurain, the five times winner of the Tour de France:

At the top of his career, Miguel Indurain had a physique that was not only abnormal when compared to statistically derived norms from the general population, but also when compared to his fellow athletes. His blood circulation had the ability to circulate 7 litres of oxygen around his body per minute, compared to the average amount of 3–4 litres of an ordinary person and the 5–6 litres of his fellow riders. Also, Indurain's lung capacity was 8 litres, compared to an average of 6 litres. In addition, Indurain's resting pulse was as low as 29 bpm, compared to a normal human's 60–80 bpm, which meant his heart would be less strained in the tough mountain stages. His VO2 max was 88 ml/kg/min; in comparison, Lance Armstrong's was 82 ml/kg/min.

(Wikipedia, 2007)

The sports world at large concerns itself with procedural fairness so that during competition athletes and teams share the same test. But unfairness prior to the contest abounds. Why worry about doping then?

I shall proceed now to one argument I think more robust in defence of the bans and two virtue-ethical considerations that support the anti-doping position.

Doping and slippery slopes

One argument, not to my knowledge explored in the copious literature on the ethics of doping, is the idea that permitting the banned substances and products that comprise doping, would be that they would lead us down a slippery slope. While one may think that this argument is straightforward enough, that we just need to go and apply it so to speak, I want to hold back. Understanding slippery slope arguments is not quite so straightforward and it is worth charting their varied conceptual geography carefully before applying them to the issue of doping.

Schauer offers the following essentialist analysis of slippery slope arguments. A 'pure' slippery slope is one where a 'particular act, seemingly innocuous when taken in isolation, may yet lead to a future host of similar but increasingly pernicious events' (1985: 361–2). Abortion and euthanasia are classic candidates for slippery slope arguments in public discussion and policy making. Against this, however, there is no reason to suppose that the future events (acts or policies) down the slope need to display similarities – indeed one might propose that they led to a whole range of different, though equally un-wished for, consequences. The vast array of proposed enhancements by those who would have no pharmacological or other technical restraints might not be captured under this conception of a slippery slope because of their heterogeneity.[6]

The excessive breadth principle can be subsumed under the latter of Bernard Williams' pair of slippery slopes distinguished thus: (1) horrible result and (2) arbitrary result slippery slope arguments. According to

Williams, the nature of the bottom of the slope enables us to determine which category a particular argument falls under. Clearly, the commonest form is the slippery slope to a horrible result argument. Walton (1992) goes further in distinguishing three types of horrible result slippery slopes: (1) thin end of the wedge or precedent arguments; (2) Sorites arguments; (3) domino effect arguments. I shall illustrate each of these arguments in relation to doping and anti-doping arguments.

In (1), the thin end of the wedge slippery slopes, allowing anabolic steroids (for example) will set a precedent that will allow further precedents (Pn) taken us to an (unspecified) problematic terminus. Is it necessary that the end point has to be bad? Of course this is its typical linguistic meaning of the phrase 'slippery slopes'. Nevertheless, one might turn the tables here and argue that the slopes might be viewed positively too (see Schubert, 2004). Perhaps a new phrase will be required to capture ineluctable slides (ascents?) to such end points. This would be somewhat analogous to the ideas of vicious/virtuous cycles. So it might be argued that the use of anabolic steroids, EPO, human growth hormone and other banned doping substances may well allow elite athletes to fulfil their Olympian dreams. *Citius, Altius, Fortius* the motto goes: faster, higher, stronger. It can present for some a legitimisation of the pursuit of limitless growth in human powers and excellences.

In (2), the Sorites idea of slippery slopes, the inability to draw clear distinctions has the effect that allowing P will not enable us to consistently deny Pn and so on. This argument has many instantiations in the literature: one allows performance enhancement by nutritional supplements, how can these rationally be distinguished? Altitude training is permitted, so hyperbaric chambers that simulate this effect cannot be banned, and if hyperbaric chambers are allowed then . . . and so on and so forth. This slope follows the form of the Sorites Paradox where taking a grain of sand from a heap does not prevent our recognising or describing the heap as such even though it is not identical with its former state.

At the heart of the problem with such arguments is the idea of conceptual vagueness. Those who wish to advocate a radically liberal stance in relation to doping might well seize upon this vagueness and apply a Sorites argument as follows: since therapeutic interventions are currently morally permissible, and there is no clear distinction between therapy and enhancement, enhancement interventions are morally permissible too. Can we really distinguish categorically between the added functionality of certain prosthetic devices and other forms of biotechnological enhancement, they might well ask? In the case of Oscar Pistorius, the champion disability athlete, the IAAF has ruled that he is precisely afforded such an advantage over an able bodied athlete. Pistorius who had both legs amputated early on in life has achieved 400m times well in excess of his competitors and sought to compete with able bodied opponents in Championship races but has been disallowed for the reason, it is alleged, that his stride length has been altered by the technology offering him an unfair advantage.[7]

In (3), the domino conception of the slippery slope, we have what others often refer to as a causal slippery slope (see, for example, Den Hartogh, 2005). Once P is allowed a causal chain will be effected allowing Pn and so on to follow, which will precipitate increasingly bad consequences.

In what ways can slippery slope arguments be used against the pro-doping lobby? Is there really an end point, a horrible result we can point to, of which we can say doping is ethically indefensible? One particular strategy adopted by proponents of doping falls clearly under the aspect of the thin end of the wedge conception of the slippery slope. While some aspects of their movement might be aimed at therapeutic effects that are undoubted goods, how would we feel if the very same lobby were to argue thereafter that there were just too many broken bones in (say) American Football (because of the new and heightened powers of their athletes) and so it was proposed that key skeletal structures such as the hip or the knee were enhanced by new construction materials such as Kevlar. And if we were to accept this would we maintain a principled position in which we could still with logical ethical authority deny the possibility of greater than 20: 20 vision for golfers or archers (despite Tiger Woods electing for such laser surgery in 2006), or artificially extended toes to lever the sprinter with reinforced feet arches to dampen the effects of the new levels of friction their legs could generate. Here pro-dopers and their typically libertarian supporters stroll half-asleep into the territory of enhancement that Kass (1997) has labelled 'repugnant'.

One strategy, therefore, to consider is the use of a therapeutically driven argument that prizes open the door with the thinnest of (morally defensible) wedges, which in principle cannot be distinguished from successive practices that we collectively feel repugnance at. While we all may recognise the repugnance, we appear to have no logical basis in denying the coherence of the first revision, and ineluctably, the later repugnant ones. I wonder how many are prepared to used therapeutic justifications to shield the more Promethean aims, less explicitly advertised. Examples of this manoeuvre can be found in medical ethics. Take for the purposes of illustration the Cognitive Enhancement Research Institute in California. Prominently on its website front page (http: //www.ceri.com/) it reads 'Do you know somebody with Alzheimer's Disease? Click to see the latest research breakthrough.' The mode is simple: therapy by front entrance, enhancement by the back door. Borgmann (1984: 36), in his discussion of the uses of technology in modern society, observed precisely this argumentative strategy more than 20 years ago:

> The main goal of these programs seems to be the domination of nature. But we must be more precise. The desire to dominate does not just spring from a lust of power, from sheer human imperialism. It is from the start connected with the aim of liberating humanity from disease, hunger, and toil and enriching life with learning, art and athletics.

Who could want to deny the powers of viral diseases that could be genetically treated? Might one want to draw the line at the transplantation of non-human capacities (sonar pathfinding)?, *in vivo* fibre optic communications backbone or anti-degeneration powers? (These would have to be non-human *ex hypothesi*.)

Nevertheless, one cannot determinately point to a precise station at which one can say 'here, this is the end we said things would naturally progress to if we allowed all and any doping'. But does this pose a problem? Well, it certainly makes it difficult to specify exactly a 'horrible result' that is supposed to be at the bottom of the slope. Equally, it makes it extremely difficult to say that if we allow precedent X it will allow practices Y or Z to follow since it is not clear how these later practices are (if at all) connected with the precedent. So it is not clear that a form of precedent setting slippery slope could be strictly used in every case against pro-dopers though it may be applicable in some.

Consider in this light, a Sorites-type slippery slope that might be used to support the lifting of doping bans. The pro-doper would have to show how the relationship between the therapeutic practices and the enhancements are indeed transitive. Or they might have to argue that the boundaries between the natural and artificial cannot be drawn sufficiently clearly since certain accepted technologies are so commonplace, such as glasses, hearing aids, prosthetic devices, vaccinations to boost the immune system and so on.

In response to this manoeuvre, which has much to recommend it, we might look first to some conceptual objections. The first was raised in relation to the natural argument. We know night from day, or orange from red, without being able to specify precisely we move from one to the other. So simply because one cannot determine a precise distinction between (say) genetic or pharmacological therapies T1, T2, T3 and enhancements E1, E2, E3 and so on, it does not follow that there are no important moral distinctions between T1 and E20. As Williams (1985) notes this kind of indeterminacy arises because of the conceptual vagueness of certain terms. Yet, the indeterminacy of so open a predicate 'heap' is not equally true of 'therapy' or 'enhancement'. The latitude they allow is not nearly as wide as this.

Instead of objecting to Pn on the grounds that Pn is morally objectionable (i.e. to depict a horrible result) one might instead, after Williams, object that the slide from P to Pn is simply morally arbitrary where it ought not to be. Here one can say, without specifying a horrible result that it would be difficult to know what, in principle, could ever be objected to. And this is, quite literally, what is troublesome. Still, the sports-libertarian might argue, 'what is wrong with arbitrariness?' Let us take one brief example. There are aspects of our lives where, as a widely shared intuition, we might think that in the absence of good reasons we ought not to discriminate among people arbitrarily. Healthcare might be considered precisely one such case. Given the ever-increasing demand for public healthcare services and products it could be argued that access to them ought typically to be governed by publicly disputable criteria such as clinical need, or potential benefit, as opposed to individual choices of an arbitrary or subjective nature.

And nothing in the pro-doping, or more broadly the pro-enhancement, position seems to allow for such objective dispute let alone prioritisation. Who does not rightly applaud advances in therapeutic medical technologies such as those from new genetically based organ regeneration to more familiar prosthetic devices? Here the ends of the interventions are clearly medically defined and the means regulated closely. This is what prevents the libertarian dopers from adopting a Sorites-type slippery slope. Where does it end though? I suggest that in the absence of a defensible *telos*, over and above the mindless mantra of more medals, more glory (the narrowly conceived *Citius, Altius, Fortius*[8]) of clearly and substantively specified ends (beyond the banner of unrestrained 'enhancement'), elite athletes, their coaches and their sports medical back-up teams alike ought to resist the potentially open-ended transformations of human nature and potentialities. For if all transformations are in principle to count as 'enhancements' then surely nothing is to count as enhancement. The very purpose of the word would fall into disuse. Thus it seems one strong argument against the pro-doping lobby generally – the arbitrary slippery slope – presents a challenge to them to show that all of what they describe as enhancements are indeed imbued with positive normative force and not merely the technological extensions of libertarianism whose conception of the good is merely an extension of individual choice and consumption.

An aretaic account of anti-doping

I have tried to show thus far that some standard arguments in favour of banning doping are either incoherent or lacking in consistency of application. I have also tried to show how we might understand slippery slopes arguments for, but in the final analysis against, doping and limitless enhancement. What might be said about a virtue-ethical account of doping and anti-doping? Well, I believe an aretaic account of what is wrong with doping and those who wish to liberalise doping products and processes will get to the heart of the matter.

The rational argument about horrible and arbitrary result slippery slopes may not convince philosophers or social scientists who think that athletes should be allowed to use any performance enhancements or indeed those athletes who wish to dope and not face sanctions or even expulsion from competition. But to limit rational argument to discussion of the rightness or wrongness of the act itself is to fail to consider the character of the doping cheat. Moreover, in aretaic ethics it is thought crucial to consider the living of good lives as an amalgam of thought, feeling and action within a relatively well-settled form of dispositions. Conceiving respect for fellow athletes is one thing, feeling it another. And virtuous action should be holistic in this regard. So we may attend not merely to what athletes think about doping, but what also they characteristically feel in relation to other athletes and their selves, which emotions are salient and why.

It is of course true that there may be many vices that attend doped athletes. Let us remind ourselves of the application of the Doctrine of the Mean, which has heuristic value even if it cannot be pressed into the service of all choices as an explanatory framework. What should we say of the praiseworthiness or culpability of the doped athlete's character? Some of these might just be a deficient – their desire to be the greatest is unhindered by reference to any rules that govern the sport. Or they may fail to feel the demands of justice; that their opponent ought to enjoy an equality of opportunity to compete and win as they do. At the other extreme, doped athletes might be thought of as vicious in their excess; the desire to emulate previous heroes may have become so strong that one becomes blinded to the demands of fair sporting competition. I want to expand, by way of example rather than by an exhaustive argument, upon two such vices that are both defects of deficiency in character; the deficiency or absence of justice that is operative (*pleonexia*) in doped athletes and the similar defect in those who have not, or not sufficient, of the quasi virtue shame (*aidos*).

The vice of *pleonexia*

In his discussion of justice as a virtue Aristotle argues that *pleonexia* is the vice that attends all acts of injustice. I shall not argue for or against that general position though I accept Williams' (1980) critique of its over-ambitious application. I am more interested in its particular application to the case of the doping cheat. First, it is typical for philosophers to distinguish two dimensions of justice: the distributional (who gets what, where, when and why) and the rectificatory (following injustice how is the matter rectified properly). Moreover, Aristotle distinguishes justice as a moral concern with 'particular justice', which is one among the virtues and related only to certain kinds of goods. In the MacIntyrean scheme we can call these external goods. Aristotle conceives of these goods as 'divisible' because as they are divided so it is the case that as one gets a portion so another cannot. MacIntyre refers to this characteristic as 'exclusivity'. They are thus typically the object of competition. With some leeway in interpretation we can think of *pleonexia* as a vice in relation to particular goods where one wants more of them, or wants more than others, or simply as greed.

As I noted in Chapter 6 on racism, it is important to follow Aristotle in distinguishing unjust acts from unjust characters. Is doping typically an act of ignorance? I shall take it that it is not. We must distinguish between an athlete who is the subject of doping in some passive sense such as the young East German athletes who were force fed illicit pharmacological enhancement under the deceit that they were nutritional supplements (Spitzer, 2006). Equally, I have considerable sympathy for the 17-year-old Romanian gymnast, Andreea Raducan, at the Sydney 2000 Olympics who took 'painkillers' on the advice of the team doctor. Subsequent tests showed that they had contained 'pseudoephedrine' a banned substance and under the strict liability ruling of doping she was expelled from the competition. Unusually, it might be thought, because the urine test showed only positive after the all-round competition Raducan was allowed to keep her medals from the floor and the vaulting competition. Perhaps this judgement displays at least some sensitivity to both distributive and rectificatory justice. Yet this irony displays the distinction: it was not suggested that Raducan's motivation was vicious merely that prior to the performance in the all-round competition an illicit substance had been found in her body and she was strictly liable for that action. It makes every sense from this perspective to say that Raducan had fallen foul of doping laws but was not herself a doping cheat.

The doping cheat is another type of character altogether. In my discussion of emotions I distinguished the episodic from those which endure over time. So too it is necessary to distinguish, as in Chapter 6, between an act that is something of a one-off, or one that has under certain conditions revealed itself, from one that is more universal and therefore thought to form part of the character of the sportsperson; that is, one which is dispositional. We can say, thus, what the doping cheat lacks and what he or she displays. He or she lacks a clear sense of justice for it is constitutive of the virtue of justice that one is habitually disposed to think, feel and judge some courses of action as just and therefore noble, while feeling revulsion at others and having the courage to resist their allures. Now the unjust person may be motivated in many ways that are not relevant to our discussion; in many different ways they may simply not care about achieving a just outcome. But the systematic nature of doping cheats – the fact that they must arrange with the help of others, the dosages of supplements, their timing, an understanding of when the active pharmaceutical agent will persist in the body and be detectable, or the duration of time they must avoid an out-of-competition test, or the other substances they must use to mask the doping substance or process – points to a systematic deception.

What is it that the doped athlete seeks to achieve? How and why should we describe him or her as pleonectic? For our purposes I want to suggest that the pleonectic doper is the one who wants not merely more, for that would simply indicate the disposition of greed. For the greedy, enough is never enough. Sparshott (1994: 188) refers to this as logically insatiable greed. It is an imperialising vice and not merely a one-off passion (Sparshott, 1994). Yet, in describing the doping cheat as pleonetic, I want to stress the connection of injustice to his or her avarice; crucially the doped athlete wants more than he or she is due. The deficit is one of not caring for justice precisely so that he or she may improperly gain the external, divisible, goods: wealth, sponsorship, fame, even honour in the form of being listed in the record books. It is to desire, avariciously, that which he or she has no right to. It is tantamount to covetousness. Williams (1980) situates one aspect of pleonexia in the heart and soul of Achilles. He wants glory and he wants it so that no one else may share it. This, it strikes me, is at least one important aspect of what the pleonectic doping cheat wants. The athlete with the vice of *pleonexia* does not simply want enough, or what is their proper reward, they want more and more than others irrespective of whether they are entitled to it by their commitment, dedication, talent, in short, not by merit.

The quasi virtue of *aidos* (or the vice of shamelessness)

In what way ought we think of shamefulness as a virtue? It is an odd idea. What has the virtuous sportsperson to feel ashamed of? On the one hand it is typical to think of modern individualistic cultures as cultures of guilt (G. Taylor, 1985). The wrongness of action is internalised to a feeling; an interiorisation of culpability and remorse for the wrong doing; for breaking a rule, or standard, or norm. Shame, it is typically said, is not so much transgression as failure and more public than private. So, as the standard account goes,[9] shame cultures are predicated on social norms such as honour. Failing to live up to the social demands that roles place upon us, we feel, when socialised into the culture, shame. We hide our face.

Why should we want to cultivate shamefulness in our athletes? Put that way, the requirement could be thought of as a perversion of an ethics of sports. Put another way, the question makes more sense: why should we wish to cultivate the capacity to feel shame? This seems much more promising. Imagine the contrary position. In contemporary elite athletics, for example, getting caught doping might be seen as little more than an occupational hazard. Charlie Francis said of Ben Johnson, that if he had simply stuck to the schedule – knowing when to come off certain drugs and doses, knowing when to apply masking agents to prevent the identification of doping substances – he would not have been caught. This manner of approaching the problem is technicist: a mere problem of timing, not one of ethics. For those who have not been taught the power of moral opprobrium, and here I am at least as much thinking of Francis as I am of Johnson, the fear of shame is not present. The fear of excommunication from the athletic community either does not register, or registers so weakly that it can be ignored. Even if felt, power diminishes in the sight of potential glory and wealth.

Shame, of course, is a powerful social regulator. When we appreciate the power of shame, of its capacity to separate us from the group, to alienate us from the communities that shape our very identities, it can indeed perform a powerful preventative function. And, we all will exhibit moral failings from time to time. Some more than others. And most, perhaps, in face of incredible rewards that are the province of some, though not all, elite sports.

Williams (1993: 87) offers a discussion of shame in Sophocles' play *Philoctetes*, which is analogous to our present concern. The cunning Odysseus is attempting to persuade Neoptolemus into a deceitful act against Philoctetes. In his sophistic strategy Odysseus appeals to Neoptolemus's virtue while at the same time attempting to assuage the power of pre-emptive shame which would prevent him from stooping low:

I know, my boy, that you are not of a nature
To say such things or use a low trick;
but it is pleasant to lay hold of victory,
so be bold

Neoptolemus's first response is what we would hope all our elite athletes would mouth:

MyLord,
I prefer to fail nobly rather than to win shabbily.

Before we cheer at his courage and the habituation of *aidos* the power of Odysseus's sophistry wins out. True to tragic Greek heroic form, he is persuaded by what he thinks is the potential glory:

All right, I'll do it, and put the shame aside.
(All cited in Williams, 1993: 87)

In this vein, but with more apparent virtue, the journalist Dag Vidar interviewed Ådne Søndrål, former Olympic skating champion and IOC member for Norway, who said that "[g]etting caught doping is the second worst crime a Norwegian can commit. In my opinion only child abuse disgusts people more. Doping is high treason against the nation." This seems to overplay the matter considerably. It should be said that the Danish scholar, Ask Vest Christiansen has said that Danish cyclists have also expressed that shame is a powerful disincentive to doping.[10] Whether this is something in a broader Scandinavian sports psyche, or the product of smaller nations with more homogeneous cultures who have always celebrated health and sports together I cannot say. On the one hand we can say that, in some cases then reports of the death of shame have been exaggerated, so to speak. Before we chide the weak-willed doper, however, there is also a word of caution about the would-be cheat. As Stewart (1892) remarks: 'If one takes credit for being ashamed, one palliates the action one is ashamed of, and is more likely to repeat it' (cited in Sparshott, 1994: 392).

It is equally true that shame has a corrosive aspect when its standards are unjustifiable. One has to only think of examples of the hegemonic force of Victorian England with its complex social codes which, among other things, prevented women even using a bicycle for fear 'it would transport them to prostitution' (Hargreaves, 1994). Equally, one thinks of honour codes in groups such as American University student fraternities or even the South African police force in the apartheid era, which, in the name of solidarity and allegiance to the group, fostered violence against women and people of colour through a large proportion of the twentieth century.

What do *pleonexia* and *aidos* point to in terms of the ethics of sport? Well, we are drawn back to the familiar pedagogical ground of Aristotle and the formation of habits: of patterns of feeling, perception, thought and action that comprise the good sportspersons and good sporting lives. Unless children are taught the import of the values of sport how will they come to feel that shame is to be avoided; how will they know what is within their reach and what beyond it; where they stand in the pantheon of mediocrity and excellence?

Here the idea of role modelling is utterly critical. One of the finest ever sports journalists, Hugh MacIlvanney, once had occasion to chastise the French footballer Thierry Henry for his tactics of "diving" (or 'simulation' in FIFA speak), a practice that has more than a family resemblance to the doping cheats. Now Henry is one of the most elegant players it has ever been my pleasure to watch on a football field. And more than that, he is regarded highly for his social responsibility outside of the game. To see him deceitfully gain a penalty kick is a sad thing indeed. Shakespeare had it just right:

> The summer's flower is to the summer sweet
> Though too itself it only live and die,
> But if that flower with base infection meet,
> The basest weed outbraves his dignity:
> For sweetest things turn sourest by their deeds:
> Lillies that fester, smell far worse than weeds.
>
> (Booth, 2000: Sonnet XCIV)

It is true, and many find unreasonable, that we hold elite sportspersons to a higher level of account than teachers or politicians. It is not only the fact of the matter that we do this but good that we do it too. Where else, in the modern age, do the masses see the morality play played out? That is the price we pay for the diminished moral resources of modernity just as it is the price the individual sportsperson pays for the grotesquely high salaries they command.

To attend to the emulative responsibilities of elite sportspersons and other virtuous considerations, is properly to be initiated into sport. This is a critical matter, as pressing as it is ancient. Often it is stories that teach us the limits. Often it is appreciation for the best standards of sporting excellence conceived of as ethically valuable practices and not mere arenas for physical excellence and the spectacles of *Citius, Altius, Fortius*; always it is about role models – exemplars of the best in us and of us. How much time is spent perfecting the forehand topspin, the head position in the sprint start, the protection of the basketball in the lay up, the perfect tuck in the somersault, the ideal timing of a hip throw? How little time perfecting ourselves; considering the appropriateness of the aims, ideals and purposes to which we strive.

Conclusion

In this chapter, I began with a consideration of the myth of Gyges' ring, I utilised some slippery slope arguments and I pointed to an illustrative example of the aretaic vocabulary that could help us understand motives for doping and anti-doping alike. At least part of what Gyges' ring teaches us, is that when people do not feel that they will be held responsible for their actions they may go to any and all lengths to achieve their (often unreflective) goals. They feel there is no power greater than their selves. They feel, perhaps, that they can bask in a glory that is not properly theirs yet feel neither ambiguity nor shame. Shame may have a chequered history, but we'd better not throw the baby out with the bath water. The shameless feel no standards beyond their own will. Character conversions are not so common outside of religion and myth, we had better attend to the cultivation of virtue and vice-aversion while these considerations have a grip on the maturing psyche of the young sportsperson.

11 Whose Prometheus?

Transhumanism, biotechnology and the moral topography of sports medicine

Introduction

The rise of sports medicine to the apex of sports science is something that I believe has not been commented upon. There are hierarchies within hierarchies. Sports medicine sits over sports science, which sits in panoramic ascendancy over what I take to be the humanities of sport: history, literature, philosophy and theology. I wish, against that hegemony, to challenge some of the more self-aggrandising possibilities of sports medicine in the final chapter of this book.

The most recent incarnation of the Promethean myth is the image of 'genetically modified athletes'.[1] Recognising limits is not, however, a prominent feature of modern medicine. Indeed it is sometimes extremely unclear where medicine begins and other social practices such as social care, welfare or education begin.[2] If, however, this conceptual inflation spreads horizontally it effects a process widely referred to as the medicalisation of everyday life. It is not the sheer spread of medicine that concerns me here, but rather its vertical ambition in transforming our very nature as humans and its impact upon our understanding of human virtue and vice.

In a recent book, the American conservative bioethicist Leon Kass has written, somewhat polemically, that

> human nature itself lies on the operating table, ready for alteration, for eugenic and neuropsychic 'enhancement', for wholesale design. In leading laboratories, academic and industrial, new creators are confidently amassing their powers, while on the street their evangelists are zealously prophesying a posthuman future.
>
> (Kass, 2002: 4)

It is against this evangelising and self-promoting backdrop that I wish to problematise the unfettered application of science and technology to the sphere of sports medicine. To do this I wish first to note elements of science derived from the English philosopher, politician and polymath, Sir Francis Bacon, from the sixteenth and seventeenth centuries, which survive and in some sense shape the hubris of modern biomedical science. Second, I wish to challenge the assumptions of transhumanism, an ideology that seeks to complete the merely 'half-baked' project of human nature (Boström, 2004). In response, I sketch out two interpretations of the myth of Promethus in Hesiod and Aeschylus that can help us see aright the moral limits of sports medicine. I conclude with a banal reminder: we are mortal beings. Our vulnerability to injury, disease and death, far from something we can overcome or eliminate, represents natural limits both for morality and medicine generally and sports medicine in particular.

Baconian science, biomedical technology and the perfection of the body

Though the Ancient Greeks and, more generally, artists throughout history have had a deep and significant aesthetic respect for the perfection of human form, the obsession with physical perfectionism arises as a moral imperative, as sociologists of the body have noted, with the increasing pervasiveness of modern technology (Shilling, 2005). In the writings of Bacon, and also Descartes, the rise of experimental philosophy (bringing together the rational and the empirical) found canonical expression in medical science. The allusion to the Baconian ideal itself belongs to Hans Jonas, whose railing against the hubris of medical technology prefigured much work in the fields of medical ethics and medical theology. Jonas wrote, as early as 1974, regarding the potential pitfalls of 'biological engineering'. Slightly less rhetorically than Kass, he argued:

> The biological control of man, especially genetic control, raises ethically questions of a wholly new kind for which neither previous praxis nor previous thought has prepared us. Since no less than the nature and image of man are at issue, prudence itself becomes our first ethical duty, and hypothetical reasoning our first responsibility.
>
> (Jonas, 1974: 141)

It will be clear that the presence of Greek myths, which raise in our imagination the proper limits of the human, cast a shadow of doubt on the uniqueness of the controlling aspects of modern biology or genetics. And despite offering two contrasting lenses with which to view biotechnology, my own posture is marked by a precautionary stance. Moreover, I will claim in the final section that there is no need for the generation of a new ethic. I claim, rather, that the moral sources for such evaluations as the proper ends of medicine and sports medicine are with us now and have been since at least the time of Plato. As Williams (1993) observed: there is no need to revive these sources since they are not dead.

It is noteworthy that the foundational drive for medical technologies in particular is one that fits with a very traditional conception of medicine as a healing art or as in the relief of suffering.

Of course the relief of suffering is a noble end associated with medicine traditionally conceived (Cassell, 1991; Edwards and McNamee, 2006; Porter, 2002). But that is neither the object of my concern nor typically those of sports medics associated with elite sports. The idea is captured brilliantly in Gerald McKenny's excellent book on bioethics, technology and the body: *To Relieve the Human Condition* (1997). It is as if the fulfilment of science's quest for domination of nature was itself to culminate in overcoming *human* nature. Now, of course, the denial or denigration of human nature is not new: early behaviouristic psychology often included a claim that human nature was no more than a myth or a hangover from a pre-scientific age, and this ideology was given further impetus in the sociobiological movements of the 1980s. Nevertheless, modern science takes the body as an object in nature, capable of precise observation and minute description. The uses of science extend not merely to intervening in, but also to re-envisioning, the body. The rise of medical technology, however, opens entire new vistas for medicine as a social practice.

Technology in medicine and sports

It is easy to think of technology as a modern social practice and to assume a particular kind of technology (such as computer technology) to represent a paradigmatic example. Nye (2006) ties technology to tool making but reminds us of the narratives in which our appreciation of those tools are rested. For example:

> In Herman Melville's *Moby Dick*, Queequeg, a South Sea harpooner visiting Nantucket, was offered a wheelbarrow to move his belongings from an inn to the dock. But he did not understand how it worked, and so, after putting all his gear into the wheel barrow he lifted it on to his shoulders. Most travellers have done something that looked equally silly to the natives, for we are all unfamiliar with some local technologies. This is another way of saying that we do not know the many routines and small narratives that underlie everyday life in other societies.
>
> (Nye, 2006: 6)

This commonplace example is a reminder of the importance of locating our views of technology historically but also brings to mind a less manipulative conception than the kind which those opposed to radical biotechnologies conjure up as counter examples. The term 'technology' has a venerable past. It derives from the conjoining of two Greek words *techne* and *logos*. *Techne* which refers to the kind of skill (practical knowledge) involved in making things. By *logos* is meant a form of reasoning aimed at understanding the nature or form of things. Although we think of the term as a modern one, it was in fact first coined by Aristotle (Mitcham, 1979) but his meaning for it was the technical skills of rhetoric; literally the *techne* of *logos* (Kass, 2002).

It is not uncommon, however, in everyday talk to slide the concept of science together with the concept of technology. Indeed, in the UK at least, sports scientists very often conflate their activities with what should properly be called sports technology.[3] Today philosophers of science clearly distinguish theory generation (science) and its application (technology), though the distinction is rather lost in the natural scientific study of sport. We could imagine then, that the domains of medical and sports technology might simply be taken to include the theoretical knowledge, practical knowledge, and the instruments and products that bring about the ends of medicine or sports respectively. If this were acceptable then their salient characteristic would be a 'means–end' structure. Technology might be thought of as the means utilised to pursue chosen ends. It would appear to follow then that technology is, in a sense, neutral. It is neither good nor bad *in itself*. Rather, its normativity is typically governed by the uses to which it is put. An example of this conceptualisation is found in the recent literature on philosophy of technology:

> Technology in its most robust sense . . . involves the *invention, development, and cognitive deployment of tools and other artifacts, brought to bear on raw materials . . . with a view to the resolution of perceived problems* . . . which, together, allow [society] to continue to function and flourish.
>
> (Hickman, 2001: 12)

An equally sympathetic account is to be found in the UN Convention on Biological Diversity (Article 2: Use of Terms) where biotechnology is defined thus:

> Biotechnology means any technological application that uses biological systems, living organisms, or derivatives thereof, to make or modify products or processes for specific use.
>
> (Wikipedia, 2006)

Less authoritatively, and even more broadly, biotechnology can also be commonsensically defined thus: 'Biotechnology is the manipulation of organisms to do practical things and to provide useful products' (Wikipedia, 2006). While such global definitions are useful as a starting point, it is important to note that they fail to distinguish ethically important characteristics of different forms of practice that fall under the headings 'technology' or 'biotechnology'.

By contrast, then, a stronger line of criticism is found especially in continental European writers who have made problematic the assumption that technology is itself a neutral means to chosen (good or bad) ends. Mitcham (1995) gives an account of this history of technological scepticism in medicine and Kapp (1877), Desauer (1927), Ortega y Gasset (1939) and Heidegger

(1977) also note more fundamental criticisms of technology as ideology where, far from being the hand-maiden of man, technology comes full circle to be his master (Foucault 1988; Habermas 1968; Marcuse 1964). Although not as radical in her writings as these latter philosophers, Lee (2003) helpfully marks the following distinction in the application of science in the form of technology whose goals are: (1) explanation; (2) prediction; and (3) control. It is the last of these aims that I want to pick up on in relation to any ethical evaluation of technologies. Nye, a historian of technology, arrives (far too swiftly for my liking) at a softer conclusion about the relations between technology and human kind. He writes: 'Stonehenge suggests the truth of Walter Benjamin's example that "technology is not the mastery of nature but of the relations between nature and man."' (2006: 7). Nevertheless, we find more classical sources that are to be interpreted less generously. Francis Bacon (1562–1626) is well known for his remarks (2000) on the development of scientific and technological methods whose aim would be 'to relieve man's estate' (i.e. of suffering/vulnerability) and likewise René Descartes (1596–1650) had wanted 'to use this knowledge [. . .] for all the purposes for which it is appropriate, and thus make ourselves, as it were, the lords and masters of nature' (2003). Of course, as C. S. Lewis pointed out in his essay, *The Abolition of Man* (1943), every time we hear the phrase 'mastery of nature' we ought to be alerted to the fact that it is some particular group that is doing the mastering for its own reasons and in light of its own version of the good, rather than the good of humanity (whatever that might look like).

Again, Lee distinguishes the types of control thus: (1) Weak: avoid the occurrence; and (2) Strong: prevent the occurrence. And the facets comprising weak or strong technological control of nature (or for my present concerns 'human nature') range from theoretical knowledge, through practical knowledge and skills, to instruments and products. Notwithstanding these cautionary considerations, I will consider biotechnology and sports technology respectively to refer to those technologies deployed to meet the ends or goals of sports medicine or sports respectively. What forms, more specifically, might this technology take? The most obvious uses by sports scientists and sports medics might be instrumentation such as hypoxic chambers (to assist the fastest recovery times for soft tissue and bone injuries[4]); gas analysers (to measure anaerobic contributions to exercise); and isokinetic strength testers or 'bod-pods' (to assess body density). Finally, the scourge of sports, many would say, fall into the category of 'technological products'. Most obvious here might be anabolic steroids, or other doping supplements such as EPO or human growth hormone. Nevertheless, it is important to note that these products are often designed, as Borgmann (1984) pointedly remarked, with medical therapies in mind. It is their use in elite sports population that is problematic, not the nature of the products themselves.

What I want to do now is to step back a little from a discussion of the enhancement mantra that governs elite sports and some sections of what is called sports medicine and consider a broader, and to my mind more problematic, application of biotechnology to enhance human nature. It is an ideology that falls under the label 'transhumanism' (TH).[5] Rather than a unified entity, TH is a broad and heterogeneous group of thinkers who give technology a grander, Promethean, aim.

What (good) is transhumanism?

A range of views fall under the label of TH.[6] The most extreme is a view according to which TH is a project to overcome the inherent limitations of human nature. Examples of these limits, which most of us take for granted as part of the human condition, are appearance, life-span, vulnerability to ageing, disease and so on. There is, however, a more extreme version of TH that sees the role of technology as one to vastly enhance both the person and his or her environment by exploiting a range of technologies including genetic engineering, cybernetics, computation and nanotechnology.

Recruitment of these various types of technology, it is hoped, will produce selves who are intelligent, immortal, etc. but who are not members of the species *Homo sapiens*. Their species type will be ambiguous, e.g. if they are cyborgs (part human, part machine). If they turn out to be wholly machines, they will lack any common genetic features with human beings. Extreme THs strongly support such developments. Less extreme THs are satisfied to augment human nature with technology where possible and where desired by the individual.

At present TH seems to command support mostly in North America, though there are some adherents from Europe (see the website of the World Transhumanism Association (WTA)). On one level it can be seen as an extension of neoliberal or libertarian thought transferred into biomedical contexts. This is because the main driver appears to be the valorisation of autonomy as expressed in economic choices of individuals. If certain technological developments enable greater defences against senescence, or if they can significantly enhance my powers of thought, speed, movement, then (as competent consumers) TH argue that anyone should be allowed to obtain them – if they can afford them of course. Sandberg attempts to give an ethical underpinning to this essentially political programme. He argues that we must consider 'morphological freedom as a right' (Sandberg, 2001).

Before TH is considered to be the product of outlandish free-thinkers who have enjoyed too much certain medico-technological products themselves, we must consider that it embodies two aims that are widely thought to be valued in the West. These are: (1) the use of technology to improve the lot of humans – work in public health, e.g. construction of sewage systems, fluoride additives to water supplies to prevent dental decay, and so on, is all work to facilitate this noble end that is shared with the entire medical enterprise; and (2) the other widely shared value is that of increased autonomy such that the individual has greater scope in governing his own life-plan.

Moreover, proponents of TH say it presents an opportunity to plan the future development of human beings, the species *Homo sapiens*. Instead of this being left to the evolutionary process and its exploitation of random mutations, TH presents a hitherto unavailable option, tailoring the development of human beings to an ideal blueprint. Typically educational, social and political reformers have been unable to carry forward their project with the kind of control and deficiency (it is said) that biologically driven technologies can.

Against transhumanism

One can ascribe to Ellul a certain prescience: without knowledge of ideologies such as TH he pointed out in 1965 that the development of technology will lead to a 'new dismembering and a complete reconstitution of the human being so that he can at least become the objective (and also the total object) of techniques' (1965: 431). One possible consequence that can be read into the grander claims of some THs is that, in effect, TH will lead to the existence of two distinct types of being, the human and the posthuman. The former are most likely to be viewed as some kind of underclass.

It is worth pursuing this argument a little. It is said that 'we' have a 'self-understanding' as human beings. This includes, for example, our essential vulnerability to disease, ageing and death. Parens (1995), in reversing the title of Nussbaum's celebrated book, captured this idea memorably when speaking of the 'goodness of fragility'. Suppose, however, that the strong TH project is realised. We are no longer so vulnerable, immortality is a real prospect. This will result in a change in our 'self-understanding'. This will have a normative element to it, most radically this may take the form of a change in what we view as a good life. Hitherto such a life would have been assumed to be finite, but now this might change.

Habermas' (2003) objection can be interpreted more or less strongly. The strongest one is that *any* change in self-understanding is a morally bad thing. But this move is not a defensible one. Consider the changes in self-understanding that have occurred over the centuries, the advent of Christianity or Islam, the intellectual revolutions that followed Copernicus and Darwin. It does not follow necessarily that any particular change in self-understanding logically entails moral decline. There are many who would advocate that this constitutes not decline but, rather, moral progress.

There are, to my mind, more telling and less abstract arguments that can be marshalled effectively against TH. These concern, in the first place, a simple argument against inequality. The second relates to the unarticulated ends of TH. What is its *telos*? What do we enhance and why? Let us consider, albeit briefly, the first consideration.

Rather than considering two species of humanities, we might (perhaps crudely) consider the two categories of economics: the rich and the poor. The former can afford to make use of TH whilst the latter will not be able to.

Given the commercialisation of elite sports one can see both the attractions (for some) and the dangers here. Mere mortals – the unenhanced poor – will get no more than a glimpse of the transhuman in competitive elite sports contexts. Note the double-binding character of this consumerism. The poor, at once removed from the possibility of choosing augmentation, end up paying for the privilege on a per-per-view basis. The weak thus pay the strong for the pleasure of their envy. By contrast, one might see less corrosive aspects of this economically driven argument. Far from being worried about it, it might be said, TH is an irrelevance, since so few will be able to make use of the technological developments even if they ever manifest themselves.

Still further, critics point out that TH rests upon some conception of the good. As seen, for one group of THs, the good is expansion of personal choice. But some critics object to what they see as consumerism of this kind. They suggest that the good cannot be equated with what people choose. With regard to the other kind of THs, those who see TH as an opportunity to enhance the general quality of life for humans, critics point out that this again presupposes some conception of the good, of what kind of traits are best to engineer into humans (disease-resistance, memory enhancement, high-speed intelligence etc.), and they disagree about precisely what 'objective goods' to try to select for installation into humans/posthumans. A further and stronger, though more abstract, objection is voiced by Habermas. It is that interfering with the process of human conception, and by implication human constitution, that deprives humans of the 'naturalness which so far has been a part of the taken-for-granted background of our self-understanding as a species' and '[g]etting used to having human life at the biotechnologically enabled disposal of our contingent preferences cannot help but change our normative self-understanding' (2003: 72). And will those TH agents (athletes and non-athletes alike), genetically and technologically modified to their autonomous heart's content, ever escape from being the objects of never ending resentment?[7]

We have seen then that there are a variety of arguments for and against TH. It will be clear that I am neither in favour of the radical nor the apparently moderate versions. It seems clear to me at least, that the project is an undesirable utopianism. We have enough problems with the human nature we struggle with let alone another nature that we neither control nor understand anywhere near as fully. It strikes me that the platitude that what is needed is nicer people not brighter ones is apposite. Perhaps that is why it is a platitude. At its heart, it seems to me, is a view of technology at the mercy of scientists generally (or in the case of athletic powers: sports *'medics'*), which is simply a case of Prometheanism. This charge is often labelled against genetic and other technologists without proper explanation. And it strikes me that the charge is not properly understood. In order that to move beyond mere slogans or name-calling, then, I shall offer two contrasting lenses through which these claims may be viewed by returning to the roots of the Promethean myth itself.

Whose Prometheus: Hesiod or Aeschylus?

In order to understand the charge of Prometheanism one might begin by asking 'What is the myth of Prometheus?' I think the better question is 'whose myth of Prometheus should we concern ourselves with?' I take my cue both from Conacher's (1980) account and also from Kerenyi's (1963) though I do not attempt fully to do justice to their theses here.[8] I merely use them for my own purpose of providing lenses to view the unrestrained enhancement ideology of TH, which it seems to me can find an easy footing in the unreflective pools of sports medicine and sports sciences more generally.

First, let us say that there is no single Greek account of Prometheus' deeds. There are at least two sources and even among these sources there are variations. The two sources, in chronology, are Hesiod and Aeschylus. In Hesiod there are two accounts: *Theogeny* and *Works and Days*. And the only full text from Aeschylus is *Prometheus Bound* though we know it to be part of a trilogy (*Prometheus Unbound, Prometheus the Firebringer*).

Theogeny is Hesiod's account of the beginning of the world. The Titans (giants) challenged Zeus and the Olympian gods for the supremacy of the world. *Works and Days* is said to be a similar account but one which celebrates the ideas that labour is the universal lot of mankind but that those willing so to do can get by. This is important to appreciate in order to evaluate the act for which Prometheus became (in)famous. Prometheus, acting against his fellow Titans, sided with Zeus and his cunning brought about the victory over the latter by the former. In consequence he was honoured by Zeus and seems to have some kind of dual nature: both God and mortal. Sometimes the two are simplistically dichotomised: Zeus as power, Prometheus as cunning reason or intellect (Conacher, 1980).

Prometheus is said to have stolen fire and to have cheated the gods out of their proper share of a sacrifice. Which came first is not always clear as there are different interpretations. But both acts, according to Kerenyi, evidence the claim that Prometheus is of deficient character. He writes:

> Prometheus, founder of the sacrifice, was a cheat and a thief: those traits are at the bottom of all the stories that deal with him. The meaning of his strange sacrifice in which the gods were cheated out of the tasty morsels is simply this: that the sacrifice offered up by men is a sacrifice of foolhardy thieves, stealers of the divinity round about them – for the world of nature that surrounds them is divine – whose temerity brings immeasurable and unforeseen misfortune upon them.
>
> (Kerenyi, 1963: xxii)

A little amplification is in order. Both Prometheus (often translated as 'foresight') and his inept brother Epimetheus (sometimes translated as 'aftersight') set out on Zeus' orders to fashion creatures to populate the Earth. Lacking wisdom (or 'foresight') Epimetheus fails to consider what qualities are necessary as he goes about making the 'animal kingdom'. Prometheus fashions mortals in the vision of the gods. Epimetheus having used all his gifts from Zeus has failed to clothe them and Prometheus watches pitifully as they shiver in the cold nights. It is here that, rebelling against Zeus' authority, Prometheus sides with mankind, and steals fire – hidden in a fennel stalk. The mortals are thus warmed.

In order to appease and honour Zeus, Prometheus reveals his disrespectful cunning. He offers him a sacrificial ox. In one half he hides the bones with a rich layering of fat which appears on the surface to be the greater and more desirable share. Under the entrails of the animal he hides in the other skin all the good meat. Zeus, apparently understanding the deception as part of the unchanging fate of mankind, accepts the lesser share.

By way of punishing Prometheus and all mortals, he withheld fire from mortals.[9] The hubris of Prometheus in particular though is captured by his punishment: he is to be chained to a tree on Mount Caucasus where an eagle will eat at his liver all day only for it to be replenished overnight for the cycle of suffering and humiliation to continue the next day and so on.

In Aeschylus we get a different interpretation of events, one that is at once more sympathetic to Prometheus. First, there is a more optimistic conception of 'human initiative' (Conacher, 1980: 13). A further aspect of this is in the fact that hope is hidden from men in Hesiod ('fortunately' it is said in Hesiod, or rather 'for their sakes') whereas in Aeschylus it is one of the gifts from Prometheus. As Conacher puts it:

> To put the point in the broadest possible terms, the Hesiodic Prometheus, by his deceptions and frustrations of Zeus in his relations with man, is presented (however 'artificially') as the indirect cause of all man's woes; the Aeschylean Prometheus, on the other hand, by his interventions on behalf of man, is presented as the saviour of mankind, without whom man would have ceased to exist and with whose help he progresses from mere subsistence to a state of civilization.
>
> (1980: 13)

Aeschylus does this by suppressing the sacrifice deception and transforms the fire-stealing act as one of daring rather than hubris. For without the deception there is no occasion for the withholding of fire, which is the consequent punishment. For fire is seen not merely as the warmth that forestalls the chill of the night but – more importantly – as the precondition of craft, trade, even civilization. But what has all this got to do with TH generally, and sports medicine more specifically?

A moral topography for sports medicine

In the rise of psychiatry, much was made of the scientism that bedevilled the then emerging profession. Disputes raged as to whether there could be

such a thing as mental illness (akin to physical illness) or whether this constituted the imposition of normative patterns of thought and action by state
powers. The more pharmacologically inclined argued that mental illness did
indeed exist but that its basis was chemical not political. Others took it to be
a case of the medicalisation of everyday life. In all of this Thomas Szasz was
(and still remains) a trenchant critic. Like Kass, Szasz has been charged with
providing powerful polemic more than patient argument. Notwithstanding
this, he once crafted the following, memorable, remark: 'Formerly, when religion was strong and science weak, men mistook magic for medicine; now,
when science is strong and religion weak, men mistake medicine for magic'
(1973: 115).

This juxtaposition of religion, magic and science is a troublesome one for
the public, no less than gullible and overcommitted athletes, who appear to
lack any kind of moral framework within which to evaluate their Herculean
efforts. Like many highly paid athletes, the models of professionalism for
sports physicians are too often dominated by Koehn's (1993) models of
expert or service-provider for fee. The hired hand goes out to the highest
bidder. But the loss of dedication to the traditional aims of medicine, let alone
the Hippocractic Oath, is palpable.

The main concern that TH raises for sports is the following, rather general,
concern: 'How are we to evaluate the enhancement agenda?' It is clear that
there are strong advocates such as Miah who want to extend autonomous
choice by athletes in ways that may easily open the door for unprincipled biomedical and sports scientists. Equally clearly there will be traditionalists,
myself included, who find the unfettered use of technology to augment
human nature utterly repellent.

One way forward is to establish better spaces of dialogue between opposing camps in order to establish what Taylor (1989) calls 'moral topography'.
I take this to be a loose application of what he had in mind in his articulation
of the moral sources of modern identity. Moral topography in sports medicine might be about drawing out the conceptual relief, and the natural and
artificial of the work of scientists therein. I use moral topography as a
metaphor for teasing out what I take to be the 'traditional' work of medicine
in the relief of suffering and the more recent (and artificial) goal of performance enhancement or the augmentation of natural abilities as opposed to the
traditional therapeutic role of medicine. This may help develop critical but
informed attitudes to, for example, the new genetic technologies that are
likely to invade elite sports over the next decade and that threaten to make
arcane the worries over steroids, EPO or human growth hormone.

Yet, in contrast to Miah (2004), and to Jonas (1974) and Kass (2002)
before him, the new biology and biotechnology or indeed the new genetics
need not require us to rethink a new ethics *ab initio*. The sources for the evaluation of medical and sports technology were revealed long ago in the
Ancient Greek writings of Plato. The historian of medicine, Edelstein (1967)
notes the Ancient Greek philosopher's task of undermining the glorification

of the body. And building upon his insight McKenny (1997) noted Plato's observations, considering the education of the Guardians so that medicine may serve rather than hinder or dominate our moral projects. In this vein we too should ask: how much attention should we devote to our bodies in the effort to optimise our capacities?; how much control should we allow physicians to exercise over our bodies?; what ends should determine what counts as a sufficiently healthy body?; what limits should we observe in our efforts to improve our bodily performance and remove causes of suffering? In short, what kinds of life shall we lead and what kinds of persons shall we become?

Elite sportsmen and women, their coaches, sports national governing bodies and no less even than sports promoters and institutions such as the IOC, the IAAF, FIFA, all have an interest in surpassing limits. Athletes are deemed to have failed if they do not 'peak' at big events breaking their own personal best times, and heights, and distances. World records must tumble at every event it seems. At this macro-level, enhanced performances are wrapped up in celebratory spectacles primarily to sell media and marketing packages. And the circus rolls on to the next event, the next town. This denial of the necessity of limits in nature by some, the desire to remove or delay their onset in the shape of disease, or burnout-syndrome, and to control these human-limiting factors by the unfettered use of biotechnology is something that should concern us all in sports. I submit that philosophers of both sport and medicine begin to press such questions of character and conduct, of ends as well as means, in the public spaces of the media as well as the gymnasium and the university so that sports do not become the vanguard of Hesiod's Promethean character and the unmooring of ethical ends.[10]

Notes

1 What is this thing called sport?

1 Phonetically pronounced: clan-ur-tid (with apologies to my Welsh-speaking friends!).
2 The conceptual core of each of these concepts is so diffuse and contested that they have often been referred to, after Gallie, as 'essentially contested concepts'. This term of art was used to depict concepts whose core meaning was contested. It seems clear to me, and as I hope to draw out in this chapter, there are enough persisting characteristics of sport that allow us to understand the concept typically even if a certain vagueness persists at its edges. That is to say, despite the many accounts of the concept of sport that exist, I see no reason to think of the concept as an essentially contested one.
3 Suits' original essay 'What is a game?' was published in 1967 and became the cornerstone of his later (1978) book *The Grasshopper: Games, Life and Utopia*. I shall comment on his account below but do not attempt to do full justice to his rich and subtle account laid out there, nor in subsequent revisions collected as an appendix in the (2005) second edition. See instead McFee (2003b).
4 Instead see Kyle (2007: 23–53) on pre-Greek athletic cultures and art notably in Mesoptamia.
5 Though in a very limited manner: £40 ($60 US dollars), a silver trophy and a hand-held computer courtesy of the sponsors.
6 See Young (1984) for a particularly sharp destruction of the myth of amateur athletic nobility in Ancient Greece.

2 Sports, persons and sportspersonship

1 This is, of course, not to say that the possibility does not exist. In one of his thought experiments Glover writes:

> Suppose we construct a robot whose 'brain' functions just like ours, although it consists of a silicon chip, Its exterior, as in science fiction films, is metallic, But, unlike any present robots, its behaviour passes any test for consciousness that we do. It does not just play chess, but appears also to read novels, fall in love, daydream and enjoy jokes. It can take part in sophisticated conversation about whether its present feeling is shame or embarrassment.
>
> Should we say that the robot really has experiences, or just that it behaves as though it does? Its behaviour gives us more evidence in favour of its consciousness than we have in the case of cats or monkeys. Against this, there is the

argument that since it is not alive it is not conscious. But perhaps restricting consciousness to things not made of the same sort of stuff as us is just a prejudice.
(Glover, 1988: 86).

2 See instead Miah (2004).
3 The most important works, for our purposes, written by Taylor between the
period 1971–84 are collected together in two volumes: C. Taylor (1985a) and
(1985b). All page references are taken from the above and not the original
sources.
4 See C. Taylor (1985a: 75–6).
5 One corollary of this point was highlighted by early English Utilitarian Jeremy
Bentham who remarked that when deciding whether or not one might harm someone or thing the question is not so much whether they can speak but whether they
can experience pain. See Midgley (1983: 203–51) *Beast and Man: The Roots of
Human Nature*, Chapter 10 'Speech and other excellences'.
6 See C. Taylor (1985a: 60–75).
7 It should be noted that Taylor does account for instances where the subject may
be said to be unaware of remorse without fully being able to articulate what it is
that one has done wrong. In such cases, one may feel an unease about a given scenario or act and only later find oneself, perhaps through the guidance of another,
to realise the proper ethical contours of the emotion.
8 Again, see Midgley (1983: 253–84), especially Chapter 11 ''On being animal as
well as rational'.
9 The notion of strong evaluation is central to Taylor's thesis here and in his later
explication of that theme in *Sources of the Self* (1991).
10 This idea is explored similarly in Kovesi (1972). See especially Chapter 2 on
'Following rules and giving reasons'.
11 This is not meant to imply that persons are *ipso facto* fully conscious of their
motives or emotions at all times.
12 A similar point is made by Williams who reminds us that modernity is partly characterised by the unprecedented degree to which we are reflectively aware of our
actions and that this self-understanding is so basic to many of the institutions of
modern life such as law, medicine or business. It is also one of the reasons why past
forms of life cannot be returned to. As he puts it: 'There is no route back from
reflectiveness' (Williams, 1985: 163–4; see also 2–3 and 156–73). See Rorty
(1976) for a discussion on the theological and legal influences of the development
of the concept of personhood which requires unified location for the attribution
of responsibility.
13 I discuss Radcliffe's personal tragedy in Chapter 9.
14 As it happens England lost the match to Germany (again) on penalties and so the
depths of his anguish were later diffused though not extinguished.
15 For a clear discussion of the notions of, and distinction between, the constitution
and institutions of games see Reddiford (1985: 41–51). However, see in contrast
Mary Midgley's comment: 'Speech is not an institution [. . .] nor is games [. . .] The
word "institution" would be best saved for things which were once instituted and
could at a pinch be disinstituted again without taking the whole human race with
them' (1974: 252). Play and games for Midgley, as for Huizinga and Berne, exist
in the cultures with whom they grew up. They are not optional extras; we need
them. Similarly, one might add to this point Lasch's remark, contrary to what
many people intuitively assert, that '[t]he degradation of sport, then, consists not
in its being taken too seriously but in its trivialization. Games derive their power
from the investment of seemingly trivial activity with serious intent' (Lasch, 1979:
195). I think Midgley and Lasch raise extremely interesting points which have
important implications for a philosophical discussion of the values of play, games

and sport. But I cannot address this issue here. Throughout the book, however, and especially in the next chapter, I shall reserve the term institution for the meaning of bureaucratic organisations that organise, control and often corrupt social practices such as sports.

16 Feitelson's work is cited but not referenced in Sutton-Smith (1974: 121).

17 It should go without saying that none of these remarks should rule out the possibility of disabled persons engaging in able-bodied sports whether adapted or otherwise.

18 To borrow the memorable phrase of my middle-distance Paralympic athlete friend David Howe.

19 Flanagan's article goes further to question in many respects the defensibility of the strong/weak distinction in ways that are not necessary for me to consider here. What I have written accords however with the interpretation that strong/weak evaluation can be translated without loss of meaning as ethical/non-ethical evaluation though I will not engage in any depth of meta-ethical dispute here as to the drawings of those or indeed the moral/ethical boundaries. I say slightly more about the scepticism of Taylor who, along with Alisdair MacIntyre and Bernard Williams, has expressed deep scepticism about the narrowness of modern morality. I take up this issue in relation to the subject of moral development in and through sport in Chapter 4.

20 I once had the dubious pleasure of receiving ski lessons at an Austrian resort. Moderately skilful in contexts where one runs, jumps, swings and throws, I found sliding and gliding all but impossible and immensely frustrating. The ski instructor felt the latter too. 'Stop thinking' he said, 'just do what is natural'. I remonstrated that (1) thinking was a professional hazard and (2) not having grown up on or near any wintry slopes the movement pattern was anything but natural to me despite his effortless élan. He remained unimpressed and I failed to warm to alpine skiing until on a short sabbatical with Sigmund Loland in Oslo, where I was taught with minimal instruction and elegant example, the two or three basic things to focus on. I achieved at least some measure of control over my wayward limbs on ontologically real slippery slopes and a small insight into the beauty of this sports form.

21 Indeed it was a mistake I made when presenting an earlier version of the paper back in 1991 at a Philosophic Society for the Study of Sport (now the International Association for the Philosophy of Sport) that was generously pointed out by Scott Kretchmar. His gentle provocation failed to get me to change my mind as a version of the piece was published (McNamee, 1992). But it seems clear to me now that Flanagan's critique is compelling and I regret not having been aware of it at the time as I do failing to take his advice.

22 Note, I am not saying that this cannot be done for I am persuaded by a lot of what appears in the Dreyfuss brothers account of the similarities of motoric and moral learning. It is just that is not the account Flanagan offers.

23 Or as a colleague remarked to me, tongue in cheek, 'is that *three* concepts: "sports", "person" and "ship"?!'

24 In sports psychology see Bredemeier and Shields (1995), and in philosophy see most recently, Feezel (2005, 83–96). I shall offer an extended critique of the whole program of psychological research in moral development and sports in Chapter 4.

25 For a critical review of which see Kretchmar (2007).

3   Sports as practices

1 See for example Arnold (1992, 1994), Brown (1991), Schneider and Butcher (1993, 1994), Gibson (1993) and Morgan (1994).

2 Later MacIntyre calls these internal goods, goods of excellence (1998) but without adding significantly to the clarity of the idea or ameliorating the charge of opaqueness.

3 A point that Gibson (1993) surprisingly ignores.

4 By which he means that moral attitudes, norms, rules and their like are the equivalent to emotions or feelings, themselves understood as pre- or non-cognitive. It is important for the virtue-ethical account of sport I am developing to note here that this view of emotion is itself a deeply flawed one and to be rejected *tout court*, and not simply by those wishing to develop or sustain a virtue-ethical account.

5 See MacIntyre (1985: 207–47).

6 For a critique of this and related communitarian theories of the situated self see Kymlicka (1989: 47–73).

7 This phrase was adopted in response to some research that suggested, in North America, the average viewer changed channels on his or her television every three minutes suggesting as much the failure to engage with the material as much as the banality of it.

8 Later in the 2004 Athens Olympics the British athlete Paula Radcliffe would suffer under similar heat conditions. I shall discuss her suffering during that race in Chapter 9.

9 See pp. 136–50.

10 One could cite any number of books on the history of sport and/or the Olympic Games. The socio-economic role played by the poets who celebrate heroic deeds in Ancient Greece is precisely part of the institutional logic of that epoch of heroic deeds that is often overlooked. For an extended discussion of the chains of compensation see Kurke (1991).

11 Morgan sets out in the last chapter in his 1994 book to discuss this very problem. He eschews alternative routes that offer solutions to intrapractice deliberations of ends such as are offered by Rawls (overlapping consensus) and Habermas (ideal-speech situations). His positive line draws first from MacIntyre (by using the practice-institution distinction to lever the internal logic of sports from external considerations) and then from Walzer (by implementing the 'liberal art of separation') so that the non-relevant considerations are 'bracketed from the deliberations of sporting communities'. What this amounts to is investing in the ongoing tradition the unavoidability of de facto authority. While this is an appealing move in many ways, it lends itself to a certain purist interpretation of the practice and a necessarily dim one of the institution. The efficacy of this distinction has already been questioned.

12 It is interesting that another of MacIntyre's critics, inspired by Hume, comes to a similar direction by way of distinguishing her own moral champion distinct from Aristotle. Baier writes:

> Virtues are those traits of character, involving both motivation and ability, to which we give approval when we reflect upon them from a point of view that has overcome the "continual contradictions" to which more partial points of view are prone. Hume's ultimate moral question is one about character: the good person is the one of whom the moral judge can say "his company is a satisfaction to me." The one who is "a safe companion, an easy friend, a gentle master, an agreeable husband, or an indulgent father."
>
> (1985: 257)

13 Again, I wish partly to alleviate Morgan from this charge on the basis of his comments, for example, that the leftists' critique often presupposes that the activity has itself no particular logic but is only an empty vessel awaiting institutionalisation of various forms. Morgan acknowledges this though he attributes the ability

of the practice to withstand the various institutional onslaughts to the practice's own awareness of its internal logic. On the one hand, I am not sure what it is for a practice to have such awareness other than through its participants, and, given my questioning of the sharpness of the distinction between sporting practices and institutions, I am not sure why we should not also include those members of the institution who are not entirely deaf and blind to the internal logic of sport.

14 The chess example is borrowed from Kolnai (1966).
15 See, for example, Peters (1966).
16 Following MacIntyre (1985) and Cooper (1975). It should be noted, though, that the *locus classicus* is Aristotle's *Nichomachean Ethics*, Book One (1980).
17 See more generally Taylor (1989: 115–26).
18 Such an idea has a long history of course. The idea captured in the evaluation – social before personal, cooperative before competitive – is to be found also in Green (1907) who writes that a pure notion of the good

> implies interest in an object which is common to all men in the proper sense, in the sense, namely, that there can be no competition for its attainment between man and man; and the only interest that satisfies this condition is the interest, under some form or other, in the perfecting of man or the realization of the powers of the human soul.
>
> (1907: 67)

19 More specifically he argues against the notion of equality of opportunity and its capacity to counteract systematically unjust distribution of goods (Singer, 1993).

4   Sport and ethical development

1 See Hampshire (1983).
2 In contemporary (sport) psychology, researchers refer to personality traits (which are considered quite fixed over time and context), omnibus dispositions (where proneness to act is more malleable) and situationally-specific traits or dispositions.
3 Although Kohlberg (1981) was initially adamant about the strong, if not perfect correlation, between thought and action, his confidence was not borne out by empirical evidence. Kohlberg (1984) and Power *et al.* (1989) attempted to explain the possible reasons for a less than perfect correlation. The idea of personal responsibility and the prevailing moral atmosphere came to be thought of as mediating influences in moral action.
4 Though, as Peters (1974: 303–35) famously observed, ought one not to *care* about duty? And if one agrees with the proposition, one ought immediately to be attuned both to the necessity of certain emotions in the appreciation and execution of one's moral duties (see especially Chapter 8 below).
5 It should be noted that Kohlberg's theory was not a unified matter. He made several revisions to his position but in this section we are merely sketching his theory in order to show its influence in sport psychological research. For more detailed exegesis see Jones and McNamee (2000).
6 What the term is taken to mean precisely is open to alternative accounts. Contrast, for example, D'Agostino (1981) and Loland and McNamee (2000).
7 A phrase I still shudder at.
8 It has been argued, with effect, that the kind of definition commonly used in sport psychological research is itself problematic – failing clearly and adequately to delineate assertion, aggression and violence – as it stands far apart from common linguistic usage and moral philosophical accounts. See Parry (1998).

9 It is clear that the many and various research publications constitute an extremely significant research programme in its totality. In order to find a shorthand for the critique we will simply refer to the corpus of work as Bredemeier and Shields while intending no disrespect to their colleagues. Second, it is extremely important to note that we hold this research in very high regard. This critique of it relates exclusively to philosophical considerations and the methodological implications that flow from the alternative theoretical conceptualisations of ethics, virtue and character that I set out here and elsewhere; see Jones and McNamee (2000) and McNamee and Jones (2000).

10 Within the philosophy of education Charles Bailey (1975) argued in a similar fashion that there was a logical connection between winning and the demonstration of superiority over an opponent. As such he argued that competitive games in particular were incompatible with moral education. For those interested in the psychological development of this point and the differentiation between task and ego-oriented individuals see McNamee *et al.* (2003).

11 Another issue with contemporary models like the one discussed here is that they do not account for reactive, 'in the heat of the moment' aggressive and/or immoral action. In sport contests, there is not always the time to think through the situation and then act in an intentional manner. There is an issue therefore about what is being predicted: one-off behaviours or patterns of responses, acts or agency/character?

12 Again, it is important to remind ourselves that their use of the term 'moral' here is theoretically guided (whether the researchers are aware of it or not) and can be traced specifically to its use in the cognitive development tradition, namely that morality is simply right action in accordance with moral principles. Likewise, morally mature agents are those who consistently and autonomously apply these moral principles. We have already shown that this is not a given, but rather a reflection of theoretical preference for one picture from a highly contested terrain.

13 This criticism might seem particularly harsh. It is important to note, however, that in their excellent, densely researched book *Character Development and Physical Activity*, limited space (Shields and Bredemeiers, 1995: 192–5) is given over to the elaboration of character and the four component virtues that are the object of my critique in the following paragraphs.

14 For suggestions of such positions see Hampshire (1983: 152):

My claim is that morality has its sources in conflict, in the divided soul and between contrary claims, and that there is no rational path that leads from these conflicts to harmony and to an assured solution, and to the normal and natural conclusion.

More generally against the theoretical systematisation of ethics see Clarke and Simpson (1989).

15 I say 'most' since psychoanalytical accounts stand out in the sharpest of contrasts. See for example Wollheim (1984: 197–225) 'The growth of moral sense' and also 'The good self and the bad self' (1993: 39–63).

16 See Guivernau and Duda (2002) for a full account of the empirical support for this point.

17 For an extended discussion of which see MacKinnon (1999: 57–90).

18 Consider the remark, which I owe to Graham McFee, that scientists should on principle treat subjects *as if* they were human beings.

19 The terms of stages ('initial', 'intermediary' and 'final') and more general inspiration are taken from Tobin (1989).

20 See Nussbaum (2001: 174–236).

21 Although the quotation is Nussbaum's, she is setting out an idea from Nancy Chodorow. It is important to note, and not merely contingent, that the philosophers and social scientists most helpful in drawing our attention to the depth and salience of the emotions in ethics are women. Moreover, this maternal aspect is not tied to the female gender in a necessary way, but merely reflects the empirical dominance of women in the care-giving, care-taking, role.

22 I explore this tension in Chapter 5.

23 According to Ryle (1972) we speak better of learning than teaching here. The point is also made by Spiecker (1999) who reminds us that character traits are better thought of as complex multi-track dispositions than simple ones. Other things being equal, glass will smash when we drop it. Persons being much more complex do not simply respond with a given act in relation to any given circumstance when they are in this intermediate stage. Notoriously, with adolescents whose value-structures are in flux, their reactions are not reliable. Equally, responses from those in the final stage of moral development are not simple, triggered, responses. Often it takes a good deal of moral maturity to see the potential clash of interests that are commonly called dilemmas.

5   Codes of conduct and trustworthy coaches

1 See Morgan (1993), Butcher and Schneider (1993) and, more recently, Allison (2005).

2 Koehn (1993), cites Annette Baier's original (1986) essay 'Trust and anti-trust' that appeared in *Ethics*. All references to that essay heretoforward are from the version of it that appears in Baier (1994) *Moral Prejudices; Essays on Ethics*.

3 These points are synthesised and amended from Dawson (1994) and Brackenridge (1994). Whether or not any code can, as Dawson asserts, offer a neutral framework seems to be highly dubious. Time and space, however, does not provide further comment.

4 The *locus classicus* of this view is Kant's *Groundwork of the Metaphysic of Morals* (1953).

5 As set out by Davis (1991).

6 The elegance itself is a little deceptive as many philosophers have noted for Kant since the 'Categorical Imperative' he took to be the cornerstone of his moral system, has not one interpretation but two. In the first instance, by wedding morality and rationality, Kant sets out what is to count as a moral rule. All moral rules, he argued, must be such that we would will all persons to act in accordance with them. It is the second interpretation of the 'Categorical Imperative' I have noted above that urges us never to treat other people as means to our ends, but rather as ends in themselves, since all human agents are worthy of our unconditional respect, because they are moral agents.

7 Any utilitarian would properly object that this negative characterisation, though it fits the utilitarian rule to minimise pain, misses entirely the corresponding rule to maximise happiness or pleasure. It should be clear that the general target here is the deontological one.

8 Since the original essay was published, there have been several revisions yet I have kept the example for its clarity. I assume that it is typical of a good many such rules. Moreover, since writing the original essay the organisation changed its name to Sports Coach UK.

9 For an account of the idea of a moral principle see Schneewind (1983). He articulates three features of a classic moral principle: relative context-freedom, unexceptionability and substantiality. To these he adds a fourth, a foundational or basic feature, which, in combination with the others gives what he calls a 'classical first principal' (1983: 114).

10 An amusing anecdote illuminates the point. I hope it does not offend my feminist friends and colleagues; it ought not. In the smash hit film *Ghostbusters* the fraudulent psychology professor Venkman has gone to see would-be client who has been citing paranormal activity in her flat (the sort of activity a code of conduct might properly comment upon) whereupon he finds her body lain on the bed with another identical figure floating invitingly above her in a provocative fashion. Venkman at first rebuffs 'I make it a rule never to go to bed with more than one person at the same time' (or something very similar) but upon further exhortations gives in with a spurious self-justification 'it's more of a guideline than a rule'!

11 I am grateful to John Lyle for this observation.

12 This is not the place for Wittgensteinian exegesis. See instead Baker and Hacker (1985) and Holtzman and Leich (1981).

13 I note though that Brackenridge (2001) argues that these are not the most important variables that predispose coaches to abuse athletes.

14 See Gambetta (1988).

15 See Chapters 6 to 9 in Baier (1994).

16 As reported by Solomon (1993: 144).

17 Though, for the untrusting, I have elsewhere explored a different and greater range of principles and rules in 'Theoretical limitations in codes of ethical conduct' (1995b).

18 I am very grateful to Graham McFee, Gordon Reddiford and Tony Skillen for their helpful comments.

6   Racism, racist acts and courageous role models

1 Perhaps the best-known advocate for the former is Warren Fraleigh's (1984) *Right Action in Sport*, while the utilitarian case is less popular, Claudio Tamburrini's (2000) *The Hand of God* is the best example of a sustained defence of a utilitarian position in sports ethics.

2 Why, it might be asked, have I indicated the age of Hill? As will become clear, the reference to Hill's age is entirely relevant to the formation of racist attitudes masked as benign humour.

7   Hubris, humility and humiliation: vice and virtue in sporting communities

1 The original focus for this chapter came predominantly from Dixon (1992). Later challenges to and revisions of his thesis are relatively unimportant for my purposes as they pertain to the notion of lop-sided defeats that are not, as I argue later, necessary to understand how weak humiliation may properly be said to be felt by sportspersons. In earlier discussion of blowout victories and defeats, Dixon (1992, 1998, 2000), Feezel (1999) and Hardman *et al.* (1996) appear to favour the idea of a simple continuum between a loss of self-esteem and humiliation (weak or strong). And this fails to capture the grammar of the emotions at hand, though it should be noted that Dixon is more dismissive of the intensity of sports' emotionality than the others. Our sense of who we are and the import we attach to projects such as sports when we are deeply committed to them has an ineradicable social dimension well captured in the phrase 'practice communities'.

2 See instead Bruckhardt (1998: 135–213) and Hatab (1991: 31–42).

3 In older shame cultures the keeping of face, or of holding to the social expectations of one's roles, is central. Yet in individualistic cultures the preservation of autonomy and integrity represent a social/moral terrain that the modernist vocabulary of universal rights is designed to promote and protect. As I have said, certain martial sports are pre-modern in certain aspects of their nature and to that degree

anachronistic. This fact opens up some latitude in terms of the possibility of imposing strong humiliation on an opponent. I am reminded, however, of the case of an elite Japanese Sumo wrestler who was involved in a motorbike accident that was publicised in the national press. So strongly did he feel that he had let down the high expectations of his sport and its code of honor (*budo* is the name given to the warrior ethic) that he offered to withdraw from his club. I am clear then, that much of what I write here is cradled in the history of Western civilisation and that the anachronism may not be felt in Eastern or Latin cultures and the tradition-bound practices that constitute them. It might be argued that my later example of Roberto Duran's over-weening machismo and subsequent humiliation entails a certain Western hegemony. Though I try to make clear why I think this is not the case, I am aware that I am at the very least open to criticism here.

4   Miller is not entirely clear here. One might assume, however, that by shame proper he means something like Aristotle's account of shame as quasi-virtue: a susceptibility to recognise and publicly show one's recognition of a moral transgression. A battery of other concepts such as awkwardness, discomfort, compassion, regret and so on have refined our appreciation of responses to minor wrongdoing. Making a virtue out of a response to wrongdoing might be beyond the bounds of reasonableness for the modern mind yet I shall attempt to carve out such a response in relation to a discussion of the ethics of doping in Chapter 11.

5   I think that this is precisely the position adopted by both Dixon (1992, 1998) and Hardman *et al.* (1996).

6   I am reminded here of Mohammad Ali when he labelled Joe Frazier as an "uncle Tom" before the first of their epic fights. He was not alone in this regard; names of former world champions such as Nasseem Hamed, Chris Eubank and Gene Tunney all trip easily off the tongue in respect of those whose mouths got the better of their manners. It is only fair to note too that Frazier was no saint. In the pre-match media banter, it was Frazier who had called Ali merely a mouthpiece for Islam. He too was made to pay for his mealy-mouthed quip. Ali was scarcely able to occupy the high ground, however, as he taunted Frazier 'nigger', while hitting him in the ensuing contest. Ali's position was that he had no right to invoke such an assault on his integrity – though he would have done well to dwell on the nature of his own racial abuse of Frazier. Not surprisingly, there is still no love lost between the two, nor their daughters who recently slogged it out in a contest more to be remembered for its hype than pugilistic excellence. I have used the male gender here and throughout the essay for no better reason than the boxing world is predominantly a male world even though this is not exclusively the case.

7   I owe this point to Keith Thompson.

8   I am grateful to Cesar Torres who first raised some disquiet about locating Duran within a discourse of Latino machismo. I later benefited from a discussion with Fernando Cervantes about this and have subsequently revised the attribution. The mere historical fact of his Latino background is an accidental and particular aspect of his hubris. I am grateful to both for their advice and correction.

9   Stories are legion of the Russian gymnastics coach Bela Karoly who initiated and sustained regimes of terror in his gymnasia and for whom the strong humiliation of his charges was part of his coaching armoury. But he is only one of many targets who might be singled out. My hunch, for which there is patchy evidence, is that this pattern of domination is not uncommon in sports where children perform at an elite level. See David (2005).

10 In the final chapter, I discuss the hubris of Prometheus in the context of sports medicine and the enhancement agenda that is prevalent in its ethos.

8 *Schadenfreude* in sports: envy, justice and self-esteem

1 I shall attempt a more balanced account of Kant's stance towards the emotions in his own virtue theory here, in contrast to the more one-sided account I gave in the original publication of this essay (McNamee, 2003b) and an earlier article on the emotion of guilt as a response to injury infliction (McNamee, 2002).
2 This is the case of the 1991 translation of the *Metaphysics of Morals*. In a footnote (91n, p. 292) to this very point, however, she notes that in the earlier 1974 translation 'affect' had been preferred to the earlier translation as 'agitation' where as 'passions' were previously labelled 'obsessions'.
3 The point may be put more generally that the emotions come in clusters (Baier, 1990: 4–5). Not surprisingly, Rorty (1988) had earlier put that observation to effect in the context of virtue theory: the virtues, she says, hunt in packs. It seems only a short leap to imagine that the vices too rarely work alone. To support this point, I shall attempt to show below that it is not justice which triggers *schadenfreude*, but envy.
4 Griffiths takes Anthony Kenny's 1963 work *Act, Emotion, Will* to be seminal here. It has found its strongest expression in the work of Robert Solomon but also is a cornerstone of Charles Taylor's theory of human agency and personhood and is central to his celebrated distinction between strong and weak evaluation.
5 It might seem reasonable to suggest that the extent to which this is the case is a hostage to the heterogeneity of emotions. Typically one might think that this propositional element may be more developed according to the complexity and/or nuance of the emotion at hand. When one feels uneasy in the dark one might say one is afraid but unable to articulate the object of the fear. Or think of long-term injured athletes who go through moods of depression without some precisely focused object as their source.
6 Philip Howard identifies *schadenfreude* as one of the black holes in English. One commentator (R. C. Trench, etymologist and author of *English Past and Present* and *On the Study of Words*) celebrates this gap, saying:

What a fearful thing it is that any language should have a word expressive of the pleasure which men feel at the calamities of others; for the existence of the word bears testimony to the existence of the thing. And yet in more than one, such a word is found: in the Greek *epikairekakia*, in the German, *Schadenfreude*.
(Retrieved at http://www.users.bigpond.com/burnside/black_holes.htm)

7 It could be argued that the comic is only a token of a wider class that might issue *Schadenfreude* vis-à-vis the trivial or insignificantly harmful.
8 As cited in Portmann (2000: 33).
9 It will probably be clear that I take my lead here from Nozick (1974: 239–46). As he puts it:

People generally judge themselves by how they fall along the most important dimensions in which they *differ* from others. People do not gain self-esteem from their common human capacities by comparing themselves to animals who lack them. (I'm pretty good; I have an opposable thumb and can speak some language) . . . self-esteem is based on *differentiating characteristics*: that's why it's called *self* esteem.
(1974: 243, emphasis thus)

10 In the introductory section of 'Envy and equality', Rawls (1972: 604) writes:

We are now ready to examine the likelihood of excusable general envy in a well-ordered society. [. . .] Now I assume that the main psychological root of the liability to envy is a lack of self-confidence in our own worth combined with a sense of impotence. [. . .] This hypothesis implies that the least favoured tend to be more envious of the better situation of the more favoured the less secure their self-respect and the greater their feeling that they cannot improve their prospects.

Here, then, we see the further conflation of related concepts, since self-confidence is not a synonym either for self-respect or self-esteem. Interestingly, in the index to Rawls's magnum opus, under 'self-esteem', it actually says, 'see self-respect'.

11 I am indebted to David Sachs' (1981) paper where a more subtle version of the relations between self-respect and self-esteem can be found.

12 The phrase 'education of the emotions' sounds odd here despite its common currency. Do we not better speak of education in and through the emotions?

13 Among the sociological theories of sport, figurational explanations of sport violence centre upon the emotions, but even there surprisingly little, beyond noting the obvious emotions of anger, excitement, and frustration, is to be found. See, for example, Dunning (1999), for a collection of essays by one of the founding fathers (*sic*) of that school of thought.

14 *Othering* is a term of art invented by feminists, I believe, to capture the manner in which non-heterosexuals are pejoratively defined as non-normal as part of a subconscious psychological process of preparing them for maltreatment or at least inequitable treatment.

9   Suffering in and for sport

1 See, however, Loland *et al.* (2005).

2 Of course, the mistake was made by philosophers for centuries so this should not be thought of as a particularly damning criticism.

3 It is worth observing that so many people mistakenly believe that pain is somehow an inescapably private event that, in so far as it happens, can only be accessed and understood by the person in pain. This position was philosophically demolished in part by Ryle's famous attack on Cartesian dualism but also by Wittgenstein's private language argument about the social and learning contexts that demand a non-private reading of these types of experiences.

4 I am grateful to Martin Lipscombe for drawing my attention to this essay.

5 I am grateful to Steve Edwards for sharing with me his thoughts on suffering and also for alerting me to his critique of Cassell's account of suffering *inter alia* with which I am in general agreement. I merely revise his analysis in a minor way in what follows. I note that he refers to Cassell's criteria as the phenomenological and intactness conditions.

6 One might say here that Edwards has not embraced theodicy from the inside. But this is not the place to argue this point.

7 I am mindful that this is 'grist to the mill' of anthropologists of sports medicine such as Howe and Waddington; part of their everyday discourses. Nevertheless, the ideas are typically ignored or pejoratively dismissed by biomedical scientists in sports.

10   Doping: slippery slopes, *pleonexia* and shame

1 Though not all of course. See, for example, Miah (2004) and Savulescu and Foddy (2007).

2 See Simon (2004) for an elaboration of this argument.

3 For an insider account of the full scale of horrors of state-sponsored doping see Spitzer (2006). For an argument that doping under medical supervision would not work in practice, let alone principle, see Holm (2007).

4 I take these examples from an article on the deployment of concepts of normality and abnormality in McNamee (2008).

5 Even with his highly functional abnormality it should still be noted that his success was also partly based on hormonal supplementation before such time as it was banned.

6 Moreover, as Sternglantz (2005) notes, Schauer undermines his case when arguing that greater linguistic precision would undermine the slippery slope and that indirect consequences often bolster slippery slope arguments. It is as if the slippery slopes would cease in a world with greater linguistic precision or when applied only to direct consequences. These views do not find support in the later literature. Schauer does, however, identify three non-slippery slope arguments where the advocate's aim is to (1) show that the bottom of a proposed slope has been arrived at; (2) show that a principle is excessively broad; (3) highlight how granting authority to X will make more likely that an undesirable outcome will be achieved. It is clear that (1) could not properly be called a slippery slope argument in itself, while (2) and (3) often play some role in slippery slope arguments.

7 The ruling, however, is contestable at a number of levels. See Edwards (2008).

8 One might also observe that among the carry-overs from Ancient Greece, this particular motto is embedded in the excesses of Imperial Rome driven the arbitrary expansion of public spectacles. One might imagine Nero standing to proclaim to his fearful but worshipping plebiscite at the games: 'more Christians, more lions, more goring!' More seriously, see Allison' s critique: 'citius, altius, fortius ad absurdum' (2005).

9 Bernard Williams, however, suggests that the typical shame culture guilt culture dichotomy is too crude. See his *Shame and Necessity* (1993: 75–102).

10 The quotation from Hanstad is from personal correspondence 3.9.2007. Christiansen's remarks were made at a conference in response to a paper I gave on anti-doping where I suggested the loss of shame in elite sports was an important factor in doping.

11 Whose Prometheus?: Transhumanism, biotechnology and the moral topography of sports medicine

1 The best known advocate for which is Andy Miah (2004).

2 With respect to health see Brülde (2001).

3 The conflation of terms gets worse than this. In my view a significant portion of what is called 'sports medicine' is not medicine at all, but more commonly sports science or sports technology. See Edwards and McNamee (2006).

4 For a debate on the pros and cons of hypoxic chambers as (il)licit uses of sports medicine see Spriggs (2005) and the collected responses by Fricker (2005), Tamburrini (2005) and Tannsjo (2005).

5 For a fuller account of the nature(s) of TH see McNamee and Edwards (2006).

6 The clearest expositor is Nick Bostrom. See his 2005b 'Transhumanist values'. See also Bostrom (2005a), and contrast with the outline of one of the movement's founding fathers Max More (More, 1996, 2005). For a more detailed summary of the purported features of TH see McNamee and Edwards (2006).

7 As Rollin (2003) remarked of those who in the future might develop, and retain the secrets of, extreme longevity.

8 A short summary of the two accounts, though with no comparison or contrast can be found in Price and Kearns (2004: 453).

9 There is some ambiguity as to whether mortals had fire before. Conacher (1980: 12) is in no doubt that Prometheus stole it back for them, which entails their prior possession of it. I set to one side, here, Hesiod's misogynistic account of the first

punishment intended for Prometheus where Zeus has Hephaestus fashion women from fire (namely Pandora) whose jar (and not 'box' as is commonly thought) contains all the portents for the suffering of mankind.

10 I am grateful to Fritz-Gregor Herrman for his insight and guidance regarding the myths of Prometheus. I am especially grateful to my colleague, Steve Edwards, with whom I have collaborated closely on issues regarding both TH – especially in the light of slippery slope arguments – (McNamee and Edwards, 2006) and also regarding the conceptual relations between medicine and sports medicine (Edwards and McNamee, 2006). This chapter is an off-shoot from those discussions and conferences which was previously presented at a conference in Prague and which was published in an earlier form in Slovenian (McNamee, 2005b) and has been significantly revised.

References

Allison, L. (2005) 'Citius, altius, fortius ad absurdum', in C. Tamburrini and T. Tannsjo (eds) *Genetic Technology and Sports: Ethical Questions*, London: Routledge, pp. 149–57.

Allport, G. (1987) *The Nature of Prejudice*, Reading, MA: Addison-Wesley.

Appiah, K. A. (1996) 'Race, culture, identity', in K. A. Appiah and A. Guttman *Color Conscious*, Princeton, NJ: Princeton University Press.

Aristotle (1980) *Nichomachean Ethics*, Oxford: Oxford University Press (trans. W. D. Ross; updated J. O. Urmson and J. L. Ackrill).

Armon-Jones, C. (1991) *Varieties of Affect*, Toronto: University of Toronto Press.

Arnold, P. (1992) 'Sport as a valued human practice', *Journal of Philosophy of Education*, 26(2): 237–56.

Arnold, P. J. (1994) 'Sport and moral education', *Journal of Moral Education*, 23(1): 75–90.

Åstrand, P. O. and Rodahl, K. (1986) *A Textbook of Work Physiology*, London: McGraw Hill.

Back, L. (1996) *New Ethnicities and Urban Culture*, London: UCL Press.

Bacon, F. (2000) *Novum Organum* (ed. L. Jardine and M. Silverhorne), Cambridge: Cambridge University Press.

Baechler, J. (1992) 'Virtue: its nature, exigency and acquisition', in J. W. Chapman and W. A. Galston (eds) *Nomos*, XXXIV: 25–48 (trans. J. Chapman).

Baier, A. C. (1985) *Postures of the Mind*, London: Methuen.

Baier, A. C. (1986) 'Trust and anti-trust', Ethics, January (96): 231–60.

Baier, A. C. (1990) 'What emotions are about', *Philosophical Perspectives*, 4: 1–29.

Baier, A. C. (1994) *Moral Prejudices: Essays on Ethics*, London: Harvard University Press.

Bailey, C. (1975) 'Games, winning and education', *Cambridge Journal of Education*, 5(1): 40–50.

Baker, G. P. and Hacker, P. M. S. (1980) *Wittgenstein: Understanding and Meaning*, Oxford: Blackwell.

Baker, G. P. and Hacker, P. M. S. (1985) *Wittgenstein: Rules, Grammar and Necessity*, Oxford: Blackwell.

Baker, J. *et al.* (2006) 'Gym users and abuse of prescription drugs', *Journal of the Royal Society of Medicine*, 99: 331–2.

Balibar, E. and Wallerstein, I. (1991) *Race, Nation, Class: Ambiguous Identities*, London: Verso.

Bambrough, R. (1968) 'Universals and family resemblances', in G. Pitcher (ed.) *Wittgenstein*, London: Methuen, pp. 186–204.

Barker, M. (1981) *The New Racism*, London: Junction Books.

Baron, M. (1995) *Kantian Ethics Almost Without Apology*, London: Cornell University Press.

Best, D. (1978) *Philosophy and Human Movement*, London: George, Allen and Unwin.

Blum, L. (2002) *'I'm Not a Racist, But . . .' The Moral Quandary of Race*, Ithaca, NY: Cornell University Press.

Bok, S. (1978) *Lying*, New York: Pantheon Books.

Booth, S. (2000) *Shakespeare's Sonnets*, Yale: Yale University Press.

Borgmann, A. (1984) *Technology and the Character of Everyday Life*, Chicago: University of Chicago Press.

Boström, N. (2004) 'Human genetic enhancements: a transhumanist perspective', *Journal of Value Inquiry*, 37(4): 493–506.

Boström, N. (2005a) 'The fable of the dragon tyrant', *Journal of Medical Ethics*, 31: 231–7.

Boström, N. (2005b) 'Transhumanist values', Online. Available at: http://www.nickbostrom.com/ethics/values.html (accessed 19 May 2005).

Brackenridge, C. (1994) 'Fair play or fair game? Child sexual abuse in sport organisations', *International Review for Sociology of Sport*, 29(3): 287–9.

Brackenridge, C. (2001) *Spoilsports: Understanding and Preventing Sexual Exploitation in Sports*, London: Routledge.

Bredemeier, B. J. (1985) 'Moral reasoning and the perceived legitimacy of intentionally injurious acts', *Journal of Sport Psychology*, 7: 110–24.

Bredemeier, B. J. (1994) 'Children's moral reasoning and their assertive, aggressive and submissive tendencies in sport and daily life', *Journal of Sport and Exercise Psychology*, 16: 1–14.

Bredemeier, B. J. and Shields, D. L. (1984a) 'Divergence in moral reasoning about sports and everyday life', *Sociology of Sport Journal*, 1: 348–57.

Bredemeier, B. J. and Shields, D. L. (1984b) 'The utility of moral stage analysis in the investigation of athletic aggression', *Sociology of Sport Journal*, 1: 138–49.

Bredemeier, B. J. and Shields, D. L. (1986a) 'Athletic aggression: an issue of contextual morality', *Sociology of Sport Journal*, 3: 15–28.

Bredemeier, B. J. and Shields, D. L. (1986b) 'Moral growth among athletes and non–athletes: a comparative analysis', *Journal of Genetic Psychology*, 147: 7–18.

Bredemeier, B. J. and Shields, D. L. (1995) 'Moral assessment in sport psychology', in J. L. Duda (ed.) *Measurement in Sport and Exercise*, Morgantown, WV: FIT, pp. 257–76.

Bredemeier, B. J., Weiss, M., Shields, D. and Cooper, B. (1986) 'The relationship of sport involvement with children's moral reasoning and aggression tendencies', *Journal of Sport Psychology*, 8: 304–18.

Bredemeier, B. J., Weiss, M., Shields, D. and Cooper, B. (1987) 'The relationship between children's legitimacy judgments and their moral reasoning, aggression tendencies and sport involvement', *Sociology of Sport Journal*, 4: 48–60

Brown, W. M. (1991) 'Practices and prudence', *Journal of the Philosophy of Sport*, 17: 71–84.

Bruckhardt, J. (1998) *The Greeks and Greek Civilization*, New York: St Martin's Press (trans S. Stern; ed. O. Murray).

Brülde, B. (2001) 'The goals of medicine: towards a unified theory', *Health Care Analysis*, 9: 1–13.

Butcher, R. and Schneider, A. (1993) 'For the love of the game', *Quest*, 45(4): 460–9.

Caillois, R. (1955) *Man, Play, and Games*, New York: The Free Press of Glencoe.

Carr, D. (1998) 'What moral educational significance has physical education? A question in need of disambiguation', in M. McNamee and S. J. Parry (eds) *Ethics and Sport*, London: Routledge, pp. 119–33.

Carrington, B. and McDonald, I. (2001) 'Whose game is it anyway? Racism in local league cricket', in B. Carrington and I. McDonald (eds) *Race, Sport and British Society*, London: Routledge, pp. 50–69.

Cassell, E. (1991) *The Nature of Suffering*, Oxford: Oxford University Press.

Clarke, S. G. and Simpson, G. (eds) (1989) *Anti-theory in Ethics and Moral Conservatism*, New York: State University of New York Press.

Coakley, J. (2001) *Sport in Society*, 7th edn, Boston: McGraw Hill.

Conacher, D. J. (1980) *Aeschylus' Prometheus Bound*, Toronto; University of Toronto Press.

Connolly, P. (2000) 'Racism and young girls' peer group relations: the experiences of South Asian girls', *Sociology*, 34: 499–519.

Connolly, W. E. (1993) *The Terms of Political Discourse*, 3rd edn, Oxford: Blackwell.

Cooper, R. (1975) *Reason and the Human Good in Aristotle*, Cambridge, MA: Harvard University Press.

D'Agostino, F. (1981) 'The ethos of games', *Journal of the Philosophy of Sport*, VIII: 7–18.

David, P. (2005) *Human Rights in Youth Sport*, London: Routledge.

Davis, N. (1991) 'Contemporary deontology', in P. Singer (ed.) *A Companion to Ethics*, Oxford: Blackwell, pp. 205–18.

Dawson, A. J. (1994) 'Professional codes of practice and ethical conduct', *Journal of Applied Philosophy*, 11(2): 145–54.

de la Chapelle A., Traskelin A. L. and Juvonen E. (1993) 'Truncated erythropoietin receptor causes dominantly inherited benign human erythrocytosis', *Proceedings of the National Academy of Sciences of the USA*, 90(10): 4495–9.

Den Hartogh, G. (2005) 'The slippery slope argument', in H. Kuhse and P. Singer (ed.) *Companion to Bioethics*, Oxford: Blackwell, pp. 280–90.

Desauer, F. (1927) *Philosofie Der Technik*, Bonn: Verlag.

Descartes, R. (2003) *Discourse on Method and Related Writings*, London: Penguin (trans. D. M. Clarke).

Dimeo, P. (2007) *A History of Drug Use in Sport: 1876–1976: Beyond Good and Evil*, London: Routledge.

Dixon, N. (1992) 'On sportsmanship and "running up the score"', *Journal of the Philosophy of Sport*, XIX: 1–13.

Dixon, N. (1998) 'Why losing by a wide margin is not in itself a disgrace: response to Hardman, Fox, McLaughlin and Zimmerman', *Journal of the Philosophy of Sport* XXV: 61–70.

Dixon, N. (2000) 'The inevitability of disappointment: a reply to Feezel', *Journal of the Philosophy of Sport*, XXVII: 93–9.

Dixon, N. (2003) 'Canadian figure skaters, French judges and realist in sports', *Journal of the Philosophy of Sport*, XXX(2): 103–16.

D'Souza, D. (1995) *The End of Racism*, New York: Free Press.

Duda, J. L. (2001) 'Achievement goal research in sport: Pushing the boundaries and clarifying some misunderstandings', in G. C. Roberts (ed.) *Advances in Motivation in Sport and Exercise*, Champaign, IL: Human Kinetics.

Duda, J. L. and Hall, H. K. (2001) 'Achievement goal theory in sport: recent extensions and future directions', in R. Singer, H. Hausenblas and C. Janelle (eds) *Handbook of Sport Psychology*, 2nd edn, New York: John Wiley and Sons, pp. 417–43.

Duda, J. L., Olson, L. K. and Templin, T. J. (1991) 'The relationship of task and ego orientation to sportsmanship attitudes and the perceived legitimacy of injurious acts', *Research Quarterly for Exercise and Sport*, 62(1): 79–87.

Dunning, E. (1999) *Sport Matters*, London: Routledge.

Edelstein, L. (1967) *Ancient Medicine*, Baltimore: John Hopkins University Press (eds O. Temkin and L. Temkin).

Edwards, S. D. (2003) 'Three concepts of suffering', *Medicine, Health Care and Philosophy*, 6: 59–66.

Edwards, S. D. (2008) 'Oscar Pistoris . . . .', *Sport, Ethics and Philosophy*, 2(2) (in press).

Edwards, S. D. and M. J. McNamee (2006) 'Why sports medicine is *not* medicine', *Health Care Analysis*, (14): 103–9.

Eichberg, H. (1990) 'Stronger, funnier, deadlier: track and field on the way to the ritual of the record's in John Marshall Carter and Arnd Krüger (eds) *Ritual and Record: Sports Records and Qualification in Pre-Modern Societies*, New York: Greenwood, pp. 123–34.

Ellington, J. W. (1994) *Immanuel Kant: Ethical Philosophy*, Cambridge: Hackett Publishing Company.

Elliott, R. K. (1974) 'Education, love of one's subject, and the love of truth', *Proceedings of the Philosophy of Education Society of Great Britain*, 8(1): 135–47.

Ellul, J. (1965) *The Technological Society*, London: Cape (trans. J. Wilkinson).

Engstrom, S. and Whiting, J. (1998) *Aristotle, Kant and the Stoics*, Cambridge: Cambridge University Press.

Erikson, E. H. (1964) *Insight and Responsibility*, New York: Norton.

Feezel, R. (1999) 'Sportsmanship and blowouts: baseball and beyond', *Journal of the Philosophy of Sport*, XXVI: 68–78.

Feezel, R. (2005) *Sport and Ethical Reflection*, Chicago: University of Illinois Press.

Flanagan, O. (1991) *Varieties of Moral Personality: Ethics and Psychological Realism*, London: Harvard University Press.

Football Against Racism in Europe (2004) 'Hill backs Big Ron', Online. Available at: http://www.farenet.org/news_article.asp?intNewsID=204 (accessed 12 September 2007).

Foucault, M. (1988) *Technologies of the Self*, London: Tavistock Publications (eds L. H. Martin, H. Gutman, and P. H. Hutton).

Fraleigh, W. P. (1984) *Right Actions in Sport*, Champaign; IL: Human Kinetics.

Frankfurt, H. (1988) *The Importance of What We Care About*, Cambridge: Cambridge University Press.

Fricker, P. (2005) 'Hypoxic air machines: commentary', *Journal of Medical Ethics*, 31: 115.

Fried, C. (1978) *Right and Wrong*, Cambridge, MA: Harvard University Press.

Fry, J. (2002) 'Coaches' accountability for pain and suffering in the athletic body', *Professional Ethics*, 9, (1–2): 5–14.

Gallie, W. B. (1956) 'Essentially contested concepts', *Proceedings of the Aristotelian Society*, LVI: 167–98.

Gambetta, D. (ed.) (1988) *Trust*, Oxford: Blackwell.

Gellner, E. (1967) 'The concept of a story', *Ratio*, 9: 49–67.

Gibson, J. H. (1993) *Performance Versus Results A Critique of Contemporary Values in Sport*, New York: State University of New York Press.

Gilligan, C. (1982) *In a Different Voice*, Cambridge, MA: Harvard University Press.

Gilroy, P. (1987) *There Ain't No Black in the Union Jack*, London: Hutchinson.

Glover, J. (1988) *I: The Philosophy and Psychology of Personal Identity*, London: Penguin.

Gough, R. W. (1998) 'Moral development research in sport and its quest for objectivity', in M. McNamee and S. J. Parry (eds) *Ethics and Sport*, London: Routledge, pp. 135–47.

Green, T. H. (1907) *Prolegomena to Ethics*, 5th edn, Oxford: Clarendon.

Griffiths, P. (1997) *What Emotions Really Are: The Problem of Psychological Categories*, Chicago: University of Chicago Press.

Guillaumin, C. (1972) *L'Ideologie raciste: Genèse et langage actuel*, The Hague: Mouton.

Guivernau, M. and Duda, J. L. (2002) 'Moral atmosphere and athletic aggressive tendencies in young soccer players', *Journal of Moral Education*, 13(1): 67–85.

Guttman, A. (1978) *From Ritual to Record*, New York: Columbia University Press.

Haan, N. (1975) 'Moral reasoning in hypothetical and actual situation of civil disobedience', *Journal of Personality and Social Psychology*, 32: 255–70.

Haan, N. (1978) 'Two moralities in action contexts: relationship to thought, ego regulation, and development', *Journal of Personality and Social Psychology*, 36: 286–305.

Haan, N. (1983) 'An interactional morality of everyday life', in N. Haan *et al.* (eds) *Social Science as Moral Inquiry*, New York: Columbia University Press, pp. 218–50.

Habermas, J. (1968) *Knowledge and Human Interests* (reprinted 1986), Cambridge: Polity.

Habermas, J. (2003) *The Future of Human Nature*, Cambridge: Polity.

Hall, S. (1992) 'New ethnicities', in J. Donald and A. Rattansi (eds) *'Race', Culture and Difference*, London: Sage, pp. 252–9.

Hampshire, S. (1983) *Morality and Conflict*, Oxford: Blackwell.

Hardman, A. *et al.* (1996) 'On sportsmanship and "running up the score": Issues of incompetence and humiliation', *Journal of the Philosophy of Sport*, XXIII: 58–69.

Hargreaves, J. (1994) *Sporting Females: Critical Issues in the History and Sociology of Women's Sports*, London: Routledge.

Harris, E. M. (2007) 'The rule of law in Athenian democracy, reflections on the judicial oath', *Ethics and Politics*, 9(1): 55–74.

Hart, H. L. A. (1955) 'Are there any natural rights', *The Philosophical Review*, 64(2): 175–91.

Hart, H. L. A. (1961) *The Concept of Law*, Oxford: Clarendon.

Hartshorne, H. and May, M. A. (1928) *Studies in the Nature of Character*, New York: Macmillan.

Hatab, L. J. (1991) 'The Greeks and the meaning of athletics', in J. Andre and R. Double (eds) *Rethinking College Athletics*, Philadelphia: Temple University Press, pp. 31–42.

Heidegger, M. (1977) *The Question Concerning Technology and Other Essays*, San Francisco: Harper Row (trans. W. Lovitt).

Herzog, D. (2000) 'Envy', in R. C. Solomon (ed.) *Wicked Pleasures*, Oxford: Rowman and Littlefield, pp. 141–60.

Hickman, L. A. (2001) *Philosophical Tools for Technological Culture: Putting Pragmatism to Work*, Bloomington: Indiana University Press.

Hoberman, J. M. (1988) 'Sport and the technological image of man', in W. J. Morgan and K. V. Meier (eds) *Philosophic Inquiry in Sport*, Champaign: IL: Human Kinetics.

Hoberman, J. M. (2005) *Testosterone Dreams: Rejuvenation, Aphrodisia, Doping*, Berkeley: University of California Press.

Holm, S. (2007) 'Doping under medical control – conceptually possible but impossible in the world of professional sports?', *Sport, Ethics and Philosophy*, 1(2): 135–45.

Holt, R. (1989) *Sport and the British*, Oxford: Clarendon Press.

Holtzman, S. and Leich, C. (eds) (1981) *Wittgenstein: to Follow a Rule*, London: Routledge and Kegan Paul.

Honda, S. (2005) 'Kendo as sport', unpublished PhD disstertation, University of Gloucestershire.

Houlihan, B. (1999) *Dying to Win*, Brussels: Council of Europe Press.

Howe, D. (2004) 'It was not a lapse: Atkinson was up to his neck in football's endemic racism', *New Statesman*, 3 May, Online. Available at: http://www.newstatesman.com/200405030005 (accessed 12 September 2007).

Howe, P. D. (2004) *Sport, Professionalism and Pain*, London: Routledge.

Huizinga, J. (1970) *Homo Ludens: a Study of the Play Element in Culture*, London: Paladin.

Illich, I. (1987) 'Some theological perspectives on pain and suffering: the meaning and management of pain', Institute for Theological Encounter with Science and Technology, Online. Available at: http://itest.slu.edu/dloads/80s/suffer.txt (accessed 13 November 2003).

Inglis, F. (1977) *The Name of the Game*, London: Heinemann.

Jacobs, J. (2001) *Choosing Character: Responsibility for Virtue and Vice*, New York: Cornell University Press.

Jonas, H. (1974) *Philosophical Essays: from Ancient Creed to Technological Man*, Chicago: University of Chicago Press.

Jones, C. and McNamee, M. J. (2000) 'Moral reasoning, moral action and the moral atmosphere of sport: some critical remarks on the limitations of the prevailing paradigm', *Sport, Education and Society*, 5(3): 131–48.

Kant, I. (1953) *Groundwork of the Metaphysic of Morals*, London: Hutchison (trans. H. J. Paton as *The Moral Law*).

Kant, I. (1974) *Anthropology from a Pragmatic Point of View*, The Hague: Nijhoff (trans. M. Gregor).

Kant, I. (1991) *The Metaphysics of Morals*, Cambridge: Cambridge University Press (trans. M. Gregor).

Kapp, F. (1877) *Grundlinien einer Philosophie der Technik*, Braunshcweig: Westermann.

Kass, L. (1997) 'The wisdom of repugnance', *New Republic*, 216: 17–26.

Kass, L. (2002) *Life, Liberty and the Defense of Dignity*, San Francisco: Encounter Books.

Kekes, J. (1989) *Moral Tradition and Individuality*, Princeton, NJ: Princeton University Press.

Kenny, A. J. (1963) *Act, Emotion, Will*, London: Routledge.

Kerenyi, C. (1963) *Prometheus*, Princeton, NJ: Princeton University Press.

Koehn, D. (1993) *The Ground of Professional Ethics*, London: Routledge.

Kohlberg, L. (1981) *Essays on Moral Development. Vol 1. The Philosophy of Moral Development*, San Francisco: Harper and Row.

Kohlberg, L. (1984) *Essays on Moral Development. Vol 2. The Psychology of Moral Development*, San Francisco: Harper and Row.

Kolnai, A. (1966) 'Games and aims', *Proceedings of the Aristotelian Society*, 66: 103–27.

Koukouris, K. (2000) 'An examination of coaches' responsibilities for premature athletic disengagement of elite Greek gymnasts', in M. J. McNamee, C. Jennings and M. Reeves (eds) *Just Leisure: Policy Ethics and Professionalism*, Brighton: LSA Publications No. 71, pp. 211–26.

Kovesi, J. (1972) *Moral Notions*, London: Routledge.

Kretchmar, R. S. (2007) 'Dualisms, dichotomies, and dead ends: limitations of analytic thinking about sport', *Sport, Ethics and Philosophy*, 1(3): 266–80.

Kurke, L. (1991) *The Traffic in Praise: Pindar and the Poetics of Social Economy*, New York: Cornell University Press.

Kyle, D. G. (2007) *Sport and Spectacle in the Ancient World*, Oxford: Blackwell.

Kymlicka, W. (1989) *Liberalism, Community and Culture*, Oxford: Clarendon.

Lasch, C. (1979) *The Culture of Nacissism*, New York: Warner Bros.

Leamon, O. (1988) 'Cheating and fair play in sport', in W. Morgan and K. V. Meier *Philosophic Inquiry in Sport*, Champaign, IL: Human Kinetics, pp. 277–82.

Lee, K. (2003) *Philosophy and Revolutions in Genetics*, London: Palgrave.

Lehman, C. (1981) 'Can cheaters play the game?', *Journal of the Philosophy of Sport*, VIII: 41–6.

Lewis, C. S. (1943) *The Abolition of Man*, Oxford: Oxford University Press.

Llanwrtyd Wells Coming Events (2007) 'Bog snorkelling', Online. Available at: http://llanwrtyd-wells.powys.org.uk/bog.html (accessed 7 June 2007).

Loland, S. (2002) *Fair play: A Moral Norm System*, London: Routledge.

Loland, S. and McNamee, M. J. (2000) 'Fair play and the ethos of sports: an eclectic philosophical framework', *Journal of the Philosophy of Sport*, XXVII: 63–80.

Loland, S. and Murray, T. H. (2007) 'Editorial: the ethics of the use of technologically constructed high-altitude environments to enhance performance in sport', *Scandinavian Journal of Medicine and Science in Sports*, 17: 193–5.

Loland, S., Skirstad, B. and Waddington, I. (eds) (2005) *Sport, Pain and Injury*, London: Routledge.

Long, J. and McNamee, M. J. (2004) 'The moral economy of racism and racist rationalisations in sport', *International Review for the Sociology of Sport*, 39(40): 405–20.

Long, J., Hylton, K., Dart, J. and Welch, M. (2000) *Part of the Game? An Examination of Racism in Grass Roots Football*, London: Kick It Out.

Long, J., Nesti, M., Carrington, B. and Gilson, N. (1997) *Crossing the Boundary: A Study of the Nature and Extent of Racism in Local League Cricket*, Leeds: Leeds Metropolitan University.

McDowell, J. (1981) 'Virtue and reason', in S. H. Holtzman and C. M. Leich (eds) *Wittgenstein: to Follow a Rule*, London: Routledge and Kegan Paul, pp. 332–3.

McFee, G. (2003a) 'Art, essence and Wittgenstein', in S. Davies and A. Sukla (eds) *Art and Essence*, Westport, CT: Praeger, pp. 17–38.

McFee, G. (2003b) *Sports, Rules and Values*, London: Routledge.

MacIntyre, A. C. (1985) *After Virtue*, London: Duckworth.

MacIntyre, A. C. (1998) *Whose Justice, Which Rationality?*, London: Duckworth.

MacIntyre, A. C. (2001) *Dependent Rational Animals*, London: Duckworth.

McKenny, G. P. (1997) *To Relieve the Human Condition*, Albany, NY: State University of New York Press.

Mackinnon, C. (1999) *Character, Virtue Theories and the Vices*, Toronto: Broadview.

McNamee, M. J. (1992) 'Physical education and the development of personhood', *Physical Education Review*, 15(1): 13–28.

McNamee, M. J. (1995a) 'Sporting practices, institutions and virtues: a critique and a restatement', *Journal of Philosophy of Sport*, XXII–XXIII: 61–82.

McNamee, M. J. (1995b) 'Sport, relativism, communality, and essential contestability, in S. Eassom (ed.) *Sport and Value* Bedford: Casper, pp. 86–119.

McNamee, M. J. (1995b) 'Theoretical limitations in codes of ethical conduct', in G. McFee *et al.* (eds) *Leisure Values, Genders, Lifestyles*, Brighton: LSA Publications, pp. 145–55.

McNamee, M. J. (1998) 'Celebrating trust: virtues and rules in the ethical conduct of sports coaches', in M. J. McNamee and S. J. Parry (eds) *Ethics and Sport*, London: Routledge, pp. 148–68.

McNamee, M. J. (2002) 'Hubris, humility and humiliation: vice and virtue in sporting communities', *Journal of the Philosophy of Sport*, 29(1): 38–53.

McNamee, M. J. (2003a) '*Schadenfreude* in sport: envy, justice and self-esteem', *Journal of the Philosophy of Sport*, 30(1): 1–16.

McNamee, M. J. (2003b) 'Is guilt a proper emotional response to the causing of an unintentional injury?', *European Journal of Sport Science*, 2(1): 1–10.

McNamee, M. J. (2005a) 'Suffering in and for sport: some philosophical remarks on a painful emotion', in S. Loland, B. Skirstad and I. Waddington (eds) *Pain and Injury in Sport*, London: Routledge, pp. 229–45.

McNamee, M. J. (2005b) 'Transhumanizem in moralna topografija sportne medicine', *Borec*, 57: 626–9 (translated in Slovenian) .

McNamee, M. J. (2007a) 'Whose Prometheus? Transhumanism, biotechnology and the moral topography of sports medicine', *Sport, Ethics and Philosophy*, 1(2): 181–94.

McNamee, M. J. (2007b) 'Nursing schadenfreude', *Medicine, Health Care and Philosophy*, 10(2): 289–99.

McNamee, M. J. (2008) 'Normality, abnormality and disability sport', *Sport, Ethics and Philosophy*, 2(2) (in press).

McNamee, M. J. and Edwards, S. D. (2006) 'Transhumanism, medical technology, and slippery slopes', *Journal of Medical Ethics*, 32: 513–18.

McNamee, M. J. and Jones, C. (2000) 'Value conflict, fair play, and a sports education worthy of the name', in M. Leicester, *et al.* (eds) *Education, Culture and Values (Vol. 4)*, London: Cassell, pp. 103–11.

McNamee, M. J., Jones, C. R. and Duda, J. L. (2003) 'Ethics, psychology and sports: back to an Aristotelian "Museum of Normalcy"', *International Journal of Sport and Health Science*, 1: 15–29.

McNamee, M. J., Oliver, S. and Wainright, P. (2007) *Research Ethics in Exercise, Health and Sport Sciences*, London: Routledge.

Macpherson, Sir William, of Cluny (1999) 'Report of the Stephen Lawrence Inquiry' (Cm 4262–I, 1999), London: Stationery Office, Online. Available at: http://www.archive.official-documents.co.uk/document/ cm42/4262/4262.htm (accessed 1 April 2004).

Mangan, J. A. (1986) *The Games Ethic and Imperialism*, Harmondsworth: Viking.

Marcuse, H. (1964) *One Dimensional Man*, Boston: Beacon Press.

Margalit, A. (1996) *The Decent Society*, London: Harvard University Press (trans. N. Goldblum).

Massara, A. (2007) 'Stain removal: on race and ethics', *Philosophy and Social Criticism*, 33: 429–528.

Melzack, R. and Torgerson, W. S. (1971) 'On the language of pain', *Anaesthesiology*, 34: 50–9.

Meyerfeld, J. (1999) *Suffering and Moral Responsibility*, Oxford: Oxford University Press.

Miah, A. (2004) *Genetically Modified Athletes*, London: Routledge.

Midgley, M. (1974) 'The game game', *Philosophy*, 49: 231–53.

Midgely, M. (1983) *Beast and Man*, Hassocks: Harvester Press.

Miles, R. (1989) *Racism*, London: Routledge.

Milgram, S. (1964) 'Group pressure and action against a person', *Journal of Abnormal and Social Psychology*, 69: 137–43.

Mill, J. S. (1859) 'On liberty', in M. Warnock (ed.) (1962) *Utilitarianism*, Glasgow: Fontana.

Mill, J. S. (1972) *Utilitarianism* (ed. M. Warnock), London: Fontana.

Miller, S. (1991) *Arete*, Berkeley: University of California Press.

Miller, W. I. (1993) *Humiliation: And Other Essays on Honor, Social Discomfort and Violence*, London: Cornell University Press.

Mitcham, C. (1979) 'Philosophy and the history of technology', in G. Bugliarello and D. B. Doner (eds) *The History and Philosophy of Technology*, London: University of Illinois Press, pp. 2477–84.

Mitcham, C. (1995) 'Philosophy and technology', in W. T Reich (ed.) *Encyclopedia of Bioethics*, London: Simon and Shuster, pp. 2477–84.

Modood, T. (1997) '"Difference", cultural racism and anti-racism', in P. Werbner and T. Modood (eds) *Debating Cultural Hybridity*, London: Zed Books, pp. 154–72.

Monaghan, L. (2001) *Bodybuilding, Drugs and Risk,* London: Routledge.

Montada, L. (1993) 'Understanding oughts by assessing moral reasoning or moral emotions', in G. G. Noam and T. Wren (eds) *The Moral Self*, London: MIT Press, pp. 292–309.

More, M. (1996) 'Transhumanism: towards a futurist philosophy', Online. Available at: http://www.maxmore.com/transhum.htm (accessed 25 September 2007).

More, M. (2005) 'Transhumanism', Online. Available at: http://www.mactonnies.com/trans.html (accessed 13 July 2005).

Morgan, W. J. (1993) 'Amateurism and professionalism as moral languages: in search of a moral image of sport', *Quest*, 45: 470–93.

Morgan, W. J. (1994) *Leftist Theories of Sport*, Chicago: University of Illinois Press.

Morgan, W. J. (1998) 'Multinational sport and literary practices and their communities: the moral salience of cultural narratives', in M. McNamee and J. Parry (eds) *Ethics and Sport*, London: Routledge, pp. 184–204.

Morgan, W. J. (2004) 'Moral antirealism, internalism, and sport', *Journal of the Philosophy of Sport*, XXXI: 61–83.

Nicholson, R. (1987) 'Drugs in sport: a reappraisal', *Institute of Medical Ethics Bulletin*, 7: 1–25.

Nilsson, P. (1993) *Fotbollen och moralen*, Stockholm: HLS Forlage.

Nozick, R. (1974) *Anarchy, State, Utopia*, Oxford: Blackwell.

Nue, J. (2002) *A Tear Is an Intellectual Thing: The Meaning of Emotion*, Oxford: Oxford University Press.

Nussbaum, M. (2001) *Upheavals of Thought: the Intelligence of the Emotions*, Cambridge: Cambridge University Press.

Nye, D. E. (2006) *Technology Matters*, Cambridge, MA: MIT Press.

Ortega y Gasset, J. (1939) 'Man the technician', in *Towards a Philosophy of History*, New York: Norton.

Parekh, B. (1995) 'The concept of national identity', *New Community*, 21: 255–68.

Parens, E. (1995) 'The goodness of fragility: on the prospects of genetic technologies aimed at the enhancement of human capacities', *Kennedy Institute of Ethics Journal*, 5(2): 131–43.

Parry, J. (1998) 'Violence and aggression in contemporary sport', in M. J. McNamee and S. J. Parry (eds) *Ethics and Sport*, London: Routledge.

Peters, R. S. (1966) *Ethics and Education*, London: Routledge and Keegan Paul.

Peters, R. S. (1974) *Psychology and Ethical Development*, London: Allen and Unwin.

Phillip, R. (2004) 'Radcliffe was a sore loser', Online. Available at: http://www.telegraph.co.uk/sport/main.jhtml?xml=/sport/2004/08/25/sorp25.xml (accessed 25 August 2004).

Piaget, J. (1932) *The Moral Judgment of the Child*, London: Routledge and Keegan Paul.

Pincoffs, E. L. (1986) *Quandaries and Virtues: Against Reductivism in Ethics*. Lawrence, KS: Kansas University Press.

Plato (1962) *Phaedrus*, London: Penguin.

Plato (1974) *Republic*, 2nd edn, London: Penguin (trans. D. Lee).

Porter, R. (2002) *Blood and Guts: a Short History of Medicine*, London: Penguin.

Portmann, J. (2000) *When Bad Things Happen to Other People*, London: Routledge.

Power, C., Higgins, A. and Kohlberg, L. (1989) *Lawrence Kohlberg's Approach to Moral Education*, New York: Columbia University Press.

Price, S. and Kearns, E. (2004) *Oxford Dictionary of Classical Myth and Religion*, Oxford: Oxford University Press.

Rawls, J. (1972) *A Theory of Justice*, Oxford: Clarendon Press.

Reddiford, G. (1985) 'Constitutions, institutions and games', *Journal of the Philosophy of Sport*, XII: 41–51.

Reid, H. (2002) *The Philosophical Athlete*, Durham, NC: Carolina Academic Press.

Rest, J. R. (1984) 'The major components of morality', in W. Kurtines and J. Gewirtz (eds) *Morality, Moral Behaviour and Moral Development*, New York: Wiley, pp. 24–40.

Roberts, G. C. (2001) 'Understanding the dynamics of motivation in physical activity: the influence of achievement goals on motivational processes', in G. C. Roberts (ed.) *Advances in Motivation in Sport and Exercise*, Champaign, IL: Human Kinetics, pp. 1–50.

Roberts, R. C. (1988) 'What an emotion is: a sketch', *The Philosophical Review*, XCVII: 183–209.

Roberts, T. (1998) 'Sporting practice protection and vulgar ethnocentricity: why won't Morgan go all the way?', *Journal of the Philosophy of Sport*, XXV: 82–102.

Rollin, B. (2003) 'Telos, value and genetic engineering', in H. W. Baillie and T. K. Casey (eds) *Is Human Nature Obsolete?*, Cambridge, MA: MIT Press, pp. 317–26.

Rorty, A. O. (1976) 'A literary postscript: characters, persons, selves, individuals', in A. O. Rorty (ed.) *The Identities of Persons*, Berkeley: University of California Press.

Rorty, A. O. (1980) *Explaining Emotion*, Berkeley: University of California Press.

Rorty, A. O. (1988) *Mind in Action: Essays in the Philosophy of Mind*, Boston: Beacon Press.

Rorty, A. O. and Wong, D. (1997) 'Aspects of identity and agency', in A. O. Rorty and D. Wong (eds) *Identity, Character and Morality*, Cambridge; MA: MIT Press, pp. 19–36.

Roth, S. and Cohen, L. J. (1986) 'Approach, avoidance, and coping with stress', *American Psychologist*, 41: 813–19.

Russell, J. S. (1999) 'Are rules all an umpire has to work with?', *Journal of the Philosophy of Sport*, XXVI: 27–49.

Russell, J. S. (2004) 'Moral realism in sport', *Journal of the Philosophy of Sport*, XXXI: 142–60.

Ryle, G. (1949) *The Concept of Mind*, London: Hutchinson.

Ryle, G. (1972) 'Can virtue be taught?' in R. F. Dearden, P. H. Hirst and R. S. Peters (eds) *Education and Reason: Part 3 of Education and the Development of Reason*, London: Routldege, pp. 44–57.

Sachs, D. (1981) 'How to distinguish self-respect from self-esteem', *Philosophy and Public Affairs*, 10: 346–60.

Sandberg, A. (2001) 'Morphological Freedom – why we not just want it but need it', paper presented to TransVision 2001 conference, Berlin, Online. Available at: http://www.nada.kth.se/~asa/Texts/MorphologicalFreedom.htm (accessed 5 October 2005).

Sandel, M. (1982) *Liberalism and the Limits of Justice*, Cambridge: Cambridge University Press.

Sansone, D. (1988) *Greek Athletics and the Genesis of Sports*, Berkeley: University of California Press.

Santayana, G. (1894) 'Philosophy on the bleachers', *Harvard Monthly*, XVIII: 181–90.

Savulescu, J. and Foddy, B. (2007) 'Performance enhancement and the spirit of sport: is there good reason to allow doping?' in R. Ashcroft *et al.* (eds) *Principles of Healthcare Ethics*, Chichester: Wiley, pp. 666–70.

Schauer, F. (1985) 'Slippery slopes', *Harvard Law Review*, 1988(99): 361–83.

Schneewind, J. B. (1983) 'Moral principles and moral knowledge', in S. Hauerwas and A. C. MacIntyre (eds) *Revisions: Changing Perspectives in Moral Philosophy*, London: University of Notre Dame Press, pp. 113–26.

Schneider, A. J. and Butcher, R. B. (1993) 'For the love of the game: A philosophical defense of amateurism', *Quest*, 45: 460–9.

Schneider, A. J. and Butcher, R. B. (1994) 'Why Olympic athletes should avoid the use and seek the elimination of performance-enhancing substances and practices from the Olympic Games', *Journal of the Philosophy of Sport*, XX–XXI: 64–81.

Schubert, L. (2004) 'Ethical implications of pharmacogenetics: do slippery slopes matter?', *Bioethics*, 18: 361–78.

Seung, T. K. (1991) 'Virtues and values: a platonic account', *Social Theory and Practice*, 17(2): 207–47.

Sherman, N. (1989) *The Fabric of Character*, Oxford: Clarendon Press.

Sherman, N. (1997) *Making a Necessity of Virtue*, Oxford: Clarendon Press.

Shields, D. L. L. and Bredemeier, B. J. L. (1995) *Character Development and Physical Activity*, Champaign, IL: Human Kinetics.

Shields, D., Gardner, D., Bredemeier, B. and Boström, A. (1995) 'Leadership, Cohesion and team norms regarding cheating and aggression', *Sociology of Sport Journal*, 12: 324–39.

Shilling, C. (2005) *The Body in Culture, Technology and Society*, London: Sage.

Simon, R. (2000) 'Internalism and internal values in sport', *Journal of the Philosophy of Sport*, XXVII: 1–16.

Simon, R. (2004a) *Fair Play*, 2nd edn, Boulder, CO: Westview Press.

Simon, R. (2004b) 'From ethnocentrism to realism: can discourse ethics bridge the gap?', *Journal of the Philosophy of Sport*, XXXI: 122–41.

Singer, P. (1993) *Practical Ethics*, Cambridge: Cambridge University Press.

Skillen, A. (1985) 'Rousseau and the fall of social man', *Philosophy*, 60: 105–22.

Solomon, R. (1976) *The Passions*, New York: Doubleday.

Solomon, R. C. (1993) *Ethics and Excellence: Co-operation and Integrity in Business*, Oxford: Oxford University Press.

Solomon, R. C. (2000) 'Introduction', in R. C. Solomon (ed.) *Wicked Pleasures*, Oxford: Rowman and Littlefield, pp. 1–17.

Solomos, J. and Back, L. (1996) *Racism and Society*, Basingstoke: Macmillan.

Sparshott, F. (1994) *Taking Life Seriously: A Study of the Argument of the Nichomachean Ethics*, Toronto: University of Toronto Press.

Spiecker, B. (1999) 'Habituation and training in early childhood', in D. Carr and J. Stuetel (eds) *Virtue Ethics and Moral Education*, London: Routledge, pp. 217–30.

Spitzer, G. (2006) 'Sport and the systematic infliction of pain: a case study of mandatory state sponsored doping in Germany', in S. Loland, B. Skirstad and I. Waddington (eds) *Sport, Pain and Injury*, London: Routledge, pp. 109–26.

Spriggs, M. (2005) 'Hypoxic air machines: performance enhancement through effective training – or cheating?', *Journal of Medical Ethics*, 31: 112–13.

Stephens, D. E., Bredemeier, B. J. and Shields, D. L. (1997) 'Construction of a measure designed to assess players' descriptions and prescriptions for moral behaviour in youth sport soccer', *International Journal of Sport Psychology*, 28: 370–90.

Sternglantz, R. (2005) 'Raining on the parade of horrible slippery slopes, faux slopes and justices: Scalia's dissent in Lawrence v Texas', *University of Pennsylvania Law Review*, 153: 1097–120.

Stornes, T. (2001) 'Sportspersonship in elite sports: on the effects of personal and environmental factors on the display of sportspersonship among elite male handball players', *European Physical Education Review*, 7(3): 283–304.

Stout, J. (1988) *Ethics After Babel*, Boston: Beacon.

Strawson, P. (1967) 'Persons', in D.F. Gustaffson, *Essays in Philosophical Psychology*, London: Macmillan, pp. 306–403.

Strawson, P. F. (1968) 'Freedom and resentment', in *Studies in the Philosophy of Thought and Action*, Oxford: Oxford University Press.

Suits, B. (1967) 'What is a game?', *Philosophy of Science*, 34(2): 148–.

Suits, B. (1978) *The Grasshopper: Games, Life and Utopia*, Toronto: University of Toronto Press.

Sutton-Smith, B. (1974) 'Towards an anthropology of play', *The Association for the Anthropological Study of Play Newsletter*, 1(2): 8–15. Reprinted in M. Hart and S. Birrell (1981) *Sport and the Socio-cultural Process*, Dubuque, IA: Brown, pp. 114–22.

Szasz, T. (1973) *The Second Sin*, London: Routledge.

Tamburrini, C. (2000) *The Hand of God*, Gothenburg: University of Gothenburg Press.

Tamburrini, C. (2005) 'Hypoxic air machines: commentary', *Journal of Medical Ethics*, 31: 114.

Tamburrini, C. (2006) 'Educational or genetic blue prints. What's the difference?', in C. Tamburrini and T. Tannsjo (eds) *Genetic Technology and Sport: Ethical Questions*, London: Routledge, pp. 82–90.

Tannsjo, T. (2005) 'Hypoxic air machines: commentary'. *Journal of Medical Ethics*, 31: 112–13.

Taylor, C. (1985a) *Human Agency and Language: Philosophical Papers 1*, Cambridge: Cambridge University Press.

Taylor, C. (1985b) *Philosophy and the Human Sciences, Volume 2*, Cambridge: Cambridge University Press.

Taylor, C. (1989) *Sources of the Self*, Cambridge: Cambridge University Press.

Taylor, G. (1985) *Pride, Shame, Guilt*, Oxford: Clarendon Press.

Tobin, B. (1989) 'An Aristotelian theory of moral development', *Journal of Philosophy of Education*, 23(1): 195–211.

Toperoff, S. (1989) *Sugar Ray Leonard*, New York: Simon Schuster.

Ture, K. and Hamilton, C. (1992) *Black Power: The Politics of Liberation*, New York: Vintage Books.

Walsh, A. and Giulianotti, R. (2007) *Ethics, Money and Sport*, London: Routledge.

Walton, D. N. (1992) *Slippery Slope Arguments*, Oxford: Clarendon.

Weil, S. (1983) 'The *Iliad* or poem or force', in A. C. MacIntyre and S. Hauerwas (eds) *Revisions*, London: University of Notre Dame Press, pp. 224–49.

Weinberger, D. A., Schwartz, G. E. and Davidson, R. J. (1979) 'Low anxious, high anxious, and repressive coping styles: psychometric patterns and behavioural and physiological responses to stress', *Journal of Abnormal Psychology*, 88: 369–80.

Wellman, D. T. (1993) *Portraits of White Racism*, 2nd edn, Cambridge: Cambridge University Press.

Whiting, B. B. (ed.) (1963) *Six Cultures: Studies of Child Rearing*, New York: Wiley and Sons.

Wieviorka, M. (1995) *The Arena of Racism*, London: Sage.

Wikipedia (2006) 'United Nations Convention on Biological Diversity', Online. Available at: http://en.wikipedia.org/wiki/Convention_on_Biological_Diversity (accessed 10 June 2006).

Wikipedia (2007) 'Miguel Indurain', Online. Available at: http://en.wikipedia.org/wiki/Indurain (accessed 21 August 2007).

Williams, B. A. O. (1973) *Problems of the Self*, Cambridge: Cambridge University Press.

Williams, B. A. O. (1980) 'Justice as a virtue', in A. O. Rorty (ed.) *Essays on Aristotle's Ethics*, Berkeley: University of California, pp. 189–99.

Williams, B. A. O. (1985) *Ethics and the Limits of Philosophy*, London: Fontana.

Williams, B. A. O. (1993) *Shame and Necessity*, Berkeley: University of California Press.

Wittgenstein, L. (1953) *Philosophical Investigations*, Oxford: Blackwell.

Wittgenstein, L. (1967) *Philosophical Investigations*, 3rd edn, Oxford: Blackwell, (trans. G. E. M. Anscombe).

Wollheim, R. (1984) *The Thread of Life*, Cambridge: Cambridge University Press.

Wollheim, R. (1993) *The Mind and its Depths*, Boston: Harvard University Press.

Young, D. C. (1984) *The Olympic Myth of Greek Amateur Athletics*, Chicago: Ares.

Index